A SCHOOL FOR TOMORROW

Jack R. Frymier

The Ohio State University

McCutchan Publishing Corporation
2526 Grove Street
Berkeley, California 94704

Contents

Preface

This is a book about a school for tomorrow. Not *the* school of tomorrow but *a* school *for* tomorrow. The book does not propose to be the answer to all of tomorrow's educational problems, but it does present a series of propositions about what schools could be like in the years ahead. It outlines an alternative to the kinds of schools that exist today.

To talk about the future is disquieting. Nobody knows exactly what tomorrow will be like. The uncertainties and inconsistencies create a discomfort that will not go away. Yet most people are future oriented. They work and "save for a rainy day." Parents deny themselves material things in order to assure their children's future. Time does indeed march on, and in spite of the latest local doom-sayers, most of us believe that tomorrow will come.

But what will tomorrow be like? What kinds of schools will we need? What roles should schoolmen play? Any consideration of the future requires at least attempts to answer such questions.

There are at least two points of view about the future. One presumes that events will unfold along the same general directions as in the past ten, fifty, or a hundred years or more. A popular song of another year maintained that "whatever will be, will be." Many people agree with this kind of fatalism. They believe that the trends evident in the world today will result in a certain kind of future. There is little doubt that we have developed fantastic capacity to project on the drawing board what tomorrow will be like if we start with today, go back to yesteryear, and then carry the projections forward in a tight, straight line. Although the fatalist acknowledges the fact that there may be variations—slight or drastic—he insists that the general outlines of tomorrow can be foreseen in terms of what exists today.

Such a conception about tomorrow is safe, but it locks people in and restricts their dreams. It denies them their capacity for exercising choice and making decisions; it fosters a dependent rather than an independent spirit. Those who are imprisoned by such fatalistic concepts are the cynics and the pessimists of today.

The second conception presumes that people can invent their tomorrows and create their futures in terms of what they hope or desire them to be. This book is based on this second point of view. While the notion of alternative futures lends itself to academic discussions, there will only be one future. The important question is: Is that future predetermined, or can it be created in terms of what we want it to be?

We have a choice to make. Do we sit back and allow the probable, predictable future to unfold, or do we go to work and create a better world? Do we maintain that "what ought to be" is simply fantasy talk, or do we reaffirm the notion that human spirit is important, even sacred, if you please, and then begin to act as if our plans and activities today will have an impact on—in fact, will create—tomorrow? We believe that the second option is both possible and desirable. Further, we also believe that principals and teachers in schools can create new and better institutions than the ones we have today. We can do it if we start to work right now.

The schools of tomorrow will become either what we make them or what we let them become. The choice is ours, and it is a choice. Either we exercise our intelligence and our will, or the decision will be made by default. This book argues that men ought to create their tomorrows. Schoolmen ought to build new conceptions of education, carefully and thoughtfully.

Education is imperative if man is to survive. The importance of the relationship of learning to life itself is apparent everywhere. Stronger, tougher organisms than man have come on the earthly scene and then disappeared from view. There is no right of survival and the human race has only one advantage: its capacity and desire to learn. Adaptability is more essential than endurance. Modifiability is more important than strength or age or anything else. When man stops learning, he also stops living.

Education and schooling are not the same. We all know that. But schools have been conceived as means to educational ends. The fact that some schools negate the attainment of educational objectives is simply proof of the point that schools and schooling absolutely must change.

This book describes propositions for change in schools initiated at the building level. The authors believe that the necessary kinds of changes cannot take place at the classroom level—there are too many practical constraints—or systemwide. The school building, with hundreds of students and dozens of professional staff, is small enough to be effective and large enough to make the changes complete. Throughout the following pages, therefore, the reader should keep four points in mind:

1. Schooling can be made both different and better.

2. The building is the most likely unit in which to bring about significant change.

3. Change will not just happen, it has to be worked at day after day.

4. Changing the parts is not enough; the "whole" must be changed.

This book represents the second phase of a four-phase developmental effort that is being undertaken by three separate agencies: the Faculty of Curriculum and Foundations at The Ohio State University; the Association for Supervision and Curriculum Development (ASCD); and the Maplewood-Richmond Heights Missouri public schools.

During the autumn of 1970, Jack Frymier wrote a paper entitled "A School For Tomorrow." The paper was presented to the Executive Council of ASCD for consideration and approval along with a proposed plan for developing the ideas further. The council approved the plan and allocated funds to begin the developmental effort. Preparation of the original paper and consideration by the council constituted phase one.

The second phase of the project took place during the latter

half of 1971 and the first six months of 1972. The senior author
invited a group of colleagues at The Ohio State University to form a
faculty seminar to discuss and develop the ideas set forth in the
original paper. Over a period of many months the group met and
worked together in an attempt to elaborate, amplify, modify, and
improve the ideas outlined in the paper. All together, six persons
participated in that working group.

During this same period, each member of the university group
invited one or two other persons from outside of the university
community to work directly with him to develop one component of
the complex of ideas in much greater detail. The fourteen persons
involved met together on three separate occasions. Each of the small
committees attempted to respond to and expand the general ideas
outlined in the original paper.

This book is the product of those developmental endeavors.
Chapter 1 is the original paper. In effect, this paper served as a
stimulus to the other writers, who attempted to honor the general
positions and philosophical premises outlined in that paper, but to go
beyond it. Chapter 2 "Purposes and Goals," was prepared by Gerald
Reagan, OSU faculty member, and Stanton Teal from California
State University, Northridge. The curriculum chapter was written by
Jack Frymier, OSU, Alfred Rasp, who works with the office of the
State Superintendent of Public Instruction in Olympia, Washington,
and Jane Wilhour, who works with the Maplewood-Richmond
Heights public schools in Missouri and at Lindenwood College. "In-
struction in a School for Tomorrow" was prepared by John B.
Hough, OSU, and Hanford Salmon who is with the Syracuse, New
York public schools. Chapter Five, "Evaluation in a School for
Tomorrow" was developed by James K. Duncan, OSU, along with
Jennings Johnson from the Rochester, Minnesota public schools,
and John Schneider, who was then a doctoral student at Ohio State.
The chapter on organization was prepared by Donald Anderson,
OSU, in collaboration with Lloyd Duvall at the Appalachian Region-
al Laboratory. The chapter on staff development was written by
Charles Galloway, OSU, and Edward Mulhern from the Montgomery
County public schools in Maryland. Finally, "From Now to Tomor-
row" was written by Jack Frymier.

Throughout the project a particular philosophic position was
taken by all the authors. Embodied in that position was the idea that
commitment to the individual learner was the central purpose of any

public school. A choice was involved here. A deliberate, rational choice that led the authors to define as the most important and ultimate end of public education the development of the rational autonomous individual. More precisely this end is defined as

the rationally autonomous individual will *choose for himself* from among available alternatives. . . . Such an individual must be able and disposed to choose for himself on the basis of standards which themselves have been *chosen*. He will be inclined to test the truth of things for himself. He must, therefore, be the sort of individual who forms his judgments and chooses what he will do on the basis of critically evaluated standards which he can appreciate and which he has accepted because the evidence and reasons support them.

The authors have elevated this end of public education over all other desirable and undesirable ends, much as the gold medal winner in Olympic competition stands above the winners of silver and bronze medals. The authors, of course, realize that the development of rational autonomous individuals does not replace other desirable educational ends, rather it becomes a priority in the authors' consideration of ends.

The authors have themselves chosen on the basis of critically evaluated standards that they appreciate and have accepted because there is *some* evidence and reason to support those standards. The authors expect others to challenge their position and propose that some other end have first priority. This book may well help others engage in an exploration of priorities and the implications of choosing particular ends as being of highest priority.

The book is developed around the choosing of the rational autonomous individual as the primary end, and the nature of the professional response to such a choice. Chapters 1 and 2 develop the rationale for the choice of a primary end and clarify the nature of that end. In chapters 3 through 5 the authors, as professional educators, outline some of the ways they believe professionals might best respond in educating children and youth toward that end. In chapters 6 and 7 professional educators outline how such an effort could be supported organizationally and how staff development could support the efforts of the professionals working toward the end of rational autonomy. The final chapter looks ahead and tries to help all who would improve the schools by examining the change problem in public education.

Phases one and two of this developmental effort have resulted in the authors' choosing for themselves a primary end for public education and elaborating some aspects of the professional response when such an end has priority. This book represents the authors' efforts at selecting and defining this end and responding professionally to the demands such a choice makes.

In phase three of this developmental effort the writing team is working with one elementary school in the Maplewood-Richmond Heights school district to implement the ideas outlined in this book in a real school. A second aspect of phase three includes the development of materials for use with professionals in the field (e.g., films, simulation materials, cassettes, pamphlets, film strips, etc.). John Belland, Robert Wagner, and Donald Cruickshank from The Ohio State University are assuming primary responsibility for that program, and they are assisted by Marcia Epstein and Jean Brown.

The fourth phase will involve dissemination of the materials through both commercial publishers and ASCD. All of the royalties from the book and other materials will go to ASCD.

Those of us who have been associated with this project have learned a lot and had a great time. We are grateful to Dean Luvern Cunningham at The Ohio State University for his continued support and encouragement; to the Association for Supervision and Curriculum Development for its commitment and support; and to the Maplewood-Richmond Heights public schools—particularly Clint Crites, Superintendent; Charles Jecmen, Principal; and the teachers at Valley Elementary School—for their confidence, cooperation, and hard work in the attempts to implement these ideas in a real school.

We also want to express our appreciation to the graduate students at The Ohio State University, Oregon State University, and The University of Texas who read the manuscripts carefully, criticized them thoughtfully, and made suggestions for their improvement. Thanks, too, to Kenneth Fishell of the University of Vermont for his comments and criticisms at one of the major working sessions of the total writing group. All of these analyses have shaped the manuscript in many ways.

Last, but not least, we are deeply grateful to Susie Parker and Louise Walldren for their meticulous care in preparing the final manuscript for publication.

Foreword

People are alike, and people are different. Both observations are true, and whatever is done to improve education must deal with both halves of that statement. For generations, however, most of our efforts at educational reform have been almost exclusively predicated on the likeness of students. There is good reason for this: proceeding under that assumption, the things that need doing are so much simpler and more familiar and carry the illusion of businesslike straightforwardness. Things can be handled objectively, managed and manipulated, organized and systematized, in the fashion characteristic of science and industry whose accomplishments our culture admires so much.

Because it is partly right that children are alike, some of these efforts get pretty fair results sometimes, and we are encouraged to continue down those paths in the hope that if we can but do it harder, more often, or more systematically, in the end we should reach the millenium. The result, as Earl Kelley once put it, is that we find ourselves with "these wonderful schools, this marvelous curriculum, these fine teachers and then: damn it all! the parents send us the wrong kids!"

There is a limit to how long we can achieve success by doing the easy thing or working harder at doing what we already know how to do. For a long time education has managed to get away with ignoring the facts of student individuality or making small concessions to give the illusion of adequate consideration. The result is an educational system in trouble, criticized for inadequacy and irrelevance by the students and society it is intended to serve.

We have run out our string. The gains we can make pursuing the same old assumptions are less and less fruitful. The nature of man and the laws of behavior cannot be set aside because they are inconvenient. What is true about people and behavior must be confronted and dealt with or inevitably those facts of life will rise to confound our very best efforts. After generations of talking about individualizing our schools, it is time to "put our money where our mouth is" and give the problem the full measure of attention it demands. That is why this is such an important book.

Dr. Frymier has a rare capacity to tackle an issue, examine its basic assumptions, and follow it through to its logical consequences. He is also able to present his case in clear and challenging terms, a quality not always appreciated by the comfortable and complacent. He is joined in this volume by a like-minded group of distinguished colleagues. Together they have asked the question, "What kind of school is called for, if we honestly apply ourselves to the problem of individualizing education?" Systematically, they have tried to examine the implications of human uniqueness for education's goals, curriculum, instruction, organization, and evaluation. The approach they have taken is long overdue, and the book they have produced is a highly provocative one.

Probably no one will find himself in complete agreement with all these authors have to say, but the conclusions they reach and the innovations they suggest will surely prove exciting and stimulating to many a troubled educator striving to make our educational system a more humane and effective instrument for human welfare. *A School for Tomorrow* is a worthy addition to the distinguished list of publications produced by ASCD.

Arthur W. Combs
October 1972

Part 1
Choosing and Defining Purposes and Goals

1

A School
for Tomorrow

Jack R. Frymier

Introduction

These are disturbing days for schoolmen. Forever admonished to change their educational ways, they have tried mightily, but apparently to no avail. After almost fifteen years of this effort, Silberman maintains that there is now a "crisis in the classroom." And so there is.

Silberman's statement describes what almost every experienced observer of the American educational scene already knows: most schools are boring, and attempts to change them have not yielded either the kind or the degree of improvement that many thoughtful persons feel must occur.

Another set of factors must now be coped with and considered. New, negative forces pressing for expression in public schools make the crisis even more acute. Because these forces are not as clearly etched in people's minds as was the launching of Sputnik, and because the motivations of many persons associated with these forces are positive in every sense of the word, the existence of a crisis is not always obvious. Even so, the crisis is real, and the forces will not go away. Educators and those concerned with schools and schooling must find ways to cope with these forces or public education will literally be dismembered: its unity of effort will be destroyed.

What I have just said is a dire prediction and must be explained. Before I proceed along that line, however, let me hasten to add that I do not think that public schools will disappear or cease to be. Public schools have been a part of our heritage and a part of our culture for a long time, and there will still be public schools a thousand years from now, if man can last that long. Once social institutions become firmly established it is almost impossible to get rid of them, whether they function in a manner consistent with the larger purposes of the society or not. How else does one explain the continued survival of the Judaism in Russia, the private school in England, or the American Legion in the United States? None of these institutions represents the mainstream of social thought in the cultures of which they are a part. Some are vigorously opposed, in fact, but they continue to survive. Certainly when an institution works to serve socially approved purposes, as the public school does, there is absolutely no reason to think that it will evaporate or go away.

However, I would guess that unless schools change dramatically in the next few years, the heart of the educational function—helping youngsters develop and learn new concepts, attitudes, and skills—may very well be assumed by other institutions in our society, and the school will be left with the residual function of containment and control. This custodial function—keeping youngsters off the streets, out of the job market, and away from the house so that parents can work—is generally assumed to be not the primary function of schools but an important subsidiary role. If other segments of society assume primary responsibility for helping children learn, schools may drift to the solely custodial functions almost without knowing it. If that occurs, schoolmen will have missed an opportunity to provide the nation and its youth better schools and better learning.

What are the forces and developments with the potential to fractionate public education? I think there are many. Let me remind the reader that I do not personally feel that the motivations of people associated with these efforts are necessarily suspect or evil. Some of them are, from my value perspective, but most are the expressions and conceptualizations of people sincerely interested in improving schools and schooling. Whether for good or evil, however, I believe the fractionating effect of these efforts has already begun and will continue.

The private school movement in the South and elsewhere is

dividing people regarding the concept and practice of public education. In some Southern communities the rise of private schools has placed the very existence of public education in jeopardy. It is hard to believe that those who argue for white supremacy and segregated schools have any real interest in the education of the young. The logic of their experience runs backward rather than forward, but the impact of their efforts on public schools is very real in many communities.

Those who advocate and support alternative and storefront schools in the northern urban areas create the same kind of impact, though to a somewhat lesser degree. The motives of these people are usually very different from those of the advocates of segregation. They simply want better education than the public schools are providing, and they see such alternative schools as vehicles toward such an end. In their view the fact that their operations may divide the community and split educators and education is beside the point.

Performance contracting is another force that has begun to fractionate the public schools. School boards have understandably been searching for new and better ways to help young people learn. When private companies promise to do the job better than public schools for the same or less money, school boards are naturally attracted. But what will it mean in five or twenty or fifty years if a commercial corporation, whose explicit intention is to make a profit, assumes primary responsibility for helping children learn to read, compute, develop social skills, or analyze values? What will that do to the public schools? What will it do to the nature of the learning that those children will experience? What if specialties develop and all the learnings are subcontracted to different commercial interests? Will it all add up in the lives and minds of the young who will be involved?

The voucher system holds the same kind of attraction and the same kind of threat, in my opinion. Theoretically it is a powerful idea. Based on the concepts of free enterprise and personal choice, it sounds good when described in abstract form. But can we ignore the fact that some people who support the notion in theory stand to gain privately if it is adopted? Can we ignore the fact that narrow and parochial interests are pushing the concept, hoping and arguing for public tax dollars to support particular ideological or religious points of view? The separation of church and state has been one of our greatest strengths since the beginning of the republic. Are we to give up such a separation for a purported financial saving, while at the same time splintering public education?

Community control, court decisions, negotiations, and learning centers built into the home are all fascinating developments on the educational scene in recent years. All are efforts to improve education, but all are pulling the schools and school people further and further apart, despite the positive intentions and noble ideals of almost everybody involved.

These are the kinds of forces that are tending to fractionate the public schools. They are part of the educational reality today. I do not deplore their development; I simply indicate their existence and what I think their impact may be during the years immediately ahead.

If my observations of the educational scene are correct (and they most certainly may not be), the question then becomes: What should schoolmen do? Three alternatives seem possible. We can assess the drift and direction of the times, accept the changes, and grab the ball and run. We can marshall our forces and defend the public schools as they are. Or we can try to change the schools from what they are to something quite different and infinitely better.

Perhaps school people ought to do what they can to hasten the demise of the public school. Perhaps its era has come and gone. Maybe we ought to turn our creative energies to conceptualizing new and better private agencies, personal operations, or completely different social institutions that can assume the many diverse functions public education now performs.

At first glance this alternative is the most attractive to me. It sounds as though it would be intellectually exciting and professionally fun. But the stakes are too high. There is much more to be lost than could possibly be gained if we go that way. In terms of my own values, I want another way.

How about choice number two, supporting and defending what schools presently do? In terms of all that we know about the weaknesses and failures of the public schools, that is hardly a good enough goal. Having said that let me quickly add that I feel the public school also has tremendous strengths. But the very strengths of the public school may be its downfall, unless we are adept and creative. Strength is not enough; the capacity to cope, adapt, and change is imperative. The public school is something like an Army tank: it possesses fantastic power and has extremely thick walls, but it is very vulnerable in spots, is extremely slow moving, and requires tremendous amounts of support and fuel.

It seems clear that the strengths and power of the public schools of yesterday are neither sufficient nor appropriate for the new and more demanding problems of today. If public schools are to survive at more than the custodial level, they must become different, better institutions than they are right now. I cast my lot with option number three. Public schools cannot abdicate their responsibility; they have to change.

Since Heraclitus we have heard that "these are changing times," and so they are. But if change is a constant factor, the pace of change is not. The world is turning faster, in the sense that many of the people of the world are experiencing more situations per given unit of time than any people have ever experienced before.

Describing the individual life as a great channel through which experience flows, Toffler reacts to the bewildering sensations that come from the pace of today's life:

For while we tend to focus on only one situation at a time, the increased rate at which situations flow past us vastly complicates the entire structure of life, multiplying the number of roles we must play and the number of choices we are forced to make. This in turn, accounts for the choking sense of complexity about contemporary life.[1]

Norman Cousins makes the same point in a different way when he maintains that "it has been more than a hundred years since 1940."[2] One hardly needs to document the fact that times change, and yet data show that schools and schooling have not changed much throughout the years. For instance, a recent advertisement in a national magazine presses the point like this: "Have students changed too much, or have the schools not changed enough?" If the implication in that question is correct, then educators have both special problems and unique opportunities in the years ahead. But what about the charge? Have the schools failed to keep pace with the times? The only honest answer to that question must be, "yes."

In a study supported by the Carnegie Corporation, Silberman describes the failures of educational reform as follows:

the reform movement has produced innumerable changes, and yet the schools themselves are largely unchanged . . . things are much the same as they had been twenty years ago, and in some respects not as good as they were forty years ago, when the last great school reform movement was at its peak.[3]

Peter Drucker approaches the point in a different way. Arguing from a purely economic point of view, he states, "There are no dumb children; there are only poor schools."[4] He adds,

teaching and learning are bound to undergo tremendous change in the next few decades. They will be transformed. Economic necessity forces us to tackle the job, no matter how great the resistance of citizens and educators. . . .
The first teacher ever, that priest in preliterate Mesopotamia who sat down outside the temple with the kids and began to draw figures with a twig in the sand, would be perfectly at home in most classrooms in the world today. Of course, there is a blackboard, but otherwise there has been little change in tools and none in respect to methods. The one new teaching tool in the intervening 8,000 years has been the printed book. And that few teachers really know how to use—or else they would not continue to lecture on what is already in the book. The priest in ancient Mesopotamia was also the first doctor. If he returned today to a modern operating room in the hospital, he would not conclude that he could do as well. Yet today's doctors are no better men than the first doctors were. They certainly are no better than the "father of medicine," Hippocrates. They stand on his shoulders. They know more and, above all, they know better. They have a different methodology. They have different tools. As a result they do entirely different things, and do them differently.[5]

Drucker's point is that educators have not developed adequate tools—concepts and artifacts—to extend and expand the impact of their effort to help young people learn. And though Silberman would argue that the problem is not simply one of increasing the efficiency of the school,[6] as Drucker implies, they both agree that today's schools must be described in static rather than dynamic terms.

Neither Silberman nor Drucker, however, are "professional schoolmen." Maybe they do not know what schools and schooling are really like. But their observations are supported by Goodlad and Klein's study of classroom practice, in which the authors state, "One conclusion stands out clearly: Many of the changes we have believed to be taking place in schooling have not been getting into classrooms; changes widely recommended for the schools over the past 15 years were blunted on school and classroom doors."[7]

My own studies of educational developments and change arrive at the same conclusion in a slightly different way: Schools have changed, but the changes have not made a significant difference in the lives and minds of those we teach.[8] Thus, even though our intentions have been noble and our efforts real, the changes have not "paid off." Schools and schooling are not keeping pace with the dramatic changes of the times.

In another place I have outlined why I feel our change efforts have not been as effective and successful as we all hoped they would be: Not only is education as a social system theoretically incapable of self-renewal and rational change, but we have asked the wrong questions, manipulated the wrong variables, and employed the wrong assumptions.[9] There is another reason, though, and it is both simpler and more profound: Children differ. Anthropologists suggest that every man is like all men in some ways, like some men in other ways, and like no other man in still other ways.[10] The same is true of children, and teachers and curriculum developers must not only be aware of the situation but also have precise and adequate information regarding the ways in which all children are alike, the ways in which some of them are alike, and the ways in which each youngster is unique.

All children are alike in that they are born; depend on others for an extended period of time; and have one heart, two kidneys, and the like. Youngsters are like some other children in terms of their sex, language patterns, developmental patterns, and immediate community environment. Each child is unique, though, in terms of his genetic pattern, the kinds of past experiences he has had, the way he sees himself, and his personal aspirations.[11]

The educator's problem is to provide the degree of similarity of program and experience that is both appropriate and possible and, at the same time, to preserve and foster individuality. It is not a simple problem, to say the least. I accept the fact that some similarity of educational experience is both appropriate and possible for all children, but I strongly suspect that many of our reform efforts have failed because we did not pay enough attention to the fact that children differ.

For example, if one looks closely at the innovations in curriculum in recent years, he is struck by the fact that we have tended to "take the old program out" and "put a new program in." It may be true, as Goodlad and Klein point out,[12] that the reason education has not been improved is that the innovations have not actually been tried—school people think they try them, but the innovations are actually not implemented all the way. Even with that reservation, there is still reason to believe that what school people have tried to do is substitute a new program, a new set of procedures, a different organizational scheme, a new something-or-other, for the old way of doing things. In thinking and working this way, what usually emerges is the classic model of experimental design: two groups of roughly similar size, socioeconomic background, ability, and age, one labeled "experimental" and the other labeled "control." The experimental group employs the new curriculum materials, the new methodology, the new something-or-other, while the control group continues in the traditional approach of the conventional curriculum. Many have criticized this way of evaluating experimental programs,[13] and rightly so, but regardless of criticism, the actual logic of experimentation has been along these lines. Even when formal and elaborate comparative evaluation has not been made, the general posture nevertheless has been one of comparing the new program with the old one, if only in crude and subjective ways.

What most frequently occurs is that one group (e.g., classroom, building, series of classrooms in different buildings, etc.) is identified as the experimental group and paired with another group of roughly similar size, socioeconomic background, ability, and age. Both groups are pretested in terms of the outcomes desired (generally achievement of some sort), then the experimental group is subjected to the special treatment, while the control group goes through their learning experience in the established way. At the end of a given period of time, both the experimental group and the control group are posttested.

Depending on the idiosyncracies and competencies of the researchers involved, along with such factors as sample size, number of variables manipulated and controlled, and the like, the typical study is of the statistical significance of the difference of the posttest means for the two groups. Graphically portrayed, such a comparison tends to look something like this.

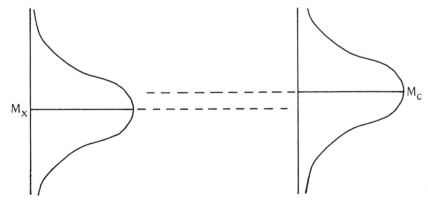

Figure 1-1. Comparison of the means of "experimental" and "control" groups

In practice the statistical significance of the difference between the means (i.e., the distance between the dotted lines) is usually determined by computing a t value or doing analysis of variance (F test), or employing some similar statistical test. Studies that have been done and the general experience of many people who work in education support the finding implicit in the diagram in figure 1: *no significant difference*. In a review of almost 300 research studies along this line, it was found that "no significant difference" is the most frequently reported research result.[14] Other studies of educational change report similar observations.[15]

If one studies the diagram in figure 1 carefully, and explores the assumptions implicit in that kind of comparison, several inferences can be made. First, by employing the experimental-control approach, what is actually being tested is a *group solution*. That is, when we take the old program out and put the new one in, what we are actually presuming is that one group solution is better than another group solution. In the same way, when we compare the new way of teaching foreign language with the traditional way, or the new physics with conventional physics, or "Words In Color" with basal reading, or team teaching with the self-contained classroom, what we have actually done is to take out one *group* approach (i.e., traditional) and substitute for it another *group* approach (i.e., modern or experimental). The assumption behind that assumption is that somewhere there must be a way of sequencing subject matter, presenting information, or organizing the school *that is best for all children*. Nonsense! There is no *one way* of doing anything in school which is best for all children, because children differ.

Some children learn best when subject matter is presented to them in such a way that they "discover" the basic constructs, the fundamental generalizations, for themselves. Other children learn better when subject matter is sequenced deductively rather than inductively, and they go from the whole to the part rather than the other way around. Some youngsters learn better when they experience things directly and concretely, other youngsters learn better vicariously or when they are told. Some students learn better when their learning experiences are spaced in short segments over an extended period of time. Other students learn better when they are completely immersed in a learning experience without interruption for a short period of time. Some learn better when they are functioning under the direct guidance and supervision of a more mature person such as the teacher, while other students learn better when they are left completely on their own. Some learners do better when they "see" a stimulus, others do better when they kinesthetically "feel" it, and still others do better when they "hear" phenomena described in spoken terms. *There is no one best way of doing anything in education,* because children differ. And it is precisely where their differences are most significant that learning is most affected, i.e., their previous experience, their concept of self, their motivation to learn, their immediate home background, and the like. Thus, there is no one best way of doing anything in education, except as it applies to a given child.

Though it is most certainly true that children are like all other children in some respects, and like some other children in other respects, it is also very true that in still other respects each child is like no other person. Those unique variations are the crucial factors that affect learning in very profound ways. If we are seriously concerned about meeting the needs of every child, as most people maintain, then we absolutely have to build a whole new concept of education for the years ahead. We need a wholly new way of thinking about learning and teaching. "A School for Tomorrow" represents my own effort to outline what I think such a school might be. In the pages that follow I have tried to think through the totality of a school. Purposes, curriculum instruction, organization, evaluation, teacher education—these and other pieces are examined in some detail. That I have not been able to "pull off" the whole thing satisfactorily does not discourage me. Hopefully these ideas will trigger other persons to generate their conceptualizations.

Purposes

Education is not without direction. The purposes or goals of education are always implicit in the endeavor if not expressly stated, and they can be ferreted out if not already there for all to see. And purposes supposedly relate directly to students' needs.

Most educational theorists make the point that the purposes of education stem primarily from three sources: [16]

1. The nature of knowledge, sometimes referred to as the disciplines. The structure, domain, and methods that are unique and peculiar to each of the various areas of scholarly inquiry are all aspects of the nature of knowledge. The ways of the poet, for

example, are different from the ways of the physicist. In like manner, the conceptual and working tools of the economist are different
from the tools of the biologist. The aspects of reality to which they
address their attention are different, as are the fundamental concepts
and associated facts with which they deal. The history of each
discipline is unique and gives it an emphasis and flavor of its own. We
can draw on these kinds of information in our attempt to determine
what students need to learn.

2. The nature of society: population patterns, demographic
data, cultural values, institutional expectations, sentiments, and
norms. Whether we use the traditional conceptualizations and data of
sociological thought, such as the *Statistical Abstract*[17] or the newer
statements, like Reich's *The Greening of America*,[18] what we know
about the nature of social institutions and their traditions and
changes represents another important source for ascertaining the
needs of students.

3. The nature of the individual's biological, physiological, and
psychological structures and functions: blood chemistry, perceptual
defenses, cognitive style, neurological processes, achievement patterns, intellectual structure, and the like.

Educators have traditionally gone to these three sources for
both information and inspiration about relating school purposes to
students' needs. Curriculum is regarded as something like a three-
legged stool: a solid base with three even supports. The seat of the
stool represents the program, with one leg rooted firmly in what we
know about the nature of knowledge, another in what we know
about the nature of society, and the third in what we know about
the nature of the individual. Such an idea is neat and understandable,
but it is as wrong as it can be.

Educational programs never actually reflect that kind of balance
and equivalent use of sources. Apparently, those who build programs
and implement curriculum subconsciously rank these sources in
hierarchical terms in their own minds, according to their own values.
Certain sources are held to be more important than others, and the
hierarchical ordering reflects this fact. Therefore, while those responsible for determining purposes and building educational programs
theoretically use the three sources of information equally, in practice, they draw on them in varying degrees. The result is that

different philosophical positions are taken that reflect the individual value systems of the people involved.[19]

For example, to presume that what we know about the nature of knowledge is of greatest worth and that what we know about society and the individual are of lesser worth will reflect a particular value judgment about what students need to learn and need to know. Let us call that assumption number one. That assumption characterizes most of the secondary schools, colleges, and universities in the United States today. These institutions are discipline oriented, and are organized and operated on the basis of subject matter concerns.

If we shift our logic and assume that what we know about the nature of society is of greatest importance, then we are operating from a very different kind of philosophical stance. Let us call this assumption two. In my experience, this is the kind of assumption that characterizes most elementary schools in the United States, where the primary concern is for the group. Cooperation, politeness, taking turns, being quiet—all social expectations—are stressed.

To presume that what we know about the nature of the individual is of greatest importance represents a very different kind of philosophical position about education. Let us call this assumption three. In my experience, there are very few classrooms or schools anywhere that reflect this ranking of curriculum sources as the basic way of meeting students' needs. Some "way-out" schools such as Summerhill are probably efforts in that direction, and individual teachers here and there implement such an assumption in their classrooms every day. By and large, however, there are very few models to which we can turn if we want to see or understand this kind of assumption in actual practice.

Because the different assumptions described above give rise to different kinds of educational purposes and goals, it is crucial to try to understand how such assumptions are actually related to students' needs. Students do have needs: academic needs, social needs, and individual needs. The question is, which needs are most pressing and most important at any given point in time?

The problem, at least in part, is one of ends and means. I want to argue that man is the end, subject matter is the means, and society is the result. I want to argue for assumption three.

Assumption number one is essentially a vocational assumption. If an individual wants to become a mathematician, he needs to study mathematics. If he wants to be a farmer, he needs to study farming.

If he wants to be an airplane pilot, physicist, poet, or plumber, he has to pursue those areas of inquiry that are directly related to his particular vocational interest.

Assumption number two, on the other hand, is essentially a cultural position. It presumes that the student needs to learn that which will enable him to become an effective, contributing member of society, and therefore the school should be an instrument of social purposes working to achieve social as opposed to individual or subject-matter ends. There can be no doubt that schools have always assumed this responsibility, but should this be the primary and overriding concern, or should it be of secondary importance? In my judgment, schools should be established and maintained by society for the purpose of serving the needs of those inside the institution rather than those outside. To argue that the school's primary purpose is to serve the needs of society is to adopt the basic logic of every totalitarian society that ever existed. While schools obviously must pay some attention to the problems of acculturation and socialization, in my opinion that should not be their primary purpose.

Thus we come to assumption number three. What does the individual really need? In physical terms, we know a lot about what people need, but when we shift to psychological or educational needs, there is a great void in what we know. All men need water, food, and oxygen, for example. We know with considerable precision, in fact, which foods and ingredients are absolutely essential to the maintenance of life. Can we conceptualize and accomplish research studies that will tell us, more specifically and accurately than we now know, which ideas, which stimuli are essential to meet the individual student's learning needs? Let us explore this problem in more detail.

The directions of the educational enterprise, or the purposes of the school, are never as neat and clear-cut as the logic of this discussion would imply. Purposes and goals always represent a blend of concerns and a mixture of values. But purposes do differ, as do practices and programs, depending on which assumption is involved. I submit that a school for tomorrow should be built on assumption number three.

If we begin by stating that what we know about the nature of the individual is most important, it follows that schools and school-men will be concerned about and teaching in the direction of individual needs. But meeting individual needs has been talked about and advocated in American education for more than a century. In the section that follows, I shall take another and, I hope, fresher look at individual needs.

Curriculum

If one begins with the premise that man is the end, it follows logically that subject matter is the means. This concept, stemming directly from assumption number three, presumes that curriculum is a means to a human end. There is nothing sacred or even worthwhile about subject matter, except as a means for answering human needs. Therefore, assumption number three suggests that the curriculum in a school for tomorrow will have a different character and be based on a different set of considerations than the curriculum in the school of today.

Let us begin the discussion of curriculum by postulating one additional thing: Life is worthwhile. Life is important. Life has value.

Life is an individual phenomenon. It is a characteristic of individual human beings. Groups do not have life. Even though we may sometimes say, "that was a dead group," or "our group came to life today," such statements are metaphorical and are made only for the purpose of communicating more effectively. Nor do the academic disciplines and fields of knowledge possess life. Whatever history or mathematics or poetry are, they are not "alive." They do not live and breathe, give birth or die, make love or war. Only men can do those things. Life is a characteristic of individual people. Life is an individual phenomenon.

Starting from the premise, then, that individual life is worthwhile, it seems reasonable and appropriate to ask: What can schools and schooling do to maintain and improve an individual's life? Whatever schools do, in other words, ought to move in the direction of life processes rather than the opposite direction. The curriculum ought to be life supporting and life enhancing, not life destroying or life diminishing.

In thinking about curriculum we should learn to employ the kinds of logic and ask the kinds of questions that persons who have worked to maintain and enhance physical life have used. But the study of curriculum as a means of preserving and enhancing intellectual and emotional life should not be subsumed under life sciences.

Many people regularly and creatively work at the business of comprehending, preserving, and improving what might be described as man's physical life. Biologists, physiologists, nutritionists, and physicians, for example, all work at perpetuating and upgrading the physical aspects of individual life. Are there basic questions they have asked, methods they have used, or research they have done that would be useful in the work of maintaining and improving intellectual and emotional life? A careful look at what these life scientists do suggests that over the years they have learned to ask certain questions about the physical aspects of life in order to determine how to maintain and improve it. Five questions, at least, seem central to their endeavors.[20]

1. What is essential in order to maintain and possibly improve physical life? What foodstuffs? What minerals? What vitamins? What ingredients or elements are absolutely essential in order to maintain physical life? Over the years researchers have identified a number of ingredients and factors, such as oxygen, protein, water, iron, and calcium, that are absolutely essential in order to maintain life. Without them the organism will deteriorate and eventually die. A by-product of the research has, of course, been the identification of nonessentials.

2. How much is essential? How much water is essential in order to maintain physical life? How much protein? How much oxygen and iron? And so on. The quantity question is the second crucial question which researchers in these fields have learned to pose.

For most of the essential ingredients it would appear that there is both an upper and a lower limit to the quantity question. For example, although the human organism has to have water in order to survive, it cannot handle 20 or 40 or 100 gallons of water a day. The body cannot consume, process, and use that much water in a limited period of time. Likewise, the human organism cannot survive for any extended period of time on a thimbleful or even a cupful of water a day. It must have more than that for life to be maintained. If he had to, an individual could probably cope with and use two or three, maybe four gallons of water every day. Likewise, a person could probably exist, for some time anyway, on as little as a quart, or perhaps even a pint, of water every day. In addition to the upper and lower limits in the quantity question, there is also an optimum amount.

3. Where are the essential ingredients found in usable form? For example, iron is essential for life to continue. But while there is iron in my pocket knife, it is of no use to me at all. I could chew on my knife all day and not get any essential iron for my body to use. In like manner, there is oxygen in sulfuric acid, but it will hurt me rather than help me if I try to get oxygen that way. In the same manner the oxygen in carbon monoxide is hurtful rather than helpful; it is not in a usable form. Thus the third question: Where can I get it?

4. How much of any essential ingredient is present within the parameters of any given source? How much iron is present in a pound of calf liver or a tablespoonful of Geritol? How much vitamin A is included in a glass of carrot juice or one soft-boiled egg? How much fat is present in a butter pat, a glass of milk, or three strips of bacon? Describing the content of essential ingredients is important if professionals hope to *prescribe* what any given individual should have to meet his needs.

5. Under what conditions will the ingestion of these essential ingredients be most helpful to individuals in maintaining and improving physical life? We know, for example, that the human organism must have oxygen, but it is also evident that every human being in the world has to have access to oxygen continuously. One can go without it for one minute, perhaps even two, but all of the oxygen in the world will not help maintain physical life once the supply has been interrupted for even a very short period of time. Therefore, the temporal conditions affecting the availability of oxygen are very important if life is to be maintained.

Time affects the individual and his fundamental needs in other ways. For instance, although the organism needs water and protein, it can survive for several hours without the former and many weeks without the latter. Eventually, however, the individual has to have both protein and water or he will die. Thus, time is one of the important condition factors affecting the maintenance and improvement of life.

Other conditions are important, too. For example, calcium, which is essential at all periods of life, is required in greater quantity during certain growth periods than at other times. Vitamin E is needed in huge amounts when an individual has been severely burned, and vitamin K is essential in greatly increased amounts if excessive bleeding is expected, e.g., during surgery.

Sequencing of intake is another factor affecting the well-being of the organism. Many persons know that if one individual drinks bourbon on an empty stomach and one eats fatty sausages for half an hour before drinking the same amount of bourbon, the results are strikingly different. Sequencing foodstuffs into the organism in one way results in one kind of impact. Sequencing them in another way results in a different kind of impact. Simultaneous consumption may result in still another form of impact.

The point is, there are conditions which are most conducive to the maintenance and improvement of physical life, and researchers have identified them. These five questions about physical life illustrate the nature of the thought processes and the types of research questions involved. Persons in education who are concerned about curriculum may be able to approach the problems and possibilities of maintaining intellectual and emotional life by asking similar questions. Educators do speak of "food for thought" and "intellectual diet" and "watered down" programs, for example, so the analogy may not be at all inappropriate. Suppose we press the same questions in curricular terms. What kind of logic will unfold?

1. What is essential for the maintenance and improvement of intellectual and emotional life? What facts? What concepts? What principles, generalizations, subject matter, or cognitive inputs are absolutely essential for intellectual and emotional life to prevail? Must every individual consume the concept of democracy, for instance, or know that two plus two equals four? Is it imperative that every human being take in factual data about quadratic equations, sentence structure, verb usage, the First Amendment to the Constitution, *Macbeth*, number theory, or time lines? What subject matter is absolutely essential to the maintenance of intellectual and emotional life?

Deciding what is essential, i.e., what ought to be taught, is relatively simple and straightforward if we start with the disciplines or with social concerns. If we start with individual concerns, however, the answers are not so readily apparent.

2. How much is essential? How many facts? How many concepts? How many generalizations or principles are absolutely essential in order to maintain intellectual and emotional life? Theoretically, the problem is similar to the problem of consumption of

physical food. There probably is such a thing as cognitive overload or stuffing, and there obviously is such a thing as stimulus deprivation. When the human organism is deprived of at least some kind of stimulation, it withers and dies. We have enough evidence from stimulus deprivation studies, such as those by Hebb[21] and Berlyne,[22] to suggest that some stimuli are absolutely essential. Or, we can throw stimuli at students so rapidly and with such volume or vividness that they cannot handle them; they get a kind of cognitive indigestion, if you please. The quantity question is real and very important.

3. Where are these essential ingredients found in usable form? We do not really know what is essential, but even if we did, we might not know where to find it. We know, for example, that a history book contains a certain kind of content, a science film contains another kind, and a mathematics workbook contains yet another. We know where such content is located in usable form, but in other areas we do not know. For example, we have little idea about what usable content is contained in an hour's counseling session or a field trip to the zoo, the bakery, or the fire house. We do not know what students get out of such experiences. Even when we do know, for example, that there are certain quantitative concepts portrayed in a mathematics book, we are not really very clear about exactly what that content is. We know something about the third question, but not much.

4. How much content is included within the parameters of any given educational unit? How many facts or concepts or principles are in this textbook as opposed to that one? What is the content of a given lecture? How many ideas and how many generalizations are contained in an hour's science film? How many facts, concepts, principles, or generalizations are present in the field trip to the zoo, the counseling session, the reprimand, or the whipping that we sometimes give young people? What is the content of the content, so to speak? What is included in the educational experience we contrive and prescribe that will, when the student has partaken of it, nurture and improve his intellectual and emotional life?

I suggest that we probably do not know much about this question either. Sometimes we have an intuition that one history book has more content in it than another, but we cannot talk about that content precisely. For example, even though our own fields are not life sciences or nutrition, most of us know more about the amount of carbohydrates or the number of calories in a soda cracker or a french fried potato than we do about the number of facts or principles in a book that we teach in our own subject matter fields.

5. Under what conditions will the consumption of certain kinds of intellectual ingredients be most conducive to optimal intellectual and emotional life? Which things should come first, and which things second? Should they be presented with pressure or with praise? Should they be accompanied by punishment or reward? Should they be apportioned over specified units of time or made available in quantity in big blocks of time?

Interestingly enough, we are apt to think that we are very knowledgeable in the "conditions" area. Most of us, for example, are not uncomfortable at all about asserting that one set of content has to precede another. That is the whole notion of scope and sequence in curriculum. We insist that this comes first, and that comes second, or that this content ought to be presented at this age level, as if we knew a lot about the conditions that are most conducive to optimum intellectual and emotional life.

We do have some ideas about these conditions questions, but the differences among individual learners are so great that many of the assumptions on which we operate are almost always wrong. For example, even if voluminous research indicated that a certain temporal pacing was most appropriate for an average learner—for example, spaced intervals of three hours a day every other day for three weeks—for some individuals it would be wholly wrong, just as consuming certain amounts of alcohol may have one kind of impact on certain people because of their physiological structure and a different impact on other people. Moreover, even though we think we know what may be appropriate for an average individual, *individuals are not averages*. I do not think we have a very good understanding about even what conditions are most appropriate to best serve the individual's intellectual and emotional life.

The five questions are: What is essential? How much is essential? Where is it found? In what quantities and under what conditions will it be most conducive to maintaining and improving intellectual and emotional life? The questions are intriguing and frustrating, but they might generate a whole new area of curriculum research if we pose them within the framework of assumption number three. It is not the purpose of this chapter to answer these questions. I do not know the answers, but I feel that the questions are very basic.

Curriculum based on assumption number three will probably be different in several specific ways. For example, in the conventional school the curriculum usually manifests itself in large pieces with relatively fixed sequences, and the number of combinations of pieces or ways of combining them is small. This is apparent, for example, with the traditional textbook (or textbook series of several grade levels) in which the curriculum "chunk" has many pages, all bound on one edge in such a way that the sequence is fairly rigidly prescribed. Because the size and the sequence restrict variation or combination of the pieces, opportunities for creativity on the part of the teacher are limited. Further, the basic organizing construct inherent in the conventional curriculum is usually a thematic or logical approach. Such an organizing principle is supposedly best for the child, but actually it represents the academic scholar's fundamental concerns.

In the school of the future, curriculum content will occur in a large number of small pieces, the sequences possible will be infinitely varied, and the number of possible combinations or permutations of pieces will be extremely large. This means that the teacher will have a genuine opportunity for creativity within the curriculum, assuring a fresh approach and an excited teacher every time. The curriculum will not become boring to the teacher as the conventional one does, because novel arrangements and different patternings will bring new insights and fresh perspectives to the teacher year after year.

The conventional school's curriculum is organized for the scholar, and the basic concern is for storage. The curriculum of a school for tomorrow will be organized for the teacher's use and the basic organizing concern will be for retrieval rather than storage. To say it another way, the conventional curriculum is organized much like a library; good for putting materials into but difficult to get them back out of. The curriculum of the future will have thousands of pieces stored in one of a variety of ways (even randomly, perhaps), but each piece will be instantly available to the teacher who needs a particular bit of subject matter to fit a particular student's particular learning need. Such a curriculum will require a different concept of instruction. In the next section we will explore some of the theoretical aspects of teacher-pupil interaction in a conventional school and in a school for the future.

Instruction

Teaching-learning situations involve teachers and students in interactive relationships within some kind of organizational context. Although contextual factors are extremely important, they will not be dealt with here. I intend to focus instead on the teacher-student relationship and to explore that relationship and its interactions in detail. The central proposition is that we must turn the whole interaction around. The logic of teaching in the conventional school is backward and wrong for a school based on the importance of the individual.

Figure 2 portrays graphically the educational process as it typically occurs in a conventional school.

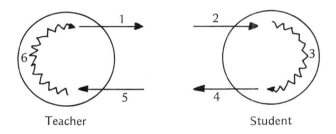

Teacher   Student

Figure 1-2. Conventional teaching-learning interaction

The logic of conventional teaching starts (point 1) in what might be called "teacher output behavior." That is, the teacher says something, or otherwise behaves in some manner that gets the teaching-learning cycle underway. "Everybody open your books to page seventy-three"; or "Betty, go to the board and write this problem down"; or "The lesson today deals with the use of the apostrophe." After the teacher output behavior occurs, the student (point 2) is expected to receive the lecture, demonstration or data, to comprehend it and give it meaning (point 3), in order to respond with the correct behavioral output (point 4). In other words, in the conventional logic of teaching and learning, teaching begins with the teacher's output behavior, and ends when correct feedback occurs (point 5).

Teaching, in the conventional sense, is defined as the extent to which the student's output behaviors follow directly from and are a function of the teacher's output behaviors. To say it another way, in the conventional school the student's response is expected to be consistent with and directly related to the stimulus the teacher provides in his own behavior at point 1. Such a model presumes that the student not only ought to but does follow the teacher's lead.

The conventional method works beautifully for "transmitting the cultural heritage" (assumption number two) or "learning about the subject from the scholar's point of view" (assumption number one), but it makes no sense at all on the basis of assumption number three, which gives primary emphasis to individual needs. Figure 3 is a graphic portrayal of a teaching-learning interaction based on the assumption that what we know about the nature of the individual is of more importance than what we know about the nature of society.

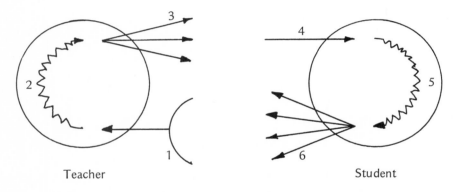

Figure 1-3. Teaching-learning interaction in a school for tomorrow

In this model the teacher's first professional act is one of intake or observational behavior (point 1). After the teacher sees, hears, or otherwise observes the student's output behavior (point 6), he then interprets the behavior (point 2) in the light of his past experience and professional training, and attempts to make sense out of the observational data that has come to him through the intake process at point 1. Following this interpretation of the student and his needs, the teacher responds (point 3). Teacher response follows from and is a function of the student as stimulus: What the teacher does comes after and is a function of the student's behavior as perceived by the teacher. Such an approach literally turns the conventional logic of teaching around.

Some might want to argue that such a reversal of logic and roles is unwarranted. Perhaps an analogy or two will help to clarify the logic involved.

Physicians, whom most would recognize as performing highly professional and important helping roles, function primarily on the basis of the interactive relationship outlined in figure 3. That is, the physician's basic task is to receive information from and about the patient (intake behavior as represented at point 1) in order to assess the problem and diagnose the patient's difficulty. Following this, the physician interprets what he sees and hears and pieces the observational data together in his mind (point 2) before he prescribes or tells the patient what to do (point 3). The effective physicians are those who are most skilled at observation and inference (diagnosis or point 2) and whose directives, decisions or prescriptions follow directly from and are precisely related to the patient's need (as manifest at point 6).

The same is true of effective waiters, architects, and others in helping roles. They work to make careful observations of the patron's or client's needs and respond in ways designed to serve those needs. The effective helper, in other words, gets his cues by observing the client's needs, and the helper's skill in meeting those needs is reflected in the appropriateness of his own output behaviors (3).

There are many other important factors about this model of teaching-learning. Going back to figure 3, we note that a variety of student output behaviors are represented by the several arrows at point 6. These several arrows are meant to describe two kinds of phenomena, both of which are important: (1) the range of behaviors that might reasonably be expected to be evident among a number of different students, and (2) the range of behavioral variables that might reasonably be expected to be found within any one student.

The conventional logic of teaching focuses on differences within the group and between groups, whereas the logic being suggested here for a school for tomorrow focuses on differences within the individual and between individuals. To point out that "Bill is different from Mary" or "Joe and John are different persons with different learning needs" is to state the obvious, but the conventional logic of teaching provides no mechanism or theoretical rationale for dealing with the obvious. Because the conventional logic of teaching begins with teacher output behavior, students are expected to receive and understand and behave in appropriate ways dictated by the teacher's own overt behaviors, regardless of the students' differences or their individual learning needs. Differences between students are important factors and can only be recognized and attended to if teachers seek to receive information about such differences and needs as the first act of professional behavior. After they recognize these differences, they will be in a position to respond in differentiated ways according to their experience and their understanding of the students' differentiated learning needs.

The second pattern of differences is equally important. Individuals differ, we know, but these differences manifest themselves through a host of important variables within each individual. For instance, ability is an important personal variable, and so is achievement, but they are not the same. Likewise, age, personality structure, motivation, and creativity are among the many important factors related to learning. All exist within every child in varying degrees. Those of us who work in education know that all these variables are important, but we usually lack the kind of experience and training necessary to cope with them either conceptually or operationally.

Suppose, for example, that we try to think about and describe variations within individuals and between individuals in a holistic way. People live and learn and function as total entities. If we are to try to comprehend the infinite range of variations that characterize all men, we need to have some way of thinking, some theoretical approach that will help us discern and comprehend the infinite range of nuances that are so important and perplexing to educators.

Suppose we start by identifying several characteristics or dimensions of individual behavior that are both important and relatively discrete. Let us begin by listing five: ability, motivation, achievement, creativity, and cognitive style. These factors are probably related, but they are usually thought of as "different" variables within the totality that we think of as the human organism. Working with just these five factors (and most persons would argue that others are equally or more important), we can begin by trying to think about each factor in a trichotomous way. When we think about ability, for example, we can try to imagine three different kinds or levels of ability, however one chooses to approach the task: High Ability, Average Ability, and Low Ability.

There is no doubt, of course, that trying to think about ability in such a simplistic, trichotomous way does a tremendous disservice to all that we know about the richness and variation in human ability. In fact, that point is the basic thesis of this entire chapter. However, as a way of trying to think about diversity in theoretical terms, the reader is encouraged to withhold his objections, for a time at least, and to try to conceptualize precise ways of thinking about people as total human beings.

For example, if we can think about three levels of ability, perhaps we can also envision three levels of motivation, three degrees of creativity, three kinds or levels of cognitive style, and three levels of achievement. All the reservations the reader has about dealing with complex phenomena in simplistic ways apply here, too. Even so, if we can withhold judgment for a bit longer, perhaps we can outline the concept in a crude but helpful way.

Starting with the five postulated variables or aspects of individual behavior, we can create a series of types of individuals, each one fundamentally different in one or more important ways. For example, a person might be envisioned as having high ability, high motivation, high achievement, high creativity, and high cognitive style. That individual would be a very different person from one characterized by high ability, low motivation, high achievement, high creativity, and high cognitive style. When just one variation is introduced into the behavioral pattern, significant differences appear. In the same way, a person of low ability, low achievement, high motivation, low creativity, and high cognitive style would be still another entirely different kind of human being, needing an entirely different kind of curriculum content and instructional style than either of the other two.

The point is, people differ. We need conceptual tools, curriculum materials, instructional procedures, organizational arrangements, and evaluative devices that will enable us to discern and comprehend the differences in important educational ways.

This line of reasoning could be developed further, but I am trying simply to outline a way of thinking about teaching and learning that turns the logic of teaching around. In addition, conceptualizing and acting on our concepts of the differences between individuals and within individuals—instead of concerning ourselves with the differences between groups and within groups—is an important step. It becomes necessary to devise both concepts and operational tools for describing and inferring from and about the many differences within and between individuals in schools. That means, of course, that the school would have to be organized differently.

Organization

If we can declare educational objectives in growth rather than control terms and have them based squarely on individuals' learning needs; if we can approach curriculum in such a way that we select and devise experiences and content that maintain and improve both the quantity and quality of intellectual and emotional life; and if we can turn the logic of teaching around so that teachers respond to students rather than insisting that students respond to teachers, then the next set of considerations we face will be organizational. Time, space, staff, materials, and resources must be so related that they give focus and power to the educational effort. That is what organization ought to be about. In a school for tomorrow the relationship of these factors would be very different from the relationship that exists in schools today.[23]

The two most conspicuous aspects of school organization today are the concept of logical equivalency and the notion of the group. The basic organizing constructs of the school presume that each teacher should work with a group, and that every teacher should get exactly the same amount of everything that every other teacher gets.

In a school organized to assure personalized instruction and individualized learning, professional personnel would be differentiated in both function and responsibility. In an elementary school, for example, there might be five master teachers, each having primary responsibility for the learning of 150 youngsters. These children would range in age from six to thirteen (all grade levels). Master teachers would be highly competent general practitioners of teaching, with doctorates and extensive training in all subject matter fields and experience with children of all ages. Their salary should be about two and one-half times the average teacher's salary. They would spend about 85 percent of their time with children in a one-to-one relationship and about 15 percent coordinating and supervising.

A typical eight-hour day (with no homework papers to correct or lesson plans to make, the school day would be extended) might be so arranged that four hours would be devoted to individual children on a twenty-minute, one-to-one basis, with children visiting the master teacher according to a planned schedule. One hour and a half might be devoted to supervisory and coordinating activities with the specialist in the school. Two hours and a half could be available for additional twenty- or thirty-minute sessions with individual children on an unscheduled basis.

By using themselves in highly focused ways with individual children, master teachers would first observe and then respond with specific suggestions and instructions. These would be based on their intimate interaction with, and knowledge of, each child. For example, they would observe student behavior in a clinical way (in a one-to-one setting, watching overt behaviors, studying particular test scores, listening to speech articulations, noting manifestations of anxiety, developing and studying case histories, watching muscular movements, etc.), and they would guide learning activities with students for subsequent specialized purposes (listening to a lecture, reading a book, participating in a discussion group for three days, building a model, visiting a given plant manager who employs a particular human relations technique with his staff, etc.). They would use dictaphones and other devices to maintain a continuous and comprehensive record of contact with each child, and these records would be available before and during each one-to-one interaction. Such teachers would not be givers of information, record keepers, scorers of tests, or graders of homework. They would be extremely sensitive and highly trained general practitioners of teaching with in-depth knowledge of the basic disciplines, and of learning, motivation, personality structure, measurement, and the fundamental learning skills.

Four groups of specialists would work under the five master teachers' direction and supervision. One group might include six persons especially competent in the areas of reading and the language arts. Two of these might be highly proficient in developmental reading and literature, two in diagnostic and remedial reading, and two in expressive communicative skills (writing, speaking, and spelling). Another group might include two persons trained in mathematics and the natural sciences, two in mathematics and the physical sciences, one registered nurse who might teach health and safety as well as serve as the school nurse, and one person trained in physical education. A third group might include eight persons with a particular competency in various areas of the creative arts and humanities. Two of these might have extensive training in music, two in art, and four in social studies and group processes. The fourth team of four persons might consist of one counseling or clinical evaluator, one psychometrician, and two instructional materials center specialists. These specialists should probably receive about the same salary as a fifth-year teacher.

The master teachers and the various specialists would require about ten secretaries (one to work for each of the master teachers, one for each of the four groups of specialists, and one for the principal) and about twenty homeroom managers who would provide continuity, a "homebase," and basic record cumulation files. Homeroom managers should be especially warm, accepting, and nurturing persons, but need not necessarily be trained beyond clerical level. These paraprofessionals should probably receive approximately half the salary of a regular teacher.

To have educators of three different levels of professional competency (i.e., master teachers, specialist teachers, and paraprofessionals) would mean that at any given time the 750 children might be dispersed this way among the various staff members: 5 children with the master teachers; 18 children with the reading and language art specialists; 12 with the math-science specialists; 8 children for a nurse-health educator; 20 with the physical educator; 40 with the music educators; 20 with the art educators; 40 with the social studies educators; 1 child with the counseling evaluator; 1 child with the psychometrist; 570 children with the homeroom managers; and 20 with the instructional materials specialists.

Evaluation

With the primary emphasis on growth rather than control, evaluation and assessment procedures will be different. In the conventional school, evaluative devices and approaches have been characterized by so-called objectivity. In the school of the future more attention will be given to so-called subjective approaches. This does not mean that objective tests and the like will not be employed. It does mean that the blind alleys that have been worked on by some persons in the measurement field will not be pursued further.

For example, any careful consideration of testing in American schools reveals that most of the evaluative devices currently used are based on the logic and assumptions of the army alpha test, which was developed more than half a century ago. The tests are pencil and paper, multiple choice, verbal, and timed. Most tests are relatively long and reflect a concern for statistical considerations rather than reality considerations. Much greater attention has been paid to reliability problems than to validity questions, even though validity is a far more crucial consideration.

In a school for tomorrow master teachers will use themselves as superbly human data processors, making clinical observations of youngsters and sorting out the nuances of individual variation with both subjective and objective approaches. In other words, they will cultivate their observational skills and spend their energies receiving and interpreting information from and about students before prescribing learning activities for each student individually.

Objective tests will be shorter, more valid, and exclusively diagnostic. They will enable teachers to identify specific achievements, motivations, learning difficulties, perceptual problems, and the like with pinpoint precision. Further, test scores will not be used either as instruments of restriction or threat, as they often are now, or as a basis for grouping students, since the fundamental organizing construct of the school will be the one-to-one relationship. Accumulations of achievement scores (e.g., the cumulative grade point average) would not reflect the logic of denial that is implicit in such operations today. The conventional marking and grading system, for instance, averages all marks together, thereby holding a student's lack of learning against him rather than against those who failed to teach him. Such assumptions would be changed.

Evaluation instruments and devices in a school for tomorrow would be shorter, mostly nonverbal and untimed, and not pencil and paper. The development of such procedures would be based upon a wedding of the clinical with the objective approach, and would open up an entirely new field of test development and research in the area of education and psychology.

Teacher Education

Having sketched an outline of a school for tomorrow, we come to the question: What would the teachers be like? It goes without saying that preservice education and inservice education for such a school would be very different from programs for the schools of today. Without doing full justice to all aspects of a completely reconceptualized approach to teacher education, let me attempt to sketch some of the characteristics of the new programs that would be possible if a school for tomorrow became a reality.

At the preservice level different kinds of preparation would be necessary for at least three different kinds of teachers: generalists, specialists, and homeroom supervisors. Because the training, responsibilities, salaries, and functions of these different types of teachers would vary so greatly, their preparation would have to vary, too.

The general practitioners of teaching, who would have primary responsibility for the education of a number of children with whom they would always relate on a one-to-one basis, should be superbly trained in all of the subject matter fields and for learners of all ages and abilities. This would require at least seven and perhaps eight years of formal education beyond high school, and such graduates would start teaching at a much higher starting salary and with much more responsibility than beginning teachers now have. Since not more than about 20 percent of a faculty would work at this master teacher level, a rigorous selection process should help both to stabilize the group in the profession and to assure its members of the elaborate professional preparation required to function at that level. That is, the extended period of training would discourage those persons who often enter the teaching field because they cannot find employment elsewhere or are merely waiting to get married or find a better job. Further, during the seven or more years spent in learning to be a master, a prospective teacher could acquire extensive experience with young people of all ages and with the totality of knowledge required, including child development, personality structure, motivation, cognitive styles, learning disabilities, intellectual processes, and the like. He should also have acquired a good grasp of several teaching fields, full understanding of the structure and intricacies of the disciplines and the interrelationships among fields of knowledge, and extensive training and experience in such areas as psychometrics, counseling, case studies, observation of individuals, and tutoring. What I am proposing is a doctoral level program (different in almost every way from the conventional doctorate in education) that would prepare a master teacher to be a superb general practitioner of teaching. As such, master teachers would be in charge of children's learning, and the specialists would work under their direct supervision and control.

Specialists would be more highly specialized than most persons with masters degrees are today. They would generally work with small groups of students in precise teaching-learning experiences as prescribed by the master teachers. They would probably work with children of all ages, but in a narrow, subject-matter field or process way; therefore their area of specialization would probably be about one full year's professional training in such things as word attack skills, psychometric testing, value analysis, number theory, speech correction, aesthetic appreciation, vocabulary development, constitutional history, and ethology.

The paraprofessional group would have much less formal training, and should be selected primarily on the basis of the kinds of people that they are: supportive, helpful, and patient.

During the time of their preparation, these teachers would all have experiences that would be primarily professional rather than academic. The intent of those responsible for their preparation should be to have these prospective teachers work hard (probably 40 or 50 hours a week in class) in laboratory and clinical situations with a minimum of term papers, lists of readings, theses, and other academic experiences. Living and working with real children and real ideas in intensive experiential situations should characterize the pre-service programs. By emphasizing professional rather than academic experiences, no downgrading of the quality of ideas or content is intended. What is intended is a deliberate emphasis on the use of knowledge as a vehicle to help children develop and grow. In other words, education is an applied field, and professional preparation should be designed to help the prospective teacher use his information and experiences to facilitate growth in other persons.

New concepts of teacher education would also be essential at the inservice education level. In general terms, a school for tomorrow would employ "Theory Y" instead of "Theory X" as a set of assumptions about motivation as it relates to teachers working to improve their professional performance.[24] In addition, a number of different assumptions about staff development would characterize the school of the future.

As schools and schoolmen presently function in their "war against ignorance," all of the troops are on the front line and none in reserve. Staff development in the school of today places about one teacher with every thirty children, but there are no extra resources in terms of staff, time, or materials to provide flexibility and resourcefulness in meeting the needs of children in their efforts to learn. And because every teacher is expected to work every day, week after week, with time out only for coffee and lunch, the opportunities for reflection and growth by the professional staff are minimized or eliminated entirely.

What is needed is a new concept of staff development in which a portion of the professional staff are purposely scheduled for a specified period of time for professional growth and development. Such a policy would increase class size slightly, but if 10 teachers in a 100-teacher school had eighteen days of inservice time to work together and plan and grow, who knows what powerful personalities and excited teachers might be interacting with youngsters day by day? The logistics of such an arrangement might vary greatly (five teachers could work together nine times during the year for two days at a time, or any other combination that seemed to make sense), but the basic principle of *scheduling* opportunities for staff development and professional growth is imperative. Further, rather than scheduling the entire school district or one building faculty for one day before school in the fall and another at mid-year, by using the concept of "professionals in reserve" it should be possible to arrange schedules so that hard-working teachers could escape from the fantastic demands of six hours of contact with classroom groups, five days a week. Small groups working together over extended periods as part of a staff development plan could undoubtedly cope with some of the very difficult problems of personal growth, materials collection and development, and meaningful visits to other institutions or experts for consultation and advice. Such a procedure would not cost any district any more money at all, but it would presume a deliberate scheduling of time for small groups of staff to learn and grow in their own varied professional ways.

Notes

1. Alvin Toffler, *Future Shock* (New York: Random House, 1970), p. 33.

2. Norman Cousins, "The Age of Acceleration," in *Issues 1968,* ed., William W. Boyer (Lawrence: University of Kansas Press, 1963), p. 3.

3. Charles E. Silberman, *Crisis in the Classroom* (New York: Random House, 1970), pp. 158-159.

4. Peter Drucker, *The Age of Discontinuity* (New York: Harper & Row, 1968), p. 347.

5. Ibid.

6. Silberman, *op. cit.*, p. 203.

7. John I. Goodlad and M. Frances Klein and Associates, *Behind the Classroom Door* (Worthington, Ohio: Charles A. Jones Publishing Co., 1970), p. 97.

8. Jack R. Frymier, *Fostering Educational Change* (Columbus, Ohio: Charles E. Merrill Publishing Co., 1969), chap. 2.

9. Ibid.

10. Clyde Kluckholm and Henry A. Murray, *Personality in Nature, Society and Culture* (New York: Alfred A. Knopf, 1948 and 1953), pp. 53-67.

11. Here and elsewhere throughout this paper I have drawn heavily on my own chapter, "Can Curriculum Meet the Needs of All Children?" in *Education for Tomorrow,* ed., Walter Lifton (New York: John Wiley & Sons, 1970).

12. Goodlad and Klein, *loc. cit.*

13. For example, see Daniel L. Stufflebeam, "Evaluation as Enlightenment for Decision Making," in *Improving Educational Assessment,* ed., Walcott H. Beatty (Washington, D.C.: Association for Supervision and Curriculum Development, 1969), pp. 41-73.

14. Frymier, *op. cit.*, app. A.

15. See Wilbur Schramm, "What We Know About Learning from Instructional Television," in *Educational Television, The Next Ten Years* (Stanford, Calif.: Institute for Communication Research), p. 54.

16. Ralph E. Tyler, *Basic Principles of Curriculum and Instruction* (Chicago: University of Chicago Press, 1950).

17. For example, Edwin G. Goldfield, ed., *Statistical Abstract of the United States,* 1961.

18. For example, Charles Reich, *The Greening of America* (New York: Random House, 1970).

19. Virgil Herrick, *Strategies for Curriculum Development* (Columbus, Ohio: Charles E. Merrill Publishing Co., 1965), chap. 1.

20. Jack R. Frymier, "Some Answers Must Be Questioned," in *The High School of the Future,* ed., William Alexander (Columbus, Oh o: Charles E. Merrill Publishing Co., 1970), chap. 2.

21. D. O. Hebb, *The Organization of Behavior* (New York: John Wiley & Sons, 1949).

22. D. E. Berlyne, *Conflict, Arousal, and Curiosity* (New York: McGraw-Hill Book Co., 1960).

23. Jack R. Frymier and Charles M. Galloway, "Personalized Teaching and Individualized Learning" in *Learning Centers: Children on Their Own,* eds., Virginia Rapport and Mary Parker (Washington, D.C., ACEI, 1970).

24. Douglas MacGregor, *The Human Side of Enterprise* (New York: McGraw-Hill Book Co., 1960).

2

Educational
Goals

What is important is that some sort of "new" school is needed. But can such a school be designed to foster the development of rationally autonomous individuals? Given the chance would we really choose such a goal?

Stanton M. Teal
Gerald M. Reagan

Introduction

In the opening chapter it was asserted that a school for tomorrow would differ from many schools of the past and present by placing greater emphasis on the individual as the center and goal of the educational enterprise. This seems appropriate, for many of us today are convinced that our schools have failed and are continuing to fail to meet individual needs, to recognize and honor diversity among students, and to develop in students a capacity and disposition for self-education. We hear demands that schools be humanized and/or that society be "deschooled." We have sympathy for many of these demands, for there is abundant evidence that schools frequently fail to achieve their professed goals, that large numbers of students are disenchanted with and alienated from educators and formal education, and that many students who are not disenchanted or alienated have nevertheless been misled and miseducated. In short, it is not surprising that the slogan of a "new humanism" for our schools has great appeal.

Some are likely to ask whether the "new humanism" or a vastly increased emphasis on the individual is in fact new or simply a new expression of a time-honored but seldom-achieved goal. We would tend to take the latter position, but this is perhaps unimportant. What is important is that some sort of "new" school is needed in which this goal is not only accepted but vigorously pursued. But to pursue a goal of schooling intelligently requires that we understand what the goal can and cannot sensibly mean. We must understand how it relates to other goals of schooling. We need to understand how the goal is and ought to be related to the procedures and practices of schooling. In brief, we need to agree about what we mean and what we do not mean when we state our goal. The pursuit of such agreement and understanding is our purpose here, and it is to this task that we now turn.

Educational Goals

Goals and Goal Statements in Education

Few writers in education would dare talk about reform of schools without some mention of the goals or aims they have for the schooling process. All that is to be done in schools, it is commonly asserted, is to be done with the goals of schooling in mind. Schooling is, or ought to be, the argument continues, a rational process directed at achieving some end. This argument makes sense to us: there are, it seems, sound reasons for thinking about, discussing, and stating goals. It also seems, however, that goal stating too often becomes either mere ritual or a process where highly emotional but unclear goals are set. Such goals are unlikely to lead to clarity and rational planning of the schooling process: rather, they are likely to mislead.

The phrases "educational goals" and "educational aims" are used frequently as if we all agreed on their meaning. This assumption of agreement does not seem warranted. There are several different sorts of "goal claims," and unless we know which sort we are discussing, we are quite likely to talk past one another. In this section, we wish to point out various things that may be intended when we talk about goals as aims of education.

General Goals as Pseudoagreements

We all recognize that in some cases we speak of general goals as aims of education that we can agree on when in fact we do not know whether accepting such goals would produce any other agreements about procedures or practices to be followed in the schools. That is, in some of our discussions of goals, the goals suggested are so general that, although everyone can accept them, there is little agreement about what we are committed to. For example, after considerable discussion and disagreement about rather specific goals, a school faculty might discover that they all agree that one of their goals should be the development of good democratic citizens. But what does this mean? Well, the phrase "good democratic citizen" clearly carries a highly positive evaluative meaning. To be in favor of good democratic citizens is like being for good government and responsible economic policy. We are all in favor of all three. But we still do not really know what someone else has in mind when he reports that he too favors good democratic citizens above any other kind. We simply do not know what the phrase means descriptively, in spite of its common use. In our imaginary school faculty it is quite possible that, although it is agreed that good citizenship is the goal, there is considerable disagreement about what such citizenship entails and what educational practices would be likely to produce it. It might be the case that among the faculty one teacher views the good demo-cratic citizen as one who never misses the weekly demonstrations on the local college campus while to another teacher the good demo-cratic citizen is one who never misses the weekly meeting of the local John Birch Society. To say that these two teachers share an educa-tional goal seems misleading.[1] What is shared is an emotional attach-ment to a word or phrase. What is *not* shared is agreement about what the word means or about the educational program suggested by the word. What seems to be agreement on goals turns out to be merely pseudoagreement.

Agreement on a highly emotional but descriptively unclear generality may be useful. It may give a group a feeling of shared purposes, togetherness, and so forth. It does not aid, however, in making clear what we wish to do and what we do not wish to do in our schools. To stop the goal-stating process with this sort of goal is to stop with pseudoagreement. "Goals" of this sort do not make clear what it is we are trying to do. Indeed such "goals" may serve to draw our attention away from important areas of disagreement.

In a project such as this it is tempting to attempt to garner support with goal statements that would generate pseudoagreement. We have at our disposal the currently popular glittering generalities: our goals might be humanizing schools and honoring individuals. If we were to assert these, and stop there, our goals would be of the same order as the social "goals" of good government and responsible economic policy. Now we do accept the goals of humanization and honoring individuals as some of the goals of school reform, but only when they are explained. In short, we hope to make clear what we will mean when we speak of our goals.

General Goals as Slogans

Some "goals" in educational writings might be better termed slogans. We do not here use the term *slogan* in any pejorative sense. We use it here as it is used in Israel Scheffler's *The Language of Education*. Scheffler speaks of slogans as "rallying symbols" for "parent doctrines" or "underlying theories." One of his examples is the slogan, "We teach children, not subjects." This slogan, according to Scheffler, was a rallying symbol for some of the doctrines of progressive education. The slogan was not intended to be a literal claim: it was intended to be a symbolic summary of some rather carefully thought-out reform doctrines. The slogan did not give rise to the doctrines; the doctrines gave rise to the slogans. So it is with some educational goal statements. They do not give rise to a particular set of educational procedures and practices but are a way of symbolically summarizing those practices.[2]

Slogan goals, it seems to us, need not present any problems as long as we recognize them for what they are. Indeed, they often seem to serve a useful purpose. They will probably be useful from time to time in the school for tomorrow project. When they are used, however, they are not to be seen as the reason that particular practices have been recommended, but rather as a way of summarizing practices that seem reasonable. In this particular chapter, we will attempt to refrain from using slogan goals. Our task here is not to come up with catchy or imaginative slogans to summarize doctrines, but rather to avoid slogans in examining proposed and possible goals that are intended in some way to guide rather than summarize educational procedures and practices.

Goals as Desired Results

A common sense way of talking about goals is that of seeing goals as desired or planned results. This seems a legitimate and important way to view goals of schooling. In this sense schooling practices and procedures are generally seen as means intended to produce the end of goal attainment. Goals in this sense range from quite specific to extremely general; we may speak of the goals of a particular lesson, a course, a particular subject matter, a school, or schooling in general. As we speak of goals as desired results in this chapter, we are speaking of goals well toward the general end of the continuum.

When we speak of general goals, it is extremely easy to move from the "desired results" usage to the "glittering generality" usage discussed above. This is true not because our goals are general but because they are not concrete. General goals are not *necessarily* abstract; nor are specific goals necessarily concrete. Concreteness and abstractness are distinct characteristics and are logically distinct from the notions of specificity and generality. A teacher who says that the goal of his lesson is to get students to "understand chapter 10" or to "learn seven new words" is being specific but not concrete. And the teacher who insists that students memorize and repeat all of the axioms of Euclidian geometry has a general but not an abstract aim.

How can we insure that our general goals are concrete? One answer to this question, we think, is to be clear about what is to be counted as evidence of goal attainment. Let us examine this in more detail.

What should be taken to count as evidence of attainment or partial attainment or progress toward attainment of some general educational goal? What should be taken as evidence that certain policies, practices, or procedures are or are not effective in leading to goal attainment? These are central questions, and they are difficult to answer when we look at some of our general goal statements, i.e., some goal statements are so general that it would be difficult to specify any particular evidence that would be useful in evaluating procedures intended to lead to the goal. What, for example, would be evidence of goal attainment when our goal is to develop good democratic citizens?

Even a less general goal statement may not be concrete enough to allow us to agree on what should count as evidence. Notice the following goal statement: "It is the goal of this school to develop law-abiding citizens." The notion of "law-abiding citizens" seems less general than that of "good citizens," but it remains difficult to say what should be taken as evidence. Will law-abiding behavior of students within the confines of the school do? Or until age 21? And does a person have to obey *every* law to be law-abiding? In short, the goal is stated in such a way that one cannot be sure what should count as evidence of attainment. The claim here is that what is meant by goal attainment must be made clear before evidence of goal attainment can be specified.

The foregoing assumes a distinction between the meaning of goal attainment and evidence of goal attainment. If we hold goal X for Johnny, what must be true of Johnny before we are willing to assert that he has in fact attained goal X? To answer this question would require a full explication of what we *mean* when we assert that someone has attained X. We should be clear about this, but we should also recognize that our evidence is often inadequate to support the full-blown assertion that Johnny has attained X. Thus, we must settle for less. Given the meaning of attainment of X, what sorts of things are we willing to treat as relevant evidence to give some support to the assertion that Johnny has attained X? Suppose that our goal is to have Johnny become (or remain) a law-abiding citizen. We observe that Johnny always obeys the local law prohibiting jaywalking. This is certainly not what we meant by our goal "law-abiding"—our claim is much more general—but the fact that Johnny does not jaywalk *is relevant evidence,* even though it is not conclusive. In many cases that is the best we can do.[3]

Basically, the point here is that general goals need to be made more concrete by specifying what the goal means and what sorts of evidence would count for or against its attainment. General goals are not useless; they are not hopelessly subjective; they need not mislead. They can be made concrete through examination and examples, and what is to count as evidence for or against their attainment can be specified. When general goals are explicated properly, they can "guide" educational practices in the sense that particular practices either do or do not produce the evidence that the goal has been or is being attained.

Goals as Principles of Procedure or Restrictions in Manner

We speak frequently of educational goals, not as desired results, but as principles to be followed or restrictions to be honored in our educational procedures *no matter what the desired results.* Some might call these "process" goals. Like desired results goals, these are important goals for educators to examine, discuss, and honor. They are quite as important as desired results goals, but they do not replace them. These process or restrictions-of-manner goals can also be either general or specific. For example, in the following passage from Scheffler's *Language of Education,* we find an argument that teaching itself involves a general restriction of manner.

But not every way of getting someone to behave according to some norm is teaching. Some such ways are purely informal and direct, operating largely by association and contact, as languages are normally learned. But not every formal and deliberate way is teaching, either. Behavior may be effectively brought into accord with norms through threats, hypnosis, bribery, drugs, lies, suggestion, and open force. Teaching may, to be sure, proceed by various methods, but some ways of getting people to do things are excluded from the standard range of the term "teaching." To teach, in the standard sense, is at some points at least to submit oneself to the understanding and independent judgment of the pupil, to his demand for reasons, to his sense of what constitutes an adequate explanation. To teach someone that such and such is the case is not merely to try to get him to believe it: deception, for example, is not a method or a mode of teaching. Teaching involves further that, if we try to get the student to believe that such and such is the case, we try also to get him to believe it for reasons that, within the limits of his capacity to grasp, are *our* reasons. Teaching, in this way, requires us to reveal our reasons to the student, and by so doing, to submit them to his evaluation and criticism.

Other restrictions of manner are quite important. For example, we want students to be treated in a humane manner, no matter what the desired results goal.

We sometimes confuse these procedural goals or restriction-of-manner goals with desired results goals. In some cases, we focus on one set of goals and ignore the other. In other cases we seem to regard only one of these sorts of goals as important. But clearly both sorts are crucial. To focus only on desired results would leave us open to many schooling practices and procedures that we ought to reject. We do not want students treated cruelly or in any demeaning fashion, no matter how effective cruel and demeaning practices may be in achieving some desired results.[4] An equally severe problem may result if we focus only on restrictions of manner. Although some may argue that schools should have only process goals, most of us believe that there should also be some educational results, some outcomes of schooling that increase the student's capacity to deal with his world. As principles of procedure, almost all of us would accept the notion of treating children humanely and fairly. But such treatment is not the desired result, but a restriction on us as we attempt to bring about the desired result. And that result is *educated* persons, not simply humanely treated persons.

Emphasis on the Individual: Ambiguous Tradition

In the history of educational thought, there is a long tradition of extolling the rights of individuals and of insisting that both the goals of schooling and the practices of schooling be concerned with the welfare of individuals. This does not mean, of course, that any society has succeeded in developing a system of schools in which these ideas have been realized. The gap between ideals or theory and educational practice is not unique to the twentieth century. The point here is that needed school reform may not demand or rest on new or novel goals of schooling, whether those goals be principles of procedure or desired results. An appeal for school reform may simply be an appeal to bring practice into line with long-standing and perhaps long-accepted goals.

Throughout our educational classics we find appeals and arguments regarding the importance of the individual in the educational process. Indeed, it would be unusual to find a major thinker in the history of Western educational thought who has not concerned himself with the problem of the individual. Certainly scholars such as Plato, Aristotle, Augustine, Comenius, Rousseau, Kant, Pestolozzi, Herbart, and Dewey have all paid attention to this problem, albeit they have arrived at a variety of different answers. Our point here is a very simple one: to see as a major question that of the role of the individual in the schooling process is in no way new or novel. It is rather a central question raised and discussed by most of our educational thinkers.

To say that most or all educational thinkers have agreed that the role of the individual in the educational process is a central question is not to say that they have agreed on the answer to the question. There is much disagreement about what it means to say that the individual is to be central in the educational process. To some it means that individual interests and needs are the source of educational goals. (This notion is discussed in detail later in this chapter.) To others it means that if there is a conflict between an individual and a group, the well-being of the individual is to take precedence unless other individuals are thereby harmed. To still others it means that there are certain individual rights that are not to be abridged under any circumstances. To some others it is a factual claim about how the young are most effectively and efficiently taught. In short, we have a long tradition of honoring the individual, at least in theory. But the content of that honoring varies widely, and simply to assert that we seek to honor the individual presents us with neither a clear principle of procedure nor a clear desired result. We have no single argument or tradition in this regard: we have many. Unless we specify more clearly what we mean by the goal of "honoring the individual," that goal is likely to be merely a slogan goal or a pseudoagreement goal.

Some might argue that although the traditional thinkers are not in agreement about the meaning of the assertion that the individual is at the center of the educational process, practicing educators are agreed. Practicing educators, it might be claimed, are on the "firing line" and know full well what this claim can and cannot sensibly mean. Whatever the initial appeal of this argument, it does not stand the test of examination. When we listen to ourselves and others talk of the importance of individuals in the schooling process, we find several distinct claims being made. Although not all claims about the importance of the individual can or will be discussed here, it does seem clear that at least the following assertions are common:

1. The assertion of efficacy. It is commonly claimed that the individual should be regarded as central because learning is most likely to occur when the educational process begins with the problems, needs, or interests of the individual. This is, of course, an empirical assertion, not a value claim as some seem to believe. Whether the assertion is true is to be determined by looking to the appropriate empirical evidence, not by an appeal to reason, common sense, or value argument.

2. The assertion of justice. Here the individual is held as central because justice demands it, because it is his right, etc. This is what we earlier called a principle of procedure or a restriction-of-manner goal. There is no necessary claim that this makes the educational process easier, more effective, or more efficient. Indeed, acceptance of this process goal may make the educational process more difficult, less effective, and less efficient in achieving other goals. In any case, this is a goal, a value principle, a claim that is not to be verified or disconfirmed on the basis of empirical evidence.

3. The assertion of the free individual as a goal. The preceding assertions have to do with the way individuals are to be treated during the educational process, no matter what the product or desired result. Here we have the claim that no matter what the procedures and practices—no matter how individuals are treated during the process—the goal is the free or autonomous individual. (Later in this chapter we shall try to spell out briefly what we mean by "the free and autonomous individual." Without some further

clarification, we again have what might be either a glittering generality or a slogan rather than a goal that might in some way guide the
schooling process.) This too is a value claim, not an empirical one.

Each of these three assertions about the importance of the
individual seems to us to be quite common. In many cases we
probably have in mind some combination of the three when we
speak of "taking the individual into account." We need not limit
ourselves to one of these assertions, but we do need to be clear about
which of the claims we are talking about. If we are not clear, we are
likely to talk past one another. If *we* assert that the individual is
central in the educational process, *you* may not know which of the
assertions we are accepting and which, if any, we are rejecting.[5]

Thus both traditional educational literature and current rhetoric
elevate the role of the individual in the educational process. Both the
rhetoric and the tradition are ambiguous. We reserve judgment on the
assertion of efficacy and accept both the assertion of justice and the
assertion of the autonomous individual as educational goals. We will
now attempt to go beyond glittering generality by making our meaning on these two goals somewhat more concrete.

Honoring the Individual: Defensible Goals

Principles of Procedure

There is a long and honorable tradition in theology, philosophy, political theory, and education that exhorts us to honor
every other individual in all our relationships. Reasons for this
prescription vary. Some assert that the prescription ought to be
followed because it is the will of god; others argue that the consequences of acting on such a principle work toward the well-being
of mankind. In short, many people agree with the principle even
though they may disagree in terms of justifying the principle. We
begin with this principle, recognizing that most will probably accept
it as a principle, even though many may disagree with any particular
justification we might offer.[6]

Let us rely on one of our major intellectual forebears for a
better statement of the principle. In *Metaphysics of Morals* Kant
speaks of the "second form of the categorical imperative." This
"imperative" is stated as follows: "Act so that you treat humanity,
whether in your own person or in that of another, always as an end

and never as a means only." If we accept this prescription, what does it suggest about goals of schooling? As educators we might accept as one of our goals working to help our society become one in which every man treats every other man as an end in himself rather than as a means to an end. This would, we think, be a noble undertaking. And although we might set up a school program with this as a goal, we would be unlikely to set up a school with the single goal of treating children as ends rather than as means. We want children to be treated as ends, but we also want them to treat others as ends long after their formal schooling has ended. In short, we can view Kant's prescription either as a principle of procedure for schools or as a desired result. As a principle of procedure it focuses our attention on how children are to be treated in schools. As a desired result, it focuses our attention on how we want every person to treat every other person, in school and out. To accept both is to accept two goals, not one. Of course we could accept the first without accepting the second; indeed, we could succeed in the first and fail in the second. Treating every child as an end in himself does not guarantee that he will come to treat others in the same way.

Let us put aside for the moment those goals that are desired results and focus on Kant's assertion as a principle of procedure. This principle, which we here accept, demands that one way of evaluating school practices and procedures is to ask whether they violate the principle. School practices and procedures may not violate this principle and yet be ineffective, i.e., this principle of procedure may be followed in school practices and yet those practices may not render the desired results. Treating children humanely does not guarantee that they will learn what we wish them to learn, or even what they wish to learn. Conversely, school practices may violate the principle of procedure and yet yield the desired results. Children may learn what we want them to learn even though we mistreat them. Principles of procedure, we hold, are necessary but not sufficient goals for a school or schooling. The same can be said for goals as desired results. Together, well-thought-out principles of procedure and desired results would be sufficient goals for schooling.

Desired Results

It is frequently asserted that a major goal of schooling is to help each individual become a free and autonomous person. One formulation of this ideal is outlined by Thomas F. Green as follows:

To imagine a man whose behavior is almost totally principled is to imagine one who has a divine-like clarity of self-knowledge and an equally penetrating insight into others. . . . he would be peculiarly at home with himself and with his world. He would be a free man.

Such a man is an ideal, of course . . . . The ideal of a man whose behavior is principled is very nearly, in fact, what the ancients meant by saying that man is a rational animal. They did not mean that men are never driven by their passions and desires. They were too familiar with the decline of Athens to believe such nonsense. They meant that men who are truly human are masters in their own house. They may hate and covet, but hate and covetousness do not rule them. This freedom and self-mastery is what we often mean by autonomy. Individuality, in its true sense, is more closely related to such autonomy than it is to nonconformity. Autonomy means "self-rule." It is, among other things, that state in which a man does *his own* thing.[7]

This goal or ideal focuses our attention not on restrictions of manner or principles of procedure, but on a desired result of schooling. How might we organize schools to make it more likely that "autonomous persons" develop? What school practices would contribute to this end, and what practices would make the development of such persons less likely? These are important and difficult questions. They are empirical questions, not ones to be answered by simply asserting that some practice is of value or by insisting that common sense will tell us that certain practices will or will not lead to this end.

We accept the notion of an autonomous person as an important and worthy goal for both the school and the wider society. (In the final section of this chapter we will attempt to explain further what we mean when we speak of the autonomous person.) We further suggest that school practices and procedures be evaluated in two ways: (1) Are the practices in accord with those principles that we accept as principles of procedure? (2) Do the practices adopted in fact lead toward the "autonomous person" result? To deal with the first question is primarily a logical matter. To deal with the second is an empirical problem. We would suggest that practices be viewed as hypotheses: particular practices are hypothesized to lead to a particular result. The desired result is the product of a value judgment. Whether given practices produce or help to produce that result is a matter of empirical fact.

In summary, we have suggested two goals. The first is a principle of procedure, the second a desired result. If these goals are accepted in a school, then (1) attempts would be made to operate the school in such a manner that every person would be treated as an end in himself and never as a means to another's end, and (2) school practices and procedures would be designed to help each student become an autonomous person.

We have not asserted that treating the child as an end in himself is the easiest or most efficient way of encouraging him to become the autonomous man. Whether such is the case is an empirical matter. We believe that the restriction in manner is based on the way the child ought to be treated, even if so treating him makes the desired result more difficult to achieve. School practices should be modified and tested to see how they do relate to the desired result, but the principle of procedure sets the boundaries within which any modifications may be made.

Our goals obviously need further explication and clarification. We have attempted to do this in the following sections, but the task is not an easy one. One approach we have taken is to ask what practices would be excluded if we accepted a certain goal. Let us now turn to that approach.

School Practices that Violate the Principle of Procedure

There are common and numerous practices in our schools that violate our principle of procedure, practices that in fact treat the child as a means to someone else's end. Extreme examples would be such things as punishing a child to set an example for a class or using children to entertain parents, teachers, or other students when so doing does not bring educational benefit to those who entertain. However common these extreme examples, they are also ones that are easily recognized and widely denounced. But many other practices, which are more subtle, are also excluded if we follow our principle of procedure. Some examples follow.

Many people concerned with contemporary problems of schooling have written about "bureaucratic goal displacement" in our schools. Goal displacement in schools occurs when noneducational goals are substituted for educational ones. Schools as organizations are means devised to pursue educational goals, i.e., schools are means intended to achieve the end of educating children. It is not unusual to find a reversal of means and ends: the education of children becomes the means to the end of maintaining and/or enhancing the organization of the school or the positions of those engaged in the education of children. When this occurs, it seems reasonable to assert that children are being treated as means rather than ends. For example, children may be required to take all sorts of national tests, give performances in the arts for the community, or follow some prescribed curriculum, not because these activities contribute to their education, but because they contribute to the enhancement of the school or those who operate the school.[8] Clearly, schools *can* be devised as a means to educate children. But just as clearly, schooling can, and sometimes does, become a means of enhancing schools, serving the purpose of educators, or pleasing parents or other community members.

A particular form of goal displacement in the classroom revolves around an insistence that rules be followed. Of course there are sensible and defensible school and classroom rules. Most classroom rules probably originate as attempts to regularize classroom procedures and to promote educational purposes. In short, rules are intended as means, as ways of maximizing the chances that any particular child will succeed in the school. Rules regarding classroom behavior may, for example, be intended to protect the rights of individuals. An instance of this would be a rule calling for relative quiet in a classroom when a teacher believes that quiet is necessary in order that no child is disadvantaged by inability to hear what his teacher or peers have to say. But whatever the reasons for rules, under the pressures of teaching it is easy for a teacher to forget that rules are intended as means and to assume that if students follow the rules the result will be what was *intended* by the rules. In short, it is easy for a teacher to insist that there be rule-following for its own sake. Even though following a rule may work an injustice in a particular case, the child is told that he must obey the rule because it is a rule. The teacher may answer the child's protests by saying "Others have followed the rule!" or "I didn't make the rules!" or "What would happen if everyone were to decide what rules to follow?" or "Just do as you are told!" Our argument is that if every child is to be viewed as an end, then rules should be seen as means only. If rule-following is insisted on for its own sake, we treat the child as a means rather than an end, and we violate our principle of procedure.

Goal displacement is a serious problem, but there are additional common violations of the imperative of treating every child as an end in himself. There are common demeaning and/or dehumanizing school and classroom practices that we all recognize and should attempt to avoid. For example, we all know there are teachers who attempt to "motivate" students through ridicule, fear, shame, or guilt. We also know of practices that afford to students none of the "due process" they would receive as a matter of course were they to be charged with a crime rather than sent to school. We recognize too that there are violations of the rights of privacy, freedom of thought and expression, and protection from the "tyranny of the majority." All such violations of the rights of students are instances of treating students as means rather than ends in themselves. Educators engaged in these violations defend themselves by asserting that the practices are necessary, or at least efficacious, in producing desired learning. Whether this is true, we hold, is beside the point. Our contention here is that such practices violate a principle of procedure and should be avoided.

Thus there are many practices in schooling which seem to violate our principle of procedure. Some of these may also make it less likely that we will achieve our desired results; others may not affect their achievement; and others may even be efficacious. In any case, the efficacy of an unjustifiable practice in producing desired results is irrelevant.

Sources of Goals

We wish to turn now to some more complex issues related both to procedures and desired results. These issues have to do with the "sources" of goals. It is commonly argued that we can arrive at and justify our goals by appeals to (1) individual differences, (2) individual needs, (3) individual interests, or (4) individual "growth." We will examine each of these appeals to see how they can help in our discussions of "individual goals" of schools.

Individuality of Students

When educators are exhorted to emphasize the individual—to make the individual their primary concern—it looks, at first glance, like a straightforward claim that once educators have adopted this value, they will know just what they should do. It looks very much like a proposed *aim* for schools and teachers, a statement that clearly prescribes what an educator should try to accomplish with his students. Yet if a teacher believes that this is a good prescription and begins to consider just what he might do in order to reach this aim, he is immediately beset with difficulties. If he had been told to emphasize "subject matter" or "social adjustment," he would probably have some sort of idea about what success would amount to. His job would be to take a student in a state of relative subject-matter deprivation or social barbarism and bring him to the point where he could be said to know the subject matter or get on well in social situations. Before a student even enters the classroom, a teacher can know what will count as evidence that a student knows when Columbus discovered America or the answer to a particular math problem. Similarly, the teacher has a good idea of the sorts of things that will count as evidence that a student has acquired certain social skills and dispositions, such as sharing, taking turns, and the like. It is not so clear just what would count as teaching success when the educator's primary purpose is to emphasize the individual or to preserve and foster individuality. There is apparently nothing in such a purpose that refers to standards "outside" the student by which to make judgments about the student's achievement. The standards of success in educating would, then, seem to lie entirely within the individual student. The teacher, in this situation, cannot know what will count as success in achieving his purposes before encountering specific individual students. Because the standards of success lie within each student, and because we know that students differ in many regards, it may be that success in educating will be unique for each student.

The problem for the educator who has decided that his aim is to foster individuality is not solved by his recognition that the standards of success in educating lie within each individual student. A teacher may very well have adopted this as a guiding principle, but then comes the actual encounter with some individual student. At this point it is up to the teacher to discover just what the student's internal standards of educational success are. If the teacher takes "knowing subject matter" as the aim, he can observe the student's achievements to date, noting what he knows and what knowledge he lacks. Then the teacher's job is to put the student in the way of experiences the teacher believes will help him learn at least some of the things that he does not already know. Similarly, if the teacher's purpose is to help the student acquire social skills and dispositions, he can observe him in various social situations, noting his skills and dispositions in terms of turn-taking, sharing, etc. Having noted those social skills the student lacks, the teacher can then involve him in situations calculated to help him develop the desired behaviors. But our teacher who aims primarily at promoting individuality is in a different sort of situation. What does he look for that will reveal where the student's educational development should lead? The answer to this question is not obvious, but several possibilities suggest themselves.

A great deal has been written about individuality in recent years. Much of the concern expressed in this writing has been centered around what the authors believe is a condition in today's world where individuality is seen as lacking. In its place, modern men are characterized as conformists, adopting modes of dress, housing, behaviors, beliefs, and values that are the same as the dress, housing, behaviors, beliefs, and values of people around them. They adopt these characteristics, not because each has critically determined that they are right, true, or somehow personally appropriate to themselves as individuals, but merely because "everyone else does it," or "everyone else believes it." Hence, when men wear wide ties and colored shirts and women wear midis or minis (or whatever the latest fashion indicates is "in"), these behaviors are seen as evidence of a failure of the individual to "be his own man." It is the "terrible sameness" of behavior and belief that is lamented. As an antidote to the sickness of conformity, it is thought that we should emphasize "difference." Individuals will, in this view, evidence their individuality by "daring to be different." The true individual will break away from the herd and take some independent action. Today's adolescents are often credited with at least having the courage to break away from old fashions and adult patterns in clothing and hairstyles, though it is often bemoaned that the styles they have adopted seem to reflect conformity to another group: their adolescent peers.

In this view individuality is equated with differentness or uniqueness as opposed to sameness. If this conception of individuality is applied as our educational aim of "promoting individuality," we see that the teacher's role is to emphasize, encourage, and bring out the "individual differences" in his students. Children are, after all, different, and a teacher who believes in promoting individuality will recognize these individual differences and seek to promote and develop them. He will not do things to make the various individual students in his charge the same as each other in spite of their differences, as various forms of "groupism" and "social adjustment" in education are seen as doing. Under the banner of promoting this sort of individuality, it is recommended that teachers ought to praise or respect what a student has done, because it is unmistakably his. Similarly, to challenge or criticize (however gently) a student's idea or his artistic production would be proscribed because the idea or product is *his,* and merely having that idea or producing that drawing is what constitutes his individuality. Obviously, the teacher must not take away a person's individuality.

On inspection this conception of individuality cannot stand up as the primary purpose of education. It fails when we realize that we have erected a conception of individuality that functions primarily to make discriminations about matters of fact into a value, a purpose to be achieved. Individuality as mere difference functions usefully when we are trying to discriminate one individual in a class from other members of that class. Hence, if we are trying to pick out the Buick from a group of cars, it will not help to be told that it is the one with wheels, since all of the members of that group share that characteristic. What is needed is to note some characteristic of the Buick that is not shared by the other members of the group, some characteristic that is uniquely the Buick's, such as "having 'portholes' in the fender." But it is important to recognize that, however useful our knowledge of this peculiar characteristic is in making the descriptive, factual distinction between Buicks and other cars, the factual difference does not by itself suggest that the difference is of value. It might be that the Buick's unique characteristic is that it has flat tires, and we would hardly take this to be a good thing for a car to have or for the Buick Motor Company to develop further in its cars. Similarly, in schooling we cannot automatically assume that unique characteristics of individual students are attributes that ought to be respected, encouraged, praised, and developed merely because they are the attributes of some student as an individual. Only the holder of an overly romanticized view of children would see them as possessed only of individual characteristics worthy of encouragement.

A further inadequacy of the conception of individuality as mere uniqueness or difference may be plainly seen if we project what would be accomplished if educators promoted it as a primary educational aim. To promote this sort of individuality in our students would be to aim for complete eccentricity. The valued product of our schools would be the person who was merely different, the more eccentric the better. Whether such a person could get anything right (e.g., speaking or writing English, solving math problems, understanding history, etc.) would not matter, or, at least, would be of secondary importance. The prime feature by which we would mark him as an "educated man" would be the extent to which he was different from other individuals. This individual would be merely a bundle of unique attributes: a kind of mixed bag of odd things.

We are arguing that there is no virtue in the mere fact of difference, but this does not mean that we do not recognize or are indifferent to the fact that individuals are different or that we believe differences are not important in the educational enterprise. We are simply pointing out that the mere factual differences between children do not, of themselves, furnish educators with tenable educational aims.[9]

Our first conception of a possible meaning for *individuality* came mainly from social critics: individuals who examine the social scene at large without limiting their concerns to the educational endeavor. Many such writers, however, function as critics of education and have, in the course of their criticism, found the schools to be lacking in their concern for the individual. Some of them suggest that schools should take promoting individuality as their primary purpose. Many of these writers avoid the "mere difference" conception of individuality and center their attention on more specific features of individuals. It has, for example, been regularly claimed that schools are too oriented to subject matter or place too much emphasis on fulfilling the needs of society. It is argued that these orientations ignore the needs, interests, and growth patterns of learners and that a proper reform of education would replace subject matter or social needs as primary purposes with attention to these neglected aspects of individual students. It is argued that if we will only concentrate our efforts in research, curriculum design, and teaching on such matters, we will have found the proper purpose of modern education. Since such things as student needs, interests, and growth patterns may be found to indicate different sorts of educational purposes, we will treat them separately in what follows.

Student Needs

Claims that the prime purpose of education is to meet pupils' needs occur everywhere. As noted above, current American school critics indicate that curricula and courses are often organized on the basis of subject-matter concerns, as seen by experts in the various disciplines. They argue, often with merit, that this is done in the absence of any knowledge of or concern for the needs of the learners who will "be exposed to" this subject matter. Teachers who are responsible for implementing this sort of curriculum adopt teaching devices calculated to get that subject matter "into" their students without much regard to the condition of any particular student. If children are eager, interested, and motivated and see the point of what they are required to learn, so much the better. The teacher should try to motivate children and explain to them the reasons for learning the subject matter. However, if the child remains uninterested or cannot see the point of his studies, it is still necessary that teacher and student work to get the prescribed subject matter into the mind of the student. In the end, such factors as the individual's interest, purposes, and experiential backgrounds are seen as things that make learning either easier or more difficult: as helps and hindrances in the job of teaching with the prime educational aim of getting knowledge into the student.

The model of education sketched above has been condemned by many critics on the grounds that it ignores the needs of individual children and has proven to be both individually and socially disastrous. Those who argue in this manner have concluded that we must abandon "subject matter" as our prime educational aim and focus our attention on meeting the needs of each individual child.

Those who advocate adoption of "meeting the needs of the individual child" as the ultimate aim of education often resort to a medical analogy to make their point. It is argued that great strides have been made in medicine because research and practice are so organized as to meet specific needs of patients. Research in biology, chemistry, physiology, and the like is organized around hypotheses that are generated with an eye to advancing knowledge in those disciplines with little attention to any immediate "payoff" in practical terms. Medical research hypotheses arise from and are directed to the solution of problems of patients. The needs of patients set the problems of the medical profession and define their successful solution. In the same way, the advancement of knowledge of the various disciplines serves as the source and standard for academic research. It is held that schools are failing to meet individual needs because they are organized to meet the requirements of academic research; hence the complaint that schools are "too academic."

When this analogy is applied directly to education, writers often urge schools to take as their primary aim "meeting the needs of individual students." Since psychology is seen as the "science of the individual," it is often to psychology that educational writers turn in their quest for this goal. The implication is that if one wants to know what children's needs are, then one should look to psychology. (In recent years, sociology and social psychology and anthropology have been vying for equal consideration as disciplines that have much to say about what the needs of our students are.) The assumption is that the needs of students may be determined through empirically based research. In short, the argument seems to be that if we can just accomplish sufficient research we will be able to find out what children need and thereby solve our age-old problems about the aims of education.

As attractive as this suggestion seems, however, there are compelling reasons that the appeal to empirical research for the discovery of individual needs cannot solve the problem of educational aims. The objections are primarily logical: that is, to think that we may determine the purposes of education by empirical research, by "needs-finding," is to misunderstand the logic of needs statements.[10]

Perhaps this may best be illustrated by returning to the medical analogy. If a doctor claims that a patient needs something (e.g., a balanced diet, a pill, or rest) he is apparently asserting a matter of fact. He is claiming that the patient currently lacks something (the treatment he needs), and that he would be likely to achieve or return to a condition of health if he got what he needed. There are two things to make explicit about the doctor's claim that his patient needs something. His claim asserts that (1) his patient is currently deficient in or lacks something, and (2) the patient's need is to remedy that deficiency. While these two points are clearly related, we will deal with them separately in order to explain some important points concerning the logic of needs claims.

The doctor's claim that his patient needs some treatment takes the general form, "X needs Y." Our first point about this claim was that "X needs Y" implies that X lacks Y. Hence, if we found that X already had gotten Y, we would withdraw the claim that X needed it. If the doctor has claimed, for example, that the patient needs vitamin C then finds out that the patient is already getting plenty of vitamin C, he will no longer say that the patient needs it. Similarly, in a school setting, if an advisor told a student that he needed to take algebra I, the advisor's claim is shown to be wrong when it is discovered that the student has already passed algebra I. Therefore, one criterion for the claim that "X needs Y" is that X lacks Y.

It would be a mistake, however, to assume that because someone lacks something, he thereby needs it. Students lack or are deficient in all sorts of things. If we found that a student lacked an expensive automobile, we would not on that account say that he needed one. Or, more drastically, if it was found that a student did not have cancer, we would not scurry around trying to find ways to infect him on the grounds that he needed it. Hence, we can say that although one criterion of "need" is that whatever is needed will be lacking, we cannot assume that whenever we discover a lack, we have discovered a need. Some lacks are needs while others are not.

This leads to our second point about the doctor's claim that his patient needs something, i.e., that the patient's need is to remedy the deficiency. Patients, when they are told that they need something (especially when what they need is uncomfortable, bothersome, or expensive), ask the doctor to explain why they need what the doctor has prescribed. In effect, they are raising a question that is appropriately asked of any claim that something is needed. That is, whenever it is claimed that "X needs Y" it is always relevant to ask what Y is needed *for*. If our doctor cannot furnish an answer to this question, that is, if the answer to the question "what is Y needed for" is "nothing," then he has failed to show that Y is needed. If our doctor has indicated that X needs to have his gall bladder removed, and then answers the patient's query concerning the purpose of such an operation with, "Oh, no purpose will be served. You just need it," then the patient may rightly conclude that he is dealing with a medicine man rather than a man of medicine.

Similarly, in a school setting, it might be claimed that a student needs phonics instruction. We (or the student) might very well ask what he needs it for. If we found that phonics would serve no purpose then we would deny that the student needed phonics. However, the claim that the student needs phonics could be supported by showing that phonics instruction would help the student learn to read. Such an answer would be acceptable, since we commonly agree that learning to read is something that would be worthwhile for the student, just as patients are likely to agree that they need treatments that will help them achieve better health.

But now we are in a position to see that we cannot bypass a

discussion of educational aims merely by conducting empirical research, that is, by observing children carefully enough to locate their
needs. The reason is that children's needs are not just "out there,"
things that can be discovered if only we will focus our attention and
energies and apply sufficiently rigorous and appropriate research.
Needs are always related to some future state of affairs that has been
deemed worthwhile. They are always needed *for* something. We
noted earlier that while needs are lacks or deficiencies, all lacks are
not needs. In order for a lack to qualify as a need, it must be shown
that giving the person what he lacks will lead to some worthwhile
purpose. Now it is clear that when we claim that "X needs Y," the
status of Y as a need depends on its being necessary for fulfilling
some purpose. Hence, we do not find purposes by merely finding
needs; we find needs only in relation to already established purposes.

Of course, this analysis should not be taken to suggest that
empirical research is irrelevant or unimportant. If we have an accepted purpose, it is surely an empirical problem to find out what
things are necessary for its achievement. When such things are found,
they will be things that students need. However, it is just as clearly a
logical mistake, the naturalistic fallacy, to suppose that we can find
our purposes by conducting empirical research on needs or anything
else. To mark something out as a need is already to have a purpose.

Thus the medical analogy is misleading when it is applied to
educational concerns. Doctors can prescribe things for patients, i.e.,
indicate that they are needed, with little dispute, because there is
great agreement about the purposes of their treatment. But there is
no such agreement about the purposes of education. Patients and
doctors are pretty well agreed on what will count as a cure. Given
this agreement on the purposes to be achieved, medical researchers
can focus their attention on finding ways to reach those purposes,
and doctors can indicate what patients need in order to reach their
common objectives. But when the analogy is shifted to schooling,
there seems to be widespread, fundamental disagreement over what
will count as "curing" our students; i.e., educating them. In this
condition, talk of meeting the needs of our students is quite empty.
Although we all agree (even the most traditional academician) that
we should meet our students' needs, that agreement is trivial because
it claims that educators should do what they ought to do. What we
ought to do is achieve our purposes, but we do not agree about what
those purposes are.

Student Interests

It was noted earlier that school critics argue that schools have ignored students' interests and that if we are to take "promoting individuality" as our prime educational aim, we must bring these student interests back into the educational picture. That is, instead of making educational decisions on the basis of the demands of subject matter or of society, we should promote individuality by promoting the interests of individual students. At the outset, however, we must recognize that the notion of "student interest" is ambiguous. In order to keep our thinking straight in this matter, it is imperative that we sort out the uses of the term.

We commonly say of a student that it would promote his interests if we could just get him to learn so-and-so. Hence, it would be in Johnny's interest if he could learn to read, calculate, and the like. In fact, it seems that whenever we make decisions about what children should learn or what activities we should have them engage in, we are always trying to select activities that will be *in the child's interest*. In this sense, "in his interests" is used to signify what would be good for the individual. If we decided that Johnny's learning to read would not be good for him, we would withdraw the claim that his learning to read was in his interest.

It should be clear, however, that if we take this as our educational aim, we have not advanced our search for values that will help direct our educational endeavors. It is a conceptual truth that educating someone always involves promoting what is good for him. Hence, it is a mere tautology to go on and suggest that the prime aim of education is to promote his interests (in this sense). Put somewhat differently, it is true that educators should promote the individual student's interests, but it is true merely because promoting the things that are in a student's interests are part of what we mean when we say that we are educating him. If we found a student who had had various experiences in school, and we agreed that none of those experiences were good for him, then we would not say that he had been educated by his school experiences. Hence, it is inconceivable that someone would recommend a curriculum for adoption in our schools and at the same time assert that this curriculum would not promote children's interests, in the sense that it would not do anything that was good for them. While it is agreed that education should promote the child's interests, this agreement disappears when we propose specific sorts of schooling that will do this. These disagreements cannot be settled by appeal to what is in the student's interests because this use of "interest" leaves the problem of aims untouched.

It should also be noted that a student may be quite bored with what is in his interest. That is, he may (and this illustrates the ambiguity) lack *interest in* things that are *in his interest*. Hence, while we may agree that it would be in Johnny's interest to learn to read, Johnny may be quite uninterested in reading.

If promoting interest in the sense of doing things that are good for students is not helpful in our search for educational aims, it might be argued that we should take our aims from things in which students are interested. But here, too, we must be careful. When we say that "X is interested in Y," we may be pointing out that X is currently showing or feeling an interest in Y. Hence, we might note that X was so interested in the lecture that he did not notice that the period had ended. Here we are indicating that X is "paying attention" in a certain way.[11] However, it is also possible to say that "X is interested in Y" without implying that X is currently showing or feeling that interest. For example, we might note that X is interested in practical politics, but is currently too busy even to think about it. It is this type of "interest" that is commonly sought on applications where the applicant is asked to list his interests. The prospective employer is not asking the applicant to list the things that promote his good or that currently engage his attention. He is asking the applicant to list activities that often absorb him: his hobbies and pastimes. This use, then, refers to the sort of disposition that X has. A teacher might say of a student that "his interest is Y" without in any way suggesting that the student is currently attending to Y. The teacher is indicating that the student has an inclination to engage in Y and does so whenever an appropriate occasion arises.

We have now distinguished two senses in which we can say that "X is interested in Y": (1) when we are asserting that X is currently attracted to and is paying attention to Y, and (2) when we are saying that X has a disposition or inclination to give attention to Y, whether or not he is currently doing so. If it is asserted that educators ought to aim at promoting what students are interested in, it will be of importance to get at just which of these senses is intended. In situation (1) the teacher would note each thing that every student happened to be interested in at each moment and attempt to promote that, while in (2) the teacher would mark out things to which each student has a rather settled tendency to give attention and seek to promote them. Having now drawn attention to these two senses in which someone can be said to be interested in something, our discussion will focus on both senses simultaneously, since our further analysis will apply equally well to either. We will follow White's conceptualization: "To feel interested in anything is to feel attracted to it, to feel inclined to give attention to it. Naturally, this also involves feeling disinclined to attend to other things . . . ."[12]

At the outset we saw that the school's job was to promote the interests of individual students, but that this was not helpful in our search for aims since it completely ignores the problem of finding criteria for those interests. But it can be argued that the students' well-being might be promoted if we would promote what students are interested in. The point of such an argument is that rather than having educators decide for the student what will be in his interest, we should assume that whatever the student is interested in will promote his interests. There is much that is initially attractive in such a proposal. It seems to be a way out of the problem of student boredom with what they do in school, and it relieves the teacher of the responsibility for trying to decide what is in any student's interests and motivating him to be interested in those things. Surely the educator's burden would be lightened if such a proposal were to be adopted.

Before adopting such a view, however, it would be well to take a second look. It may be that our seemingly perennial frustrations, which are apparently overcome by this proposal, are leading us to jump too hastily to its side. First, it seems clear that students often are not interested in things that are manifestly in their interests. For example, a child may be so interested in games that he is not interested in learning to read or an adolescent may be so interested in playing sex games that he is not interested in learning science. It also seems obvious that students are often interested in things that are not in their interests, such as crime, pornography, and torturing animals or other students. The educator's task is to make the important interesting, not simply to make the interesting important. Such realizations point to the question of why existing interests should be considered as valuable. To assume that they are is to commit the naturalistic fallacy of assuming that because something is, it is worthwhile.[13]

The proposal that educators should promote only existing interests implies that the teacher has no responsibility for directing interests or trying to form new interests. This view ignores the fact that interests are socially acquired and that if the teacher abdicates responsibility here and individual interests are taken to be educational aims, interest-forming is left to other mind-forming agencies of society. There seems little reason to opt for a position that accords advertisers, peer groups, governments, and the like, the right to influence interests but suggests that teachers are treading on forbidden ground when they enter this domain. There is surely something odd in suggesting that it is proper for those in the marketplace to interest students in buying the objects of the latest fad but improper for educators to attempt to interest students in critically analyzing the claims of the admen. The effect of such a suggestion is to leave the determination of educational aims (student interests) up to everyone but educators!

Of course, we could arbitrarily define education as "promoting existing student interests." This move, however, would be attempting to settle the serious value problems of education by definition, when what is needed is serious sustained analysis and reasoned argument. Such a tactic would accomplish little, because the definition has few adherents and because it ignores the very real value-problems in education.

Since education involves promoting what is in the students' interests, educators must discriminate between interests that have educational relevance and those that do not. This judgment will be made on the basis of educational aims. Consequently, existing interests *per se* cannot be aims. The schools' problem is often to interest students in things they are not now interested in, that is, to stimulate new interests. For example, it is often thought that the schools have a responsibility to help students develop "concern for others," "ability to sustain interest," and "care for clarity," and even to stimulate interests in subjects of which the students currently are not aware.

In accomplishing educational aims, current student interests are surely important. Current interests may function as a way of "getting into" subjects, or as a psychological condition of student motivation. For example, a student may currently be interested in some noneducational activity (such as learning how to buy and pay for things.) His interest in that activity may lead him to engage in learning to count, calculate, and the like, and that, in turn, may lead to an interest in mathematics itself without the further support of the original interest. Perhaps a student's educational interest in something may lead him to other educational interests. In either case, the educator's concern with what the student is interested in has to do with methods and motivation rather than aims. The problem of aims still remains. Educators must continue to decide which existing student interests should be stimulated and encouraged, which new interests should be introduced, and which educational attainments should be harnessed to existing interests.

Student Growth

If student needs and interests fail to provide us with the aims for education, it is often suggested that if we will but aim at promoting individual student growth, we will at last have found a viable educational aim that can give meaning to our belief in promoting individuality.

If it is true that our schools have too often made decisions about what to teach, as well as how and when to teach it, on the basis of what various subjects seem logically to require or on the basis of the requirements of society, then taking the promotion of individual growth as our educational aim seems to be just the antidote we have been seeking to cure those educational ills. The image of the schools as basing decisions on "external" concerns (the disciplines or the needs of society) is commonly characterized by metaphors that ignore the individual student and his individual characteristics that might influence the course of his schooling. Prominent among such metaphors are those of "shaping" and "molding." The home of such metaphors is in the work of the artist who shapes or molds his medium to his preconceived design. The medium, such as clay, is seen as quite malleable, and its final shape depends almost entirely on the artist's plan and skill in executing his design.

The school analogy suggested by these metaphors is obvious. Without going into great detail, we will make explicit the important features of education to which the analogy calls attention. The first thing to notice is the importance of determining clear, well-formulated aims. To *mold* something after the fashion of the artist is commonly seen as acting to bring unformed material to fit a preconceived design. Teachers cannot, on this view, merely muddle around aimlessly with their material. Rather, they must know clearly what they want to make of their students. Once the aims are determined, educators will be able to determine what subjects and activities they should present to their students in order to reach their aims. Arguments about which subjects or methods are best are essentially fruitless until one knows what the subjects and methods are supposed to achieve.

It is also important to note that the artist's aim or plan does not come from the clay with which he works. Such aims are formulated according to the criteria of artistic excellence without regard to the nature of individual lumps of clay. The artist will wish to mold his clay so that the final product of his efforts will be judged as good according to those standards of esthetic excellence. Similarly, the criteria of the educators' aims lie in the standards of excellence of education, not within individual students.

The shaping and molding metaphors also emphasize the indispensable importance of the teacher's role. After all, it is teaching (the actions of the teacher) that brings about the desired result (the educated person). Conversely, the child is seen as basically plastic and passive in deciding what, when, and how things will be learned. His role is to accept the teacher's prescriptions and handling just as the clay "accepts" the artist's design and handling. Just as the artist brings about the desired result by controlling his medium in particular ways, the teacher brings about the educated person primarily as a result of the exercise of proper, skillful control of students.

As a corollary, the prime responsibility for success or failure in educating lies with the educator. In the artistic realm, we seldom praise or blame the clay for the final form it takes; rather, while we do engage in the evaluation of the product, the artist is held accountable for its final form. Of course, it is recognized that some of the individual materials with which the artist or educator may have to work could be sufficiently defective to defeat even the best efforts of the most skillful.

To aim at promoting the growth of individual students is to oppose the image of schooling suggested by the shaping and molding metaphors. The emphasis on individual growth points to just those places where the analogies suggested by those metaphors are weak or break down. Let us proceed directly to an analysis of the concept of growth. By noting how the term *growth* is used in educational contexts and by comparing it with the educational analogies suggested by the shaping and molding metaphors, we will be able to see just what is involved in taking growth as our educational aim.

The natural home of the concept of growth is in the physical development of organisms. This is illustrated by the fact that the "gardening" analogy is so often used in the context of educational discussions of growth. We will use this same gardening analogy to help unravel some of the various strands involved in the growth ideal.

In the gardening analogy, school children are likened to the seeds and plants in a garden (the school), growing to their full flower under the care of an attentive gardener (the teacher). As Scheffler describes it:

> There is an obvious analogy between the growing child and the growing plant, between the gardener and the teacher. In both cases, the developing organism goes through phases that are relatively independent of the efforts of gardener or teacher. In both cases, however, the development may be helped or hindered by these efforts. For both, the work of caring for such development would seem to depend on knowledge of the laws regulating the succession of phases. In neither case is the gardener or the teacher indispensable to the development of the organism and, after they leave, the organism continues to mature. They are both concerned to help the organism flourish, to care for its welfare by providing optimum conditions for the operation of the laws of nature. The growth metaphor in itself thus embodies a modest conception of the teacher's role, which is to study and then indirectly to help the development of the child, rather than to shape him to some preconceived form. . . .[14]

The first point of contrast between the molding and growth metaphors is that while the clay will become any form whatever in the hands of a skillful artist, the gardener *cannot* take a plant or seed and make it into whatever he chooses. The tomato seed will become a tomato plant, no matter what other plans the gardener has or how skillful he is in his attempts to make it into something else. While this point may be made in various ways, it is clear that the seed contains within itself an "essential nature" or "potentiality" that cannot be changed by a gardener's actions. The gardener's first job is to discover the essential nature of each of his seeds, i.e., what potentiality it has. Similarly, the teacher-gardener must study the individual children with whom he works to discover their inborn potentials or essential natures. Not every seed has the potential to become the same kind of plant, and not every child will have the potential to develop into the same thing. For example, some children have among their "potentials" the potential to become scientists or mathematicians. Others may lack this potential but have other potentials that are lacking in the prospective mathematician or scientist, e.g., the manual dexterity needed to become a surgeon or cabinetmaker. In short, some children are "naturally good" with their minds while others are similarly good with their hands. Others are "born" artists, while still others have inborn potentials for working with people and may be born leaders or teachers. Emphasizing these differences, we may see the aims of education as lying within each student. The educator's role is to assist the development of individual potentials, to help the student actualize his potentials. Instead of attempting to determine educational aims without regard to individual students, he will study each student carefully in order to discover his potentials.

The second point of contrast between these two powerful metaphors is that any changes in the clay are due entirely to the artist's actions, but the transformations in a plant proceed, in a measure, independently of the attention of the gardener. Plants may grow without the help of any gardener at all. The image of the child in these two analogies is quite different. On the one hand, there is the plastic, passive child who "develops" according to the way he is controlled by adults. On the other hand, we have the image of a child who develops primarily on his own toward an end inherent in his own makeup. The actions of teachers may only thwart or help in this development.

The child grows on his own, and this growth occurs in rather definite stages. Just as the gardener must understand the stages of development his plants go through so that he may know when to take appropriate measures to help them reach their full potentials, the teacher must understand the laws of child growth. We know, for example, that it is fruitless to try to teach a child to walk before certain physiological developments have occurred. Therefore, the teacher must possess a sufficiently detailed knowledge of the laws of growth to know when the necessary developmental conditions have occurred in individual children to ensure that his assistance will be rendered at the point when each child is ready for it.[15]

As we have noted, the strength of the growth metaphor lies in the fact that it counters what are obvious points of breakdown in the molding metaphor. We recognize that individual students are not like clay in several respects. Clay is wholly dependent on the artist's actions for whatever transformations it goes through, but children *do* change independently of adult actions. Jokes about putting bricks on a child's head to keep him from growing out of his clothes are just that—jokes. Similarly, children are not completely malleable or capable of fitting into any mold. Put somewhat differently, children are capable of selecting and rejecting various molds that educators might attempt to fit them into. Consequently, teachers cannot mold children to preestablished forms after the fashion of the artist. Similarly, some of the changes that we observe in children do seem to occur in regular, predictable ways. Further, while the molding metaphor generally ignores the differences between children, the growth metaphor emphasizes their differences. In fact, those differences figure importantly in the determination of aims, since, as we have noted, growth-aims are seen in terms of developing individual potentials.

Not only does the molding metaphor break down in the above ways, but the image of schooling it projects is often subject to moral objections. The main point of such objections may be clarified by noting that the artist may squeeze or pound on his clay or do whatever he deems necessary to bring his clay to the appropriate form without any moral qualms. When such a model is shifted from a person's dealings with inanimate materials to a teacher's relations with students, it suggests a thoroughgoing authoritarianism. Hence, if such actions as pounding and squeezing were taken by a teacher in order to bring his students to some desired state, we would likely arise in moral indignation. After all, educating is subject to ethical restrictions of manner that are ignored by the molding and shaping metaphors. The recommended emphasis on promoting individual growth counters this neglect by specific implications concerning the role of educators in relation to individual students. Instead of imposing preestablished aims on students, the teacher must derive aims from individual students' natures. Instead of acting as an all-powerful molder of students, the educator is characterized as a helper.

It should be clear at this point why the promotion of individual growth will be an attractive and powerful idea in a society that professes democratic forms and values and takes note of the actual "facts of child development." Since we seem to have established a case for growth-aims as a likely candidate for giving specific meaning to the proposed educational aim of promoting individuality, it would be well to turn an analytical eye to "growth." In this way we may be able to see if the concept of growth is capable of furnishing sufficient direction for the educational enterprise. Our analysis will proceed by returning to the specific features of the growth metaphor that we noted earlier and by attempting to see more precisely what they involve in educational terms.

The first feature of growth we noted was that children are held to have individual potentialities or essential natures after the fashion of seeds. That is, whatever a human infant will become is already present as "pure potentiality" in his nature. The educator must study each child carefully to discover his individual potentials in the same way that the gardener must determine what his seedlings potentially are. This study is necessary because the gardener—and analogously the teacher—cannot treat all seeds and plants in the same way if he hopes to bring each of them to full maturity.

However, it must be clear that something happens to our analogy when we shift from the arena of biology to that of child development. Just as children are not completely malleable like clay, neither are they like acorns, which will develop into oak trees in spite of human interference. While the growth metaphor is useful for purposes of calling attention to the fact of individual variability in contexts where educators and other adults are ignoring it almost completely, it seems to err in other important ways. That is, it attributes too little to the power of social influence. For example, without denying completely the possibility of genetic factors having something to do with intelligence, it does seem clear now that social factors play a much more important role. We now believe that physical and human environments are the crucial determinants in the development of human abilities and dispositions. It seems that the best we can safely say at this point is that a human child is potentially a human adult. That is, we can safely say that they will not turn into alligators, chickens, or chimps. But discovering this sort of potential does not solve our aims problems; rather, it sets the problems. It is, of course, one feature of the human condition that the range of human adult types a child may grow to be is large indeed. And within that range lie many types that are not worth encouraging because they seem intrinsically evil or conflict with other types that seem worthwhile. Individuals are potentially warlike or peaceful, killers or priests, admen or educators, creators or destroyers of beauty. The potentialities of human children may be turned to good or ill. Surely educational aims should pick out potentials worthy of development, and for this reason we cannot aim at developing *all* potentials.

The previous argument has been based on potentialities as

judged from their outcomes, from what we know individuals can turn into because humans have turned into such things in the past. But it might be argued that some individuals have turned into monstrosities because of the inappropriate treatments we have given them. Hence, just as an acorn may develop into a deformed oak tree if it is handled in a way that violates what its nature requires, a child may develop into a "deformed" adult because we have not accorded him the treatment that his nature requires. This is just the sort of view expressed by Rousseau in *Emile*. In this view, children are naturally good, and it is the upbringing by the society, including teachers, that produces bad men. Various growth theories differ on what sort of treatment children require. They range from an essentially "hands-off" policy to one where the teacher is seen as a more active facilitator of whatever growth patterns the child exhibits. In either case, however, each child is seen as having an essential nature or real self that is good and that "unfolds" according to the laws of growth. Children will, it is believed, turn out well if adults will stop imposing their values, beliefs, and behaviors on them and, instead, allow or help them to grow naturally.[16]

Again, however, we may see that this view neglects the importance of the social in child development. If we could somehow omit all social influences from the individual we would not be left with a naturally noble individual. Rather, we would have an individual with formless fears, impulses, and desires. The "noble savage" turns out to be just a savage.

We might also examine this idea from the perspective of the teacher who assumes that each child has an essentially good nature containing potentialities to be developed. This teacher faces the problem of determining what that nature *is* in order to help it unfold. What will our teacher look for? What are the clues of natural potential for something?[17] Possibly the teacher should look to existing interests or desires. In our analysis of "interests" as aims, however, we have already seen compelling reasons why this way of guiding educational practice is inadequate. A further problem arises if we take existing interests as indicators of innate potentials or essential natures. It seems obvious that the interests children exhibit are, at least in large measure, the results of previous social experience. If the teacher is to make valid inferences about a child's true self or natural potential, he must be in a position to sort out the results of previous social conditioning and experience from the displays of the student's true nature. But this seems quite impossible. For example, if a child exhibits an interest in reading, how is the teacher to know whether the child has an inherent potential for reading or whether he is merely interested in reading because his parents read, because an older sibling has received familial recognition for his reading achievements, or because his peers are all reading and he wants to be "in" with them? On its face, this looks like a silly sort of thing to worry about. Since they consider reading to be a worthwhile thing to be interested in, most teachers are just quite thankful for the fact that the child has the interest and ability, and they go ahead and capitalize on it in their instruction. But if we are operating within the doctrine that teachers should assist in the development of the child's true self or essential nature, then a teacher cannot be satisfied with the mere display of an interest. He must also determine if that interest "comes from" the child's true self. It would be a violation of this educational doctrine to promote the child's interest in reading if that interest was not an outgrowth of the child's nature but an interest brought about by social conditioning. For example, modern advertising methods have succeeded in giving adults and children a wide range of interests, from owning a particular doll to smelling nice by using various perfumes and deodorants. But it seems difficult to argue that these interests are connected in any meaningful way with anyone's essential nature. Yet knowing just which interests are and which are not developments coming from an individual's essential nature is just what is required by this doctrine. Since we lack a way of making such discriminations, the "essential nature" criterion places the teacher in an impossible position.

Another feature of the growth idea was seen to be that some changes observed in children occur quite independently of adult actions. Further, it was noted that these changes seem to occur in definite stages or phases analogous to the development of plants from seeds to mature adult members of their species. The analogy seems quite appropriate when we are considering the biological maturation of children. It would be a mistake for an adult to expect mastery of any act by a child in whom the prerequisite muscular development had not occurred. But the import of knowledge of such maturational stages for teaching seems to be essentially negative. It will tell us what *cannot* be done rather than what *should* be done. Once a certain level of maturation has occurred, we are still left with the problem of determining just what acts to teach. Just because a child has the physical ability to perform an act does not authorize our teaching him to do it for the simple reason that not all things of which individuals are capable are worthwhile. Hence, while knowledge of the stages of maturation may be quite helpful in devising procedures and sequences of instruction for individual children (especially in early childhood education), such knowledge does not advance our quest for educational aims.

The observation of stages in the growth of individuals has not been limited to the level of biological maturation. Under the influence of the biological metaphor, there have developed various influential theories of human growth indicating stages of social, emotional, cognitive, and more recently, moral development. It seems clear that many of these theories are mixtures of empirical findings and "advice." Rather than scientifically examining and explaining changes found in children in different cultures and social groups, these theories *assume* certain social ideologies and present evidence and guidance in the task of bringing children to some chosen ideal of maturity. Theories of child development of this sort are, therefore, *technologies* for achieving ends that are assumed but seldom argued or justified.

R. F. Dearden puts the problem most succinctly:

Whether we do or do not agree with the chosen ideal which is the central organizing principle, however, it is clear that a "science" of child development which goes beyond cultural anthropology, and therefore cultural relativity, ceases simply to be science and becomes a sustained attempt at ethical persuasion, rich in favoured recommendations. One result of this is a chronic unclarity as to the *grounds* on which this or that is being argued. Another result is that the recipients of the advice are never quite sure whether what is required of them is attention to the latest findings of empirical research, or some kind of personal ideological conversion. The truth, of course, is that both are required.[18]

We do not mean to argue that all "growth" theories are subject to such objections. Maslow, for example, clearly recognizes the ethic built into his theory of self-actualization though the ethic remains vague and unjustified.[19]

Piaget and Kohlberg explicitly attempt justification of the ethics embedded in their theories of intellectual and moral development.[20] While it would certainly be appropriate to our task here, an adequate analysis would surely constitute at least a chapter, if not a book, on its own. We hope it will be sufficient to remind the reader of the sorts of fundamental philosophical questions that should be asked of such theories:

1. Do they commit the naturalistic fallacy of trying to infer judgments of value from empirical claims?

2. Are their justifications of the value hierarchy implied in their stages adequate?

3. Are their recommended "treatments" or procedures justified?[21]

In the preceding pages we have critically analyzed the ideas of individual "needs," "interests," and "growth" as sources of educational goals. Although we have been quite critical of many assertions commonly made about these ideas, it has not been our intent to suggest that these concepts have no use in educational theory. Our purpose was to see if such concepts might furnish us with content for the aim of promoting individuality. While the analysis has found each of these concepts to be lacking in this regard, it would be a mistake to conclude that they have no place in educational thought and practice. Rather, in pointing out that needs, interests, and growth cannot mark out educational aims, we hope to indicate what sorts of conceptual work these concepts might fruitfully perform. For some years now philosophers have been at work patiently analyzing these and other crucial concepts that have come to be used in an unguarded and often extravagant manner that obscures intelligent insights into educational problems. These analyses have served to untangle the logic of these terms and to help us see more clearly just how they relate to education. In this chapter we have tried to examine these concepts, carrying out in a survey manner some of the work just referred to. Perforce, ours has not been an in-depth analysis, and we have had to leave many of the conceptual puzzles untouched. The reader who wishes to explore these matters further is encouraged to consult the sources listed in our bibliography.

One point should be clear from our analysis, however. While the various candidates for educational aims we have examined have failed *as aims,* they do suggest implications for the conduct of schooling. Slogans about the school's obligation to meet children's needs, further their interests, and promote their growth have all been seen as attempts to counter certain existing school practices, policies, and assumptions. As such, these slogans point to principles of school procedure and practice. Emphasis on such slogans in educational discourse may be taken as attacks on authoritarian methods of handling subject matter and students, the bureaucratic tendency in

schools toward goal displacement, and the schools' implicit or explicit demands for conformity and obedience on the part of students
(and often teachers). What they show is a common concern for the
individual student as a developing person. Hence, while they fail as
educational aims, the authors hold that such concepts are probably
necessary to elucidate the nature of the education of children as
distinct from merely controlling, manipulating, or baby-sitting them.

Some expansion of the above point seems to be in order. Earlier
in the chapter we distinguished among several kinds of goal statements. Two that we accepted as useful were (1) goals as principles of
procedure, and (2) goals as desired results. Our analysis in this section leads us to three conclusions:

1. Much of what has been written and said about individual
needs, interests, and growth has been at the slogan level.
2. Examining these slogans in an attempt to spell out desired
results does not appear promising.
3. The concern with individual needs, interests, and growth
seems supportive of and closely related to the principles-of-procedure
or restriction-of-manner goal argued for in the first part of this chapter: in a school for tomorrow every child ought to be treated always
as an end in himself, not as a means to other ends.

Thus, although we do not believe that exhortations to honor individual interests, needs, and growth will lead us to defensible desired
results goals, we do hold that they call our attention to the question
of principles of procedure or restrictions of manner.

All the chapters in this book indicate great concern that there
be a renewed emphasis on the individual in the proposed school for
tomorrow. This concern encompasses what we have called principles
of procedure. But it goes beyond such principles to include attention
to a desired result. We have called this goal the "autonomous individual." In the final section we will attempt to summarize some of
the ideas about this ideal.

The Autonomous Individual as Educational Goal

Our thesis, briefly stated, is that in a school for tomorrow the
desired result is a rationally autonomous individual and that this
result cannot be achieved if the schooling is exclusively entertain-

ment, conditioning, training, indoctrination, and/or brainwashing. Nor is this end likely to be reached by a program that ignores individual needs, interests, and developmental patterns. Schooling that relies on modes of teaching such as conditioning and indoctrination[22] or ignores student interests and needs may produce graduates who are well-informed, patient, diligent, conforming, and obedient, but it is not likely to result in rationally autonomous individuals.

What do we mean by rationally autonomous individuals? Our desired result could be held to be just another slogan amenable to the same criticisms that have been leveled at other proposed aims. Indeed, we may find that it will usefully function in that manner for the idea of a school for tomorrow. But our problem here is not to provide this book with a rallying cry; it is to see what is implied in this concept and to examine it critically in order to see whether it is justifiable.

Earlier in this chapter we indicated several things that cannot serve as aims of education. It may be worth noting that these could not be what we mean when we suggest the development of the rationally autonomous person as an important aim of education. To review, we do *not* mean a person who treats himself or others as a means, one who is merely unique or different, or one who is guided only by his momentary wants, interests, and desires. It is perhaps necessary to point this out again, because the idea of the autonomous person is sometimes misunderstood as signifying the sort of individual who "does his own thing," whatever that is. We have argued, however, that our commitment to education obligates us to promote what is worthwhile rather than simply those things that may be the object of interest and desire on the part of individuals. Those involved in education ought to be concerned for the *quality* of the individual produced. To promote the goal of the autonomous individual is not thereby to promote the goal of individuals suited to live in a state of anarchy.

Although it may be helpful to indicate what we do *not* mean by the autonomous individual, clearly this is not sufficient. We will now attempt to indicate in a more positive manner what we do mean. The remainder of this essay will be devoted to an attempt to capture, at least in outline, the main features of the concept of the rationally autonomous individual and to suggest the lines of justification for such a concept as a central educational aim.

The first obvious characteristic of the rationally autonomous person is that he is not dependent on others. In the face of pressures, directives, and prescriptions for him to behave or think in certain ways, he will not merely conform, obey, or believe in the way indicated. When confronted with new problems and issues, he will not wait to be told what to do or blindly follow what others are doing or believing. Autonomy indicates that the individual will *choose for himself*. But the notion of choosing presents a serious problem for us, because it is unclear what is involved. We have a tendency to use the term *choice* to apply to different states of affairs, not all of which seem compatible with autonomy. Perhaps specific examples will help clarify the matter.

As Vance Packard reported in *The Hidden Persuaders*, the widespread use of "Madison Avenue" techniques of persuasion have led many individuals to buy one product as opposed to others that are equally available. We sometimes say of those individuals (and they almost invariably say of themselves) that they chose to buy the product in question, even in cases where they made no comparative study of the various alternatives and have no clear reasons for their choices. The paradigm case of this can be seen in certain tests showing that in the absence of "brand names" consumers are unable to differentiate between their "chosen" product and other brands of similar type, and, in the face of this, they still cling to the belief that their brand is best. This is quite different from the case of the individual who is able to assess various features of competing products and to select the one that meets objective standards of excellence. While we often describe both states of affairs as "choice," it seems clear that the claim to autonomy can be upheld only in the latter case. In order to differentiate these cases, it will be useful to say that in the former case the individual *opts* for what he selects. In that way we may reserve the term *chooses* for the latter case, which is compatible with autonomy.

We are now in a position to say more precisely that the rationally autonomous individual will *choose for himself* from among available alternatives. But our case of choice also allows us to notice other features that clarify rational autonomy even further. In describing the state of affairs we have called "choice," explicit reference was made to "objective standards." While such a reference is sufficiently clear to mark off the second case from the first, which would more accurately be described as opting on the basis of whim, prejudice or mere personal preference, more needs to be said about objective standards.

In the first place, standards are "objective" in the sense that they refer to the object being judged rather than to the individual subject doing the judging. When someone says, for example, that "heroin is good" in the face of the overwhelming evidence of its dangerous and damaging consequences, he is apparently not asserting something about the heroin itself. He is saying something about himself, i.e., "I like heroin." The "standard" he is using is *subjective* in that it states something about him rather than the heroin. *Objective* standards, when used to judge, would state something about the heroin itself.[23]

Up to this point we have said that the rationally autonomous person is one who chooses for himself on the basis of judgments according to objective standards. But this is not yet sufficient. It is quite possible for individuals to possess those characteristics and still fail to be rationally autonomous. For example, the person who has been *indoctrinated* could also be said to choose for himself on the basis of objective standards. Yet we would not say of him that he was rationally autonomous. The reason for withholding that description is that the indoctrinated man has not *chosen* the standards he uses. True, he believes those standards and can produce reasons and arguments for them. But those reasons and arguments are used merely to defend his position and persuade others. They are not used to determine the truth or rightness of the standards themselves. The standards are his in the sense that he has them, uses them, and believes in them. But they are his master because he has been given them rather than having chosen them. He has no inclination to change them on the basis of other arguments or evidence.[24]

While such a person can make his own choices, in a significant sense they are not his choices because the standards he uses have not been rationally chosen by him. We come then to another characteristic that seems necessary for saying that an individual is rationally autonomous: the standards that are the basis for choice must themselves have been chosen. The autonomous individual will be inclined to test the truth of things for himself. He must, therefore, be the sort of individual who forms his judgments and chooses what he will do on the basis of critically evaluated standards that he appreciates and accepts because they are supported by evidence and reason.

In rather sketchy form, this is a general description of what we mean by the "rationally autonomous individual." There is no magic in the label: some might choose to call our ideal simply "the free man" or "the educated man." Clearly there is little new in our ideal:

whatever we name it, it has a long and honored history. We do not claim originality, but we do claim that this ideal is too often rejected, forgotten, or ignored in programs of schooling. As we talk of a school for tomorrow that attempts to bring about a renewed emphasis on the individual, we will do well to keep this ideal or desired result in mind. Schools may be inadequate instruments for achieving this result, but a school for tomorrow is one place to start, one place where the young might *begin* to become rationally autonomous persons.

Notes

1. Our common attachment to such "goal terms" leads some to suggest that we have essential agreement and need not spend too much effort in "goal-finding." Myron Lieberman argued that the problem in American education was not one of goal finding because, "the American people are in substantial agreement that the purposes of education are the development of critical thinking, effective communication, creative skills, and social, civic, and occupational competence." (*The Future of Public Education* (Chicago: University of Chicago Press, 1960), p. 17.)

2. Scheffler also shows that slogans sometimes become dissociated from their parent doctrines and become "doctrines" in their own right. When this occurs, i.e., when the slogan is seen as a literal claim or doctrine, it should be evaluated as such. Dissociated slogans are likely to lead to the pseudoagreements discussed above.

3. Our biases may show here, but this seems to be a problem with some who see "behavioral objectives" as a royal road to educational salvation. Behavioral objectives, it appears, are not objectives or goals at all. They are statements describing the evidence of goal or objective attainment. It is important to state what is to count as evidence of goal attainment, but evidence of attainment and attainment are not the same thing.

4. The analogy of our legal system may be useful here. In our legal system we are not concerned with results alone but insist that in arriving at results we honor all sorts of restrictions of manner, e.g., rights of individuals and due process.

5. We should also notice that "making the individual central" is rhetoric that is not limited to systems we would describe as democratic. Alfredo Rocco, in describing the role of individuals in the fascist state, said,

For we, too, maintain the necessity of safeguarding the conditions that make for the free development of the individual; we too believe that the oppression of the individual personality can find no place in the modern state. . . . Our concept of liberty is that the individual must be allowed to develop his personality in behalf of the state. . . . (From a speech delivered by Rocco at Perugia, Italy, on August 30, 1925, reprinted in Carl Cohen, *Communism, Fascism and Democracy* (New York: Random House, 1962), p. 344.)

6. We do not mean to claim that the principle should be accepted because most or many people do accept it. Such a claim would be an example of *ad populum* fallacy. We are simply saying that most people support this principle at least verbally.

7. Thomas F. Green, *The Activities of Teaching* (New York: McGraw-Hill Book Co., 1971), pp. 168-69.

8. This is not intended as an argument against exams, performances, or curricular prescriptions. These all have educational uses. The question here is whether certain educational practices are adopted not to further education, but to further other interests of various concerned groups.

9. This is not intended as a suggestion that educators need not recognize and take into account individual differences. We are unlikely to achieve our aims without such recognition. Our point is that these differences are not the source of our educational aims or goals.

10. For an excellent detailed discussion of this, see B. Paul Komisar, " 'Need' and the Needs Curriculum" in B. O. Smith and R. H. Ennis, *Language and Concepts in Education* (Chicago: Rand McNally & Co., 1961), chap. 2.

11. We cannot, however, equate interest with attention, since one can pay attention to Y, when he is commanded to do so, without being interested in Y. An excellent discussion of this may be found in A. R. White, *The Philosophy of Mind* (New York: Random House, 1967), pp. 82-86.

12. White, *op. cit.*, p. 84.

13. We are not claiming that no existing interests are worthwhile. The fallacy lies in assuming that just because an interest exists, it is worthwhile. An existing interest could very well be valuable, but its value must be justified separately. Whether it is a good thing to promote Johnny's interest in pulling the wings off butterflies, depends on considerations other than the mere fact that he is interested in it. It is at least conceivable that we could find reasons or circumstances that would make us deem such interests as worthwhile.

14. Israel Scheffler, *The Language of Education* (Springfield, Ill.: Charles C. Thomas, 1960), p. 49.

15. The teacher's role with regard to readiness suggested by the growth metaphor has been interpreted in two basic ways. One interpretation suggests that teachers should wait almost passively for the marks of readiness to occur on their own. Another, perhaps more prevalent interpretation, indicates that the teacher should provide an environment that stimulates and encourages readiness.

16. The view that children have essentially good natures is opposed to some formulations of the molding metaphor. The ideas of shaping and molding have, historically, been quite amenable in cultures that have emphasized original sin and the corresponding view that children naturally have evil natures that must be controlled and trained in the ways of right and good.

17. Of course, potentials do not exist in the abstract. A potential is always for something in particular. While we sometimes say that someone has "great potential," the context usually makes it clear what it is for.

18. R. F. Dearden, *The Philosophy of Primary Education* (New York: Humanities Press, 1968), pp. 28-29. A more detailed analysis of many of the ideas addressed in this chapter may be found in Dearden's book.

19. See, for example, Abraham Maslow, *Motivation and Personality* (New York: Harper & Row, 1954).

20. See Jean Piaget, *The Moral Judgment of the Child* (London: Routledge & Kegan Paul, 1932); J. Flavell, *The Developmental Theory of Jean Piaget* (Princeton, N.J.: Van Nostrand, 1963); H. Furth, *Piaget and Knowledge* (Englewood Cliffs, N.J.: Prentice-Hall, 1969); idem, *Piaget for Teachers* (Englewood Cliffs, N.J.: Prentice-Hall, 1970); Lawrence Kohlberg, "Early Education: A Developmental View," *Child Development* 39 (1968); idem, "Development of Moral Character and Ideology," in *Review of Child Development Research*, vol. 1, ed. M. L. Hoffman (New York: Russell Sage Foundation, 1964); idem, "Stage and Sequence: The Cognitive-Developmental Approach to Socialization," in *Handbook of Socialization*, ed. D. Goslin (Chicago: Rand McNally & Co., 1968); L. Kohlberg and E. Turiel, "Moral Development and Moral Education," in G. S. Lesser, *Psychology and Educational Practice* (Chicago: Scott, Foresman & Co., 1971).

21. For more extended and detailed philosophical assessments

of growth and developmental theories, see R. F. Dearden, *The Philosophy of Primary Education* (New York: Humanities Press, 1968); R. S. Peters, ed., *Perspectives on Plowden* (New York: Humanities Press, 1969); R. S. Peters and P. H. Hirst, *The Logic of Education* (London: Routledge & Kegan Paul, 1970); D. W. Hamlyn, "The Logical and Psychological Aspects of Learning," in *The Concept of Education,* ed. R. S. Peters (New York: Humanities Press, 1967); and T. Mischel, ed., *Psychological and Epistemological Issues in the Development of Concepts* (New York: Academic Press, 1970).

22. For a discussion of the various modes of teaching, see Green, *op. cit.,* pp. 21-39.

23. For another way of putting this same point, see Green, *op. cit.,* pp. 173-184. In Green's account the distinction is between preferences and judgments, between prizing and appraising. Preferring or prizing are subjective: a claim to prefer or prize is a claim about the person making the claim. A judgment, on the other hand, is not a claim simply about the "judge," but is addressed to that which is being judged. Green further claims, and we concur, that although judgments are in this sense objective, they are never conclusive: reasonable men may disagree on matters of judgment. To say then that judgments are objective is not to say that there is only one correct answer to a question of judgment.

24. For a further discussion of this point, see Green, *op. cit.,* pp. 27-33, 41-56.

References

Archambault, Reginald D. "The Concept of Need and its Relation to Certain Aspects of Educational Theory." *Harvard Educational Review* 27 (Winter 1957).

Bailey, C. "The Notion of Development and Moral Education." *Proceedings of the Annual Conference of the Philosophy of Education Society of Great Britain,* 3 (1969).

Beek, C. M., Crittenden, B. S. and Sullivan, E. V., eds. *Moral Education: Interdisciplinary Approaches.* Toronto: University of Toronto Press, 1971.

Best, Edward. "The Suppressed Premiss in Educational Psychology." In *Psychological Concepts in Education,* edited by B. Paul Komisar and C. J. B. Macmillan. Chicago: Rand McNally & Co., 1967, pp. 1-13.

Black, Max. "Education as Art and Discipline." *Ethics* 54, no. 4

(1944): 290-94. Reprinted in Israel Scheffler, ed., *Philosophy and Education*. 2d ed. Boston: Allyn & Bacon, 1966, pp. 39-46.

Brown, L. M. *General Philosophy in Education*. New York: McGraw-Hill Book Co., 1966.

Dearden, R. F. *The Philosophy of Primary Education*. New York: Humanities Press, 1968.

———, Hirst, P. H. and Peters, R. S., eds. *Education and the Development of Reason*. London: Routledge & Kegan Paul, 1972.

Ennis, Robert H. "Readiness to Master a Principle." In *Psychological Concepts in Education*, edited by B. Paul Komisar and C. J. B. Macmillan. Chicago: Rand McNally & Co., 1967, pp. 51-59.

Flew, Anthony. "What is Indoctrination?" *Studies in Philosophy and Education* 4, no. 2 (Spring 1966).

Frankena, William K. *Three Historical Philosophies of Education*. Glenview, Ill.: Scott, Foresman & Co., 1965.

Green, Thomas F. *The Activities of Teaching*. New York: McGraw-Hill Book Co., 1971.

———. "A Topology of the Teaching Concept." *Studies in Philosophy and Education* 3, no. 4 (Winter 1964-65): 284-320.

———. "Teaching, Acting, and Behaving." *Harvard Educational Review* 34 (Fall 1964): 507-24.

Hirst, Paul H., and Peters, Richard S. *The Logic of Education*. London: Routledge & Kegan Paul, 1970.

Komisar, B. Paul. "Teaching: Act and Enterprise." In *Concepts of Teaching: Philosophical Essays*, edited by C. J. B. Macmillan and Thomas W. Nelson. Chicago: Rand McNally & Co., 1968, pp. 63-88.

———. " 'Need' and the Needs Curriculum." In *Language and Concepts in Education*, edited by B. Othanel Smith and Robert H. Ennis. Chicago: Rand McNally & Co., 1961, pp. 24-42.

——— and McClellan, James E. "The Logic of Educational Slogans." In *Language and Concepts in Education*, edited by B. Othanel Smith and Robert H. Ennis. Chicago: Rand McNally & Co., 1961.

Macmillan, C. J. B. "The Concept of Adjustment." In *Psychological Concepts in Education*, edited by B. Paul Komisar and C. J. B. Macmillan. Chicago: Rand McNally & Co., 1967, pp. 60-71.

Martin, Jane R., ed. *Readings in the Philosophy of Education: A Study of Curriculum*. Boston: Allyn & Bacon, 1970.

Oakeshott, Michael. "Education: The Engagement and Its Frustration." *Proceedings of Annual Conference of the Philosophy of Education Society of Great Britain,* 5, no. 1 (1970): 43-76.

Olford, J. E. "The Concept of Creativity." *Proceedings of the Annual Conference of Philosophy of Education Society of Great Britain.* 5, no. 1 (1971): pp. 77-95. Reply by R. K. Elliott, ibid., pp. 97-104.

Passmore, John. "On Teaching to be Critical." In *The Concept of Education,* edited by R. S. Peters. New York: Humanities Press, 1967, pp. 192-211.

Perry, Leslie R. "What Is an Educational Situation?" In *Philosophical Analysis and Education,* edited by Reginald D. Archambault. New York: Humanities Press, 1965, pp. 59-86.

Peters, Richard S. "What Is an Educational Process?" In *The Concept of Education,* edited by R. S. Peters. New York: Humanities Press, 1967, pp. 1-23.

_____ . *Ethics and Education.* Chicago: Scott, Foresman & Co., 1967.

_____ . "The Concept of Character." In *Psychological Concepts in Education,* edited by B. Paul Komisar and C. J. B. Macmillan. Chicago: Rand McNally & Co., 1967, pp. 72-83.

_____ . " 'Mental Health' as an Educational Aim." In T. H. B. Hallins, *Aims in Education.* Manchester: Manchester University Press, 1964, pp. 71-90.

_____ . "Education as Initiation." In *Philosophical Analysis and Education,* edited by Reginald D. Archambault. New York: Humanities Press, 1965, pp. 87-111.

_____ . "Aims of Education—A Conceptual Inquiry." In *Philosophy and Education: Proceedings of The International Seminar, March 23-25.* Toronto: Ontario Institute for Studies in Education, 1966, pp. 1-16.

_____ . *Authority, Responsibility and Education.* London: George Allen & Unwin, 1959.

Scheffler, Israel. "Philosophical Models of Teaching." *Harvard Educational Review,* 35, no. 2 (Spring 1965): 131-43.

_____ . *The Language of Education.* Springfield, Ill.: Charles C. Thomas, 1960.

Soltis, Jonas F. *An Introduction to the Analysis of Educational Concepts.* Reading, Mass.: Addison-Wesley Publishing Co., 1968.

Steinberg, Ira S. *Educational Myths and Realities.* Reading, Mass.: Addison-Wesley Publishing Co., 1968.

White, Alan R. *The Philosophy of Mind.* New York: Random House, 1967.

Wilson, John B. "Comment on Flew's 'What is Indoctrination?' "
    Studies in Philosophy and Education 4, no. 4 (Summer 1966).
Wilson, John, Williams, Norman, and Sugarman, Barry. *Introduction
    to Moral Education.* Baltimore, Md.: Penguin Books, 1967.
Wilson, P. S. *Interest and Discipline in Education.* London: Rout-
    ledge & Kegan Paul, 1971.

Part 2
Choosing and Defining Professional Means for Attaining Goals

3

Curriculum

Some "new" conception of a curriculum will be needed in a school for tomorrow. But how would a curriculum be conceived if the primary goal of such a school was that of fostering the development of rationally autonomous individuals. What kind of a curriculum would we and our students choose?

Jack R. Frymier
Jane Wilhour
Alfred Rasp

Man Shapes and Is Shaped by His Environment

Human behavior is a function of the interaction of the individual with his environment. The individual has both a time span and a life space, and he lives and functions in an environmental setting.

Man is a part of the universe, yet apart from the universe. As part of the natural phenomena of the universe, man interacts with his environment and is profoundly affected by both the nature and quality of those interactive efforts. He looks at the stars and writes sonnets and songs. He pollutes rivers and air and gets ill and complains. By deliberate and unconscious endeavor, he creates and recreates environmental artifacts, which in turn affect the way he thinks, acts, and feels. Probably no organism but man has evolved to the point of exercising such extensive control of those aspects of the universe with which he interacts. The result is that man shapes and is shaped by his environment day after day.

To illustrate, let us consider Winston Churchill's ideas about reconstructing the House of Commons during the height of the Second World War as described by Ways:

The old house had been blasted by a German bomb, and the question was how it should be reconstructed. A more spacious chamber, perhaps? One with a semi-circular arrangement of comfortable chairs and useful desks, such as many of the world's parliaments enjoyed? Churchill thought not. What he wanted, essentially, was a replica of the old House with its rows of facing benches that symbolically expressed the party structure, emphasizing the contrasting roles of the Government and the Opposition. The new House, like the old, should have far fewer seats than there were members, so that in an ordinary ill-attended session speakers would not be discouraged by addressing empty benches. On great occasions, members flocking in would be crowded standing in the aisles, thus encasing debate and decision with visible signs of gravity and urgency.[1]

Churchill's argument might be summarized as "we shape our buildings, and afterwards our buildings shape us." Thus, man shapes his environment, is shaped by it in turn.

Social institutions such as schools, which are conceived by men and maintained by men, are part of man's environment. Beliefs and assumptions, which are made by men and held by men, are also part of man's environment, and so are curricula. And man is imprisoned by the institutions he builds, the assumptions he holds, and the curricula he creates. Men tend to get "locked in" by their own beliefs and ways of doing things. They know that they ought to hold themselves open to propositions and possibilities of change, but the general course of events is such that the forces for conserving existing institutions and existing beliefs yield ground slowly to the forces of change.

Man affects what is around him, and is affected in return. That point is simple and yet profound. It is so obvious that it hardly seems worth making, but it is so important that those who are environment builders—*curriculum construction* is the term we usually employ—must grasp its significance or lose their own sense of perspective.

At this point let us return to the basic premise of this book about a school for tomorrow: children differ. We have built our proposition on the anthropologists' generalization that every man is like every other man in some ways, like some men in other ways, and like no other man in still other ways. Deducing directly from that generalization, each child is like all other children in some respects, like some children in other respects, and like no other child in still other respects. The differences, as well as the existing similarities, form the framework within which the curriculum worker must function. The responsibility of a school for tomorrow will be to meet the needs of each child. Therefore, curriculum developers must have precise information about the areas in which all children are alike, the areas in which some of them are similar, and the areas in which each youngster is unique. In other words, it is presumed that each student will have educational needs in common with all children and with some children, and still other educational needs that are unique to him as a purposive, functioning individual.

The concept of "need," which is very common in education, requires some explanation. It is clearly related to the discussion above, but because adequate theoretical distinctions are not always made, what people *want,* what people *ought to have,* and what people *need* are often talked about as if they were synonymous. For example, to note that a given individual wants to be a farmer, a pilot, or a baseball player is not to say that he needs or ought to be a farmer, pilot, or baseball player. Likewise, to be aware of the fact that a particular person wants to take drugs; to study a foreign language, ancient history, or modern mathematics; or to go fishing, ride a bicycle, or cook spaghetti is insufficient evidence to presume that he needs or ought to do those things. In the same way, what an individual needs may not be what he wants at all. The person with a severely gangrenous foot, for example, needs to have his leg amputated if he is to survive, but he probably does not want to lose his leg. The alcoholic who wants a drink actually should have no alcohol at all, but he probably does need some other substances in order to maintain and improve his physical, intellectual, and emotional life.

Perhaps it would be useful to suggest a simple matrix as a way to encourage thinking about this problem. Suppose we begin by postulating that wants, needs, and oughts are different facets of human existence. That notion might be disproven over time, but at the moment there seems to be sufficient general evidence that those words refer to different degrees of imperativeness as far as the human condition and life itself are involved. Further, let us also postulate that some things can be thought of in the positive sense ("I want this," "he needs that," etc.), and other phenomena can be categorized as detrimental or negative as far as life itself is concerned. Using such a conceptual process suggests the following matrix as a guide to thought about human needs.

Using this simple matrix as a conceptualizing framework, it immediately becomes apparent that there are varying degrees of imperativeness reflected in each of the cells. If we can think of the cells as categorically different rather than points along a continuum, we

	Must Have	Makes No Difference	Dare Not Have
Wants	3	4	5
Oughts	2	4	6
Needs	1	4	7

might be able to use the framework as a sorting bin for the knowledge bits and range of experiences usually included in what is generally described as "curriculum." For example, if we take "parts of speech" as an illustration and ask ourselves where it goes in the matrix, it becomes evident that some students want to learn about the parts of speech and some do not want to learn about them. Some teachers would argue strongly that all children ought to learn the parts of speech; others would argue just as strongly against it on the ground that requiring such experiences for all students generates negative feelings about communication and language. Finally, it would be very difficult to demonstrate experimentally or even experientially that parts of speech are necessary, since millions of people communicate reasonably well without ever having encountered the notion of "parts of speech." Among those who have learned the parts of speech, it has helped some and been detrimental to others, so it cannot be concluded that such information dare not be experienced. The point is, determining the worthwhileness, appropriateness, and imperativeness of curriculum is not simply a matter of seeking consensus, although that might be one point at which to start.

To compound the problem, consider for a moment what happens when pathological factors become apparent. A person who is addicted to drugs, for example, physically "needs" a substance that is obviously detrimental to him both physically and psychologically. But that does not negate the fact that he "needs" the drug, and needs it badly. The fact that consuming or partaking of an addicting drug denies the individual his rational, autonomous individuality—his capacity to consider factual data and make rational decisions, his capacity to exercise personal choices, etc.—makes the problem even more complex. As another example, it is easy to recognize the fact that an emotionally disturbed youngster or a child who is deaf or blind has different wants, oughts, and needs from children who are more typical in the statistical sense.

The point is, curriculum is one aspect of a learner's environment. Given the premise that man shapes and is shaped by his environment as he interacts with it, curriculum workers in a school for tomorrow must reflect an awareness of and knowledge about the similarities and differences among and between students. Furthermore, this awareness and knowledge must manifest itself directly in terms of the characteristic aspects of curriculum itself. That is, curriculum must be so conceptualized and administered that the differences and similarities—the wants, oughts, and needs—can be dealt with creatively and effectively. That is not a simple problem, to be sure.

Given this general exploration of some of the factors that must be considered, let us shift our attention to an examination of the theoretical aspects of curriculum itself.

A Definition of Curriculum

For our purposes, the elements essential in curriculum are actors, artifacts and operations.[2] The choice of terms is intentional. Actors are people, but the term *actors* implies more than *people*. Artifacts are things, but more is implied by the term *artifacts* than by *things*. Similarly, *operations* implies more than *processes*. These implications can be summed up under the ideas of intent, purpose, and ends: qualities assumed inherent in the elements of curriculum.

We are proposing that actors, artifacts, and operations be considered as the basic ingredients of curriculum. Examination of these concepts may help clarify their nature and justify this position.

The term *actors* refers to those people directly involved: students, teachers, materials producers, supervisors, and administrators. (Many others are not directly involved but affect curriculum indirectly, and often profoundly, e.g., school board members, publishers, parents, and legislators.) One purpose of the term is to define some people inside curriculum and others outside, thus helping to establish a bounded concept. An actor then, is an element within curriculum, and the term implies intent or purpose and direct involvement.

Artifacts refers to "products of human workmanship." For our purposes this term applies to what we normally think of as "subject matter" or "content." This implies the notion that ideas are products of human workmanship. Ideas, however, are typically represented by things, such as textbooks or films. This assumes that any kind of symbolic representation of ideational phenomena can be considered an artifact. Like *actors, artifacts* implies purpose or intent: made or used for a reason.

Artifacts are bounded with respect to curriculum by the relationship they have to actors. In other words, an artifact becomes a curriculum artifact because of its relationship to a person directly involved in curriculum.

An *operation* is a process involving modifications over time in actors and artifacts or in their relationships. That Johnny knows "7 x 6 = 42," when at some prior time he did not, is after-the-fact evidence of the existence of an operation. The teacher teaching Johnny "7 x 6 = 42" is also evidence of an operation. An infinite variety of groupings of actors and artifacts may be involved.

If it is assumed that a curriculum event includes actors, artifacts, and operations, then it is important to conceptualize a way of thinking about curriculum that will illustrate the reality in action. Suppose we recast our conceptualizations so that the individual learner is separated from the other actors in curriculum and so identified that we can more clearly comprehend exactly what happens to him while he is interacting with the environment. That is, the individual learner is a part of a curriculum event, but we also need to understand how he interacts with the other people and things in his learning environment. Let us so formulate our theoretical considerations that the individual learner is highlighted and more conspicuous as a unique, purposive organism interacting with the things and people around him.

The theory being outlined here presumes that time and space are fundamental aspects of human existence. That is, temporal and spatial phenomena are presumed to be basic dimensions of human behavior and must be accounted for and incorporated in any valid and useful theory of curriculum. It is further assumed that human behavior is a function of the interaction of the individual with his environment and that the environment can be differentiated according to what impinges on the individual at a given moment and what affects him over a longer period of time. Likewise, the environment can be differentiated in terms of what is smaller and more proximal to the individual and what is larger and more distal from the individual.

Assuming that behavior is a function of the individual's interaction with his environment, we might represent this concept symbolically as: $I \rightleftarrows O$ in which I = individual, $\rightleftarrows$ = interaction, and O = environment.

Assuming further that environment can be differentiated in terms of both time and space, let us now suggest that the symbolic representation of this concept might be portrayed as: $\boxed{I \rightleftarrows O}$ in which I = individual; $\rightleftarrows$ = interaction; O = immediate, close environment; and $\boxed{}$ = long term, more distant environment.

We now have included within our paradigm four factors directly derived from the basic dimensions of time and space. For the purposes of this paper $\boxed{}$ shall be defined as context, O shall be defined as other people or artifacts within the context (e.g., teachers, other students, books, etc.), $\rightleftarrows$ shall be defined as the interactive relationship between the individual and other people or between the individual and artifacts, and I shall be defined as the being and the behavior of the learner. In the pages which follow, these aspects of the paradigm are described in more detail, beginning with the notion of context.

Context

The context is the ordered aspect of the environment that is characterized as being larger in size and/or longer in duration than the immediate instances, particular people, or specific things with which the individual interacts. In this sense, its most typical form is an institution, an institutionalized idea, or a social system of one kind or another.

For example, "library" is a bigger concept than "book," "librarian," "book borrower," or even "book lending." Furthermore, it transcends in both time and space the immediate people, events, and artifacts that are involved. As such, its order—i.e., its organization and precisely defined interrelationships, including its history, policies, practices, and purposes—allows and hopefully enables those who function within its parameters to use the context as a continuing framework for interaction with the other people and artifacts represented here as O.[3] In other words, an outstanding characteristic of any context is the extent to which order prevails. Order brings security. The ability to predict with reasonable assurance what will or will not happen under a given set of circumstances increases the individual's capacity to exert control over his environment. Order also enables the individual to interact with his environment more efficiently and more effectively. Random behavior is minimized.

Organization means that access, retrieval, storage, and manipulation of the elements of the larger whole are simpler, easier, and faster because of the ordered nature of the context.

In social situations characterized by revolution or riot, for example, order disappears. Even if the revolutionary force itself is highly organized and rigidly disciplined, i.e., very "ordered," it generates disorder by its actions. Thus people are less able to predict and control their environment and their lives. An accident, a carcinoma, and a revolution are all deviations from the generic organization of the phenomenon and are thus pathological, disorderly, and disintegrative. Life as a process and as a complex, interrelated set of phenomena is order-creating, order-reproducing, and order-assuring. The individual constantly strives to "make sense out of," i.e., to organize and bring order to, his experiences. As Combs and Syngg say, "the basic motivation of the individual is to maintain and to enhance the self."[4] That is, the basic inclination of the organism is to preserve the organization of body tissues and personal experiences that makes up the individual and to improve that ordered entity over time. Order without freedom is death, but freedom without order is chaos.

Five theoretical dimensions of social systems have been identified as useful constructs in describing the notion of "context" more precisely.[5] They are goal, domain, function, confidence, and record. Each of these theoretical constructs is outlined and illustrated below.

1. The goal dimension refers to the purposes or objectives for which the context was established or has evolved. Goals give direction to the context. Whether they are explicit or implied, specific or general, and universally understood or evident to only a few, goals are the part of the context related to the aims or intentions of those working within the context.

2. The domain dimension refers to the segment of reality that has been singled out for special attention by those working within the context. Thus, a library is primarily concerned with books; banks deal with money; restaurants concern themselves with food; contractors build houses, commercial buildings, and so forth; scientists accomplish research in their fields of scholarly inquiry; and our government, in this country at least, governs according to the areas of authority that have been defined by the concept of federalism practiced in the United States today. Every context has a geographical space, an area, a set of reality factors, a domain within which it operates.

3. The function dimension refers to the unique operations inherent in each of the various contexts identified. In the context of government, for example, the basic functions are making, executing, and reviewing laws and their execution. In science the methods of science reflect the function dimension: formulating hypotheses, devising experiments to test the hypotheses, and inferring from the data whether the hypotheses are refuted or supported. In industry somebody plans, somebody produces, and somebody evaluates whether the plan was appropriate and sound and whether it was effected satisfactorily. Sometimes subsystems within the context accomplish the various functions, and sometimes the functions are accomplished by separate bodies, each with its own sphere of authority.

4. The confidence dimension refers to the nature of the interactions that occur within the system as it functions to keep the enterprise on target and on course. Contexts possessing integrity— that is, systems that are complete and concerned with truth—function in such a way that they use the data created during the evaluative phase of the operation as a substantive basis for positive change. The confidence dimension does not presume that men must be basically "good" for the system to work; it presumes that "error will out" and that the system will process evaluative data and use it as a basis for systematic and continuous change. The concept of "checks and balances" in our government represents an instance of the confidence dimension in that particular context. Replication in the field of science or quality control in industrial production represent the concept in another way. Monitoring efforts by "watch dog" committees, by such groups as the Pure Food and Drug Administration, or by referees and umpires in athletic contests reflect the confidence dimension in other kinds of situations.

5. The record dimension refers to the "printout" that results from every context in operation. The balance sheet in business, the scientific report in the academic world, and the printed laws and court decisions in government all represent tangible evidence generated by the system in the course of its operation. Data in the record dimension reflect the soundness of policies, the effectiveness of management, and the appropriateness of decisions. In the main, the record represents a kind of residue from the system's functioning that can be used as a basis for making interpretations about the context and its operations.

For the purpose of this paper, those contexts characterized by clear statements of goals, differentiation in terms of domain and function, use of evaluative data as a basis for establishing confidence and fostering change, and a systematic way of recording the nature of those accomplishments are considered "open" contexts. Those lacking the above characteristics are considered "closed" systems. It has not been described extensively here, but one can readily conceive of systems or contexts that are ordered and organized and ones that are disordered or disorganized and perhaps even disintegrating. Given these considerations and depending on the extent to which order or disorder exists and the extent to which the system is open or closed, we can envision four different kinds of contexts: (1) open and ordered, (2) open and disordered, (3) closed and ordered, and (4) closed and disordered.

In summary, a context represents an ordered and ordering system, which may be open or closed, and which reflects five basic dimensions: (1) there are goals; (2) the contexts can be spatially differentiated from one another in terms of the domains involved; (3) the functions include planning, doing, and evaluating; (4) there are ways in which evaluative data are used as corrective feedback; and (5) a tangible, apparent, and communicable record is generated from the operations of the context.

Individual

Returning to our basic postulates of time and space, let us now attempt to generate a theory of human behavior as a function of these postulations. For example, suppose that we deduce from our basic assumptions of time and space two fundamental aspects of human personality that we designate "attitudinal dimensions." One would be a temporal dimension and the other a spatial dimension. For purposes of discussion, assume further that these two dimensions are orthogonally related to one another, and their intersection creates a kind of behavioral vector that causes individuals to behave in certain kinds of ways.

The temporal dimension presumes a past-future orientation. The spatial dimension presumes a self-others orientation. Graphically described, these two dimensions might look something like figure 3-1.

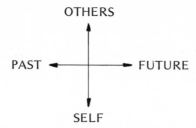

Figure 3-1. Temporal and spatial dimensions of personality

Depending on the nature of the intersection and the strength of the dimensions, we can predict four different, "unbalanced" types of behavioral vectors and a fifth, "balanced" type.

Type 1. Future-others oriented

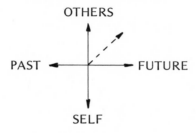

Type 2. Past-self oriented

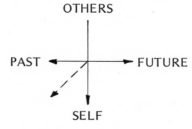

Type 3. Future-self oriented

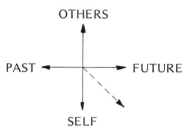

Type 4. Past-others oriented

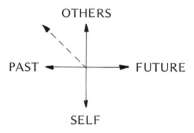

Type 5. Balanced

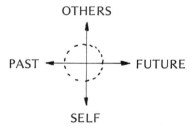

The type one vector portrays a person (future-others oriented) who might be thought of as a philanthropist or humanist, while type two (past-self oriented) might best be described as a misanthropist or fascist. A type three person (future-self oriented) would probably be thought of as opportunistic or selfish, while type four (past-others oriented) might be described as a sentimentalist. Type five would be a "typical" or "normal" individual, at least in the statistical sense.

Figure 2 portrays these same concepts in a slightly more elaborate way.

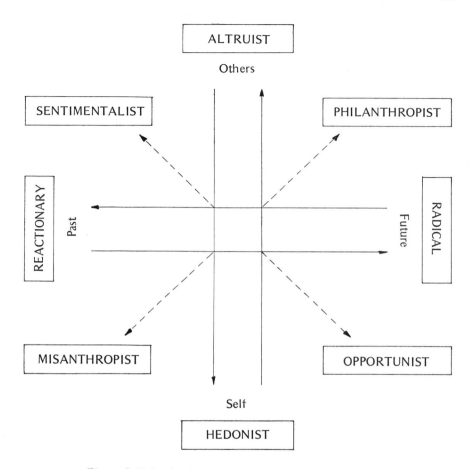

Figure 2. Behavioral vectors resulting from interaction of
attitudinal dimensions

In figure 2 it becomes apparent that if we conceptualize the temporal
and spatial aspects of human existence as basic attitudinal dimensions, we can predict nine different types of behavior vectors—
altruistic, philanthropic, radical, opportunistic, hedonistic, misan-
thropic, reactionary, sentimental, and "normal"—an expansion of
our original typology outlined above. The labels are arbitrary and
probably not precise, but the logic is obvious, and it suggests a way
of thinking about human behavior in both temporal and spatial
terms.

The concepts outlined here could apply to the I (individual) in our original paradigm: $\boxed{\text{I} \longrightarrow \text{O}}$ but it could also apply to the O (immediate environment) when it represented another person rather than an artifact, per se.

Interactive Relationships

In our paradigm the symbol $\longleftrightarrow$ portrays the interactive relationship that exists between an individual and another individual or an artifact. Theoretically, several kinds of interactive relationships can be identified:

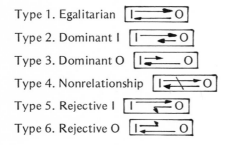

Type 1. Egalitarian

Type 2. Dominant I

Type 3. Dominant O

Type 4. Nonrelationship

Type 5. Rejective I

Type 6. Rejective O

In the first type, the equal length arrows suggest an egalitarian relationship. In the second type, the uneven length favoring the I suggests that the individual dominates the other individual or the artifacts involved. The uneven length of arrows in the third type suggests a relationship in which the other individual or artifact dominates I, while the fourth type suggests a situation in which there is no interactive relationship, even though I and O may be physically close. In the fifth and sixth instances we can envision situations in which one person is interacting positively while the other person or artifact is rejecting the interactive relationship somehow. Other possibilities could also be invented.

Considering these various possibilities, let us return to our initial portrayal of five types of individual; philanthropist, misanthropist, opportunist, sentimentalist, and "normal." Ignoring the other possibilities for the moment, and assuming for the time being that O represents another person rather than an artifact, let us press our concept of interactive relationships still further. (For the sake of simplicity and in an effort to "make sense" out of a very complex set of phenomena by dealing with only a portion of the totality, the other four types will not be dealt with here.) That is, in the discussion above we have postulated that the intersection of attitudinal dimensions within an individual would result in the formation of a certain type of behavioral vector for that person. Let us now extend those concepts and hypothesize about the various kinds of relationships that might develop if the behavioral vectors of two persons came together in an interactive way.

It is extremely difficult to describe graphically, but perhaps we can imagine the attitudinal dimensions and the resulting behavioral vector for one person as existing on a single two-dimensional plane. If so, we might also imagine the attitudinal dimensions and the resulting behavioral vector for another person as existing on a different plane. If we brought these two planes together at right angles, we would have a three-dimensional portrayal of human interactions. The idea can be more easily understood if we hold one hand in front of ourselves in a vertical plane, hold the other hand in front of ourselves in a horizontal plane, then bring the two hands together until they intersect between the fingers. Or, we could portray the same interaction by taking two sheets of paper, cutting a slot halfway across each sheet, and then bringing the two papers together so that we get two intersecting planes at right angles to each other.

If we now return to our previous discussion, perhaps we will be in a position to theorize about the nature of interactive relationships between people in a more precise way. Let us assume, for example, that the attitudinal dimensions with their resultant behavior vector for one person (i.e., I) could be drawn out on a piece of paper or drawn on the palm of the hand held in a vertical plane, and we could further assume that the attitudinal dimensions and associated behavioral vector for the other person (i.e., O) could be drawn on another piece of paper or on the palm of the hand held in a horizontal plane. Our paradigm suggests that if we bring these two together in an interactive relationship, as represented by the intersecting pieces of paper held at right angles or the intersecting hands, we can predict a whole series of different kinds of interactive relationships depending on the attitudinal dimensions and resulting behavioral vectors of the two individuals involved.

In theoretical terms, there would be at least twenty-five different kinds of interactive relationships possible, starting with the five basic types described above (i.e., philanthropist, opportunist, misanthropist, sentimentalist, and normal). Listed below are the twenty-five kinds of relationships that can be deduced directly from our paradigm.

1. $I_p - O_p$
2. $I_p - O_o$
3. $I_p - O_m$
4. $I_p - O_s$
5. $I_p - O_n$

6. $I_o - O_p$
7. $I_o - O_o$
8. $I_o - O_m$
9. $I_o - O_s$
10. $I_o - O_n$

11. $I_m - O_p$
12. $I_m - O_o$

13. $I_m - O_m$
14. $I_m - O_s$
15. $I_m - O_n$

16. $I_s - O_p$
17. $I_s - O_o$
18. $I_s - O_m$
19. $I_s - O_s$
20. $I_s - O_n$

21. $I_n - O_p$
22. $I_n - O_o$
23. $I_n - O_m$
24. $I_n - O_s$
25. $I_n - O_n$

Suppose that we now add to our considerations another set of factors that affect learning, i.e., information about accomplishment. A learner uses information as feedback to adjust his approach to the task, to pace events, or, in a variety of ways, to accomplish whatever it is that he is attempting to learn. And information about accomplishment affects how and when and what a student learns.

Furthermore, information as feedback comes both from the learner (I) and from others (O). Likewise, the information generally connotes positive (+), negative (-), or neutral (0) feeling tone. That is, praise, reproof, or nonjudgmental data become available to a learner relative to his learning efforts. Given these basic considerations, we can now conceptualize nine different types of qualitative relationships: ++, +0, +-, 0+, 00, 0-, -+, -0, and --.

The ++ pertains to an interactive relationship in which feedback about accomplishment is personally detected by the learner to be positive and is seen by another person (e.g., teacher) and reported to the learner as positive. For example, if a student working at the problem of balancing a chemical equation feels that he is making progress and mastering the task, and his teacher also reports to him that he is accomplishing the resolution of this problem, this would be a ++ type interactive relationship.

A +0 type interactive relationship represents a situation in which the learner feels he is mastering the learning task and is getting nonjudgmental comments and specific information about his efforts from his teacher, e.g., "You have two hydrogens here and two hydrogens there, four oxygens here and four oxygens there." A -+ type relationship represents a situation in which the learner feels he is making errors or in some way not mastering the task at hand, but his teacher sees the situation differently and tells him he is doing very well. The reader can envision the other possibilities that have been described in theoretical terms. They will not all be illustrated here. The point is that these nine types of relationships suggest, in effect, nine kinds of qualitative interactions that could occur for each of the twenty-five types of interactive relationships described earlier.

For example, we can conceive of an interactive relationship between a philanthropic individual (I_p) and a philanthropic teacher (O_p) that is perceived by the individual student as positive and also reported to be positive by the teacher to the student. Symbolically, such an interactive relationship might be portrayed as: $+I_p +O_p$. Carrying this logic further, we could envisage nine different types of interactive relationships between a philanthropic I and a philanthropic O as follows:

$$+I_p +O_p \qquad\qquad 0I_p -O_p$$
$$+I_p 0O_p \qquad\qquad -I_p +O_p$$
$$+I_p -O_p \qquad\qquad -I_p 0O_p$$
$$0I_p +O_p \qquad\qquad -I_p -O_p$$
$$0I_p 0O_p$$

The same logic would apply to each of the twenty-five types of interactive relationships described above. The 225 theoretically possible interactive relationships will not be listed here, but there is no question that a host of curriculum research hypotheses might be generated by a careful study of such a listing.

Artifacts

Thus far in this chapter we have explored the notions of context, individual, and interaction portrayed in our paradigm. The paradigm, of course, presumes that behavior is a function of the interaction of the individual with his environment. Environment has been further presumed to mean what is immediate and close up and what is long-term and more distant as represented by the notion of "context."

In the sections above dealing with the individual and interactive relationships, the immediate environment was assumed to be another person, and therefore the same factors applied to both parties to the relationship. But individuals also interact with artifacts, and a theory of curriculum must take into account an individual's interactions with the artifacts of his environment.

In general terms, there are three important aspects of artifacts to be considered: (1) the extent to which they are perceived, (2) the extent to which they are valued, and (3) the extent to which they are mastered. Each of these aspects is explored below.

Artifacts in one's environment may be perceived or not perceived.[7] Three aspects of perception seem particularly important:

1. The artifact must be a part of the learner's perceptual field and be differentiated sufficiently to be seen as figure against ground. In other words, the artifact must be perceptually "grasped," that is, clearly seen, felt, or heard.

2. Significance or meaning must be attributed to the artifact by the learner. He must understand what the artifact is for; it must have personal meaning for him.

3. The artifact must be perceived accurately and not distorted; the perception must be consistent with the reality involved.

If the artifact does not lie within the learner's perceptual field and is not perceptually "grasped," or if no meaning is attributed to it, or if the perception is inaccurate or incorrect, the artifact has not been perceived.

After an individual has become aware of an artifact he may come to value it, to want it or desire it. He may sense the potential for a productive interaction with the artifact; thus a goal emerges. "I need that typewriter." "I want to read that book." The goal gives direction to the individual; thus values give direction to human behavior.

Finally, as a result of perceiving an artifact and seeing it as valuable and worthwhile, the individual interacts with the artifact in such a way that eventually he masters or fails to master it. Mastery means that the artifact as perceived is manipulated by the individual in the direction of the goal, and the goal is achieved. That is, the task is accomplished, the problem solved, or the product produced.

Given these aspects of an interactive relationship with an artifact, it becomes evident that we can identify a variety of different kinds of relationships. For example, we can imagine a situation in which the artifact is clearly perceived, valued, and mastered. Or, we can envision a situation in which the artifact is clearly perceived and valued but not mastered. Carrying the logic further, we can also imagine a situation in which the artifact is perceived and mastered but not valued or one in which it is perceived but neither valued nor mastered.

In a hypothetical sense, it might very well be that those four possible types of interactive relationships between an individual and an artifact represent situations in which there would be differing degrees of motivation:

Perceived	Valued	Mastered
Perceived	Valued	Not mastered
Perceived	Not valued	Mastered
Perceived	Not valued	Not mastered

It seems that the first instance probably represents the greatest motivation and the last instance the least, but that hypothesis needs to be tested experimentally. When an individual interacts with an artifact in his immediate environment, the nature of that interactive relationship is reflected in the extent to which the artifact is perceived, valued, and mastered. Artifacts that are not perceived obviously do not affect learning in that they cannot be valued nor can they be mastered.

To this point we have discussed curriculum artifacts in terms of how they might be perceived by the individual learner. Artifacts can also be described in terms of their reality characteristics, however, and from a teacher's point of view. It seems appropriate to think about curriculum artifacts from a phenomenological perspective, i.e., in terms of the extent to which they are perceived, valued, and mastered, but it is equally appropriate to identify and describe artifacts in terms of how they might be organized and stored or used. The following section, therefore, proceeds from an "external" rather than an "internal" or perceptual point of view. It is assumed that students must perceive artifacts—i.e., interpret the stimulus, attribute meaning to the reality—if learning is to occur, but teachers need to have other theoretical handles with which to grasp artifacts if they are to be effective in helping children learn.

Characteristics of Curriculum Artifacts

There are a number of identifiable attributes of curriculum artifacts that may be useful for teachers intent on "meeting the needs of the individual child," i.e., for helping students become rational, autonomous individuals. For example, curriculum artifacts vary in size, quantity, quality, flexibility, intention, organizing constructs, utility, significance, adaptability, degree of compulsion associated with them, and the like. If the curriculum in a school for tomorrow is to be growth-oriented rather than control-oriented, and if curriculum is actually to serve the individual learner's needs, then the artifacts and their use will probably be characterized in very different ways from those curriculum artifacts found in most schools today.

If one studied the theoretical aspects of curriculum in today's schools, it is probably safe to say that he would find that curriculum artifacts show up in large pieces, with fixed sequences, organized in terms of the scholar's interests, and difficult to adapt or modify sequentially, spatially, or otherwise. Let us examine some of these ideas to see if we can gain insights about how curriculum in a school for tomorrow might and ought to be different.

The most obvious example of a curriculum artifact in use in today's schools is the textbook. Textbooks represent fairly large "chunks" of stimulus material-information. They may have anywhere from a few to several hundred pages of information. Furthermore, the sequencing of stimulus material in the textbook is relatively inflexible; the pages are glued along one edge, sewn together, and numbered sequentially from the front of the book to the back.

Adapting curriculum material to fit the varying needs of different children is difficult when the curriculum artifacts are characterized in the ways described above. Starting from the premise that children are different, a series of criteria might be developed that could be applied to curriculum artifacts in a school for tomorrow. The following criteria might be a useful set with which to begin:

1. Materials should be in small rather than large pieces.
2. Sequencing and patterning of materials should be as variable as possible.
3. There should be far more stimulus material than any student could interact with in any given period of time.

4. Materials should be so stored that they are instantaneously available to the teacher or to the learner.

5. Materials should be highly valid.

6. Materials should be varied in form.

7. Materials should be organized and stored in terms of readability, interest, topic, point of view, and the like.

8. Materials should be available and manipulable for "study."

Perhaps an exploration of these criteria would illustrate their usefulness and relevance to curriculum workers interested in developing curriculum artifacts for children who differ in terms of ability, interest, experience, personality, creativity, and otherwise. The above list of criteria is certainly not complete, but it may at least be a useful beginning.

If we start with the assumption that children are different, a school for tomorrow will need a large number of curriculum artifacts—far more than any particular student might be expected to use—simply because of the fact that students with different abilities, different interests, different experiences, different personalities, and other differences would inevitably need different curriculum materials. Therefore, the range of materials available in a school for tomorrow would, of necessity, be extensive. Finding a reasonably precise fit between a given learner's "needs" and the artifacts available would require that the breadth of stimulus material, i.e., the number of "pieces," be very great.

Next, if we continue to honor the uniqueness of each learner as a fundamental proposition, it will obviously be necessary to have this range of stimulus material available in such a form that different topics, different facts, and different arrangements of artifactual material would be possible in order to meet the needs of the individual learners. In practical terms, this means that variable sequencing and patterning of materials would be a must, which would be possible only if the materials themselves were available in relatively small, discrete pieces. Arranging hundreds of bits of information (e.g., facts, concepts, illustrations, etc.) in textbook form "locks" the sequence in and limits the amount of information available to what can be included in a reasonable size. Separating stimulus material in such a way that each "piece" is relatively small (e.g., one page or a single concept film), coupled with the notion of having far more material than any given learner could conceivably cope with, means that a teacher could select from a broad array of artifacts the particular curriculum "pieces" that would be most helpful to a particular student at a given time.

Curriculum artifacts in a school for tomorrow will have to be highly valid; that is, accurate, truthful, and descriptive of the reality involved. Curriculum materials in today's schools have been diluted and distorted through the efforts of school people to make them "acceptable" to the community or sufficiently abbreviated that a large number of "brief" descriptions can be included in a textbook or other form intended for all students in a particular classroom, grade level, school district, or state system. Working in ways that are designed to get textbooks "adopted" tends to force scholars to slight controversial areas, ignore important but more complex topics, or "water down" the content in any one of a multitude of ways. For example, tomorrow's learners must get at the facts of pollution and the reality of continued economic growth, but those problems get slighted today because they may offend certain community "leaders," irritate particular taxpayers or "ruffle the feathers" of certain groups.

Because learners are different, the form of artifacts must also differ. Some children probably learn best when they see, others when they hear, others when they feel, and still others when they experience in a particular pattern or sequence of ways. In practical terms, this means that a school for tomorrow must have stimulus material, i.e., curriculum artifacts, in a variety of media and forms: printed verbal material, graphics, films, music, objects, and so on.

Another consideration is that artifacts ought to be available and manipulable so that students can pick them up, handle them, underline them, put them in their notebooks, and the like. Experience suggests that the "fleetingness" of some materials stands in the way of children's learning. Students need an opportunity to examine, to ponder, to ask questions about, to draw pictures and make notations from curriculum materials, if possible. Or, if the materials are in film form, say, they need the chance to view the film two or three or half a dozen times. Storing curriculum materials in abstract form on a computer may be theoretically possible and practical, but employing the computer that way for the basic aspects of curriculum denies the child an opportunity to handle materials physically, to sequence things in his own mind or on the table in front of him, or to contemplate by underlining and writing notes to himself alongside the particular concept or fact. Such considerations mean that real objects and actual printed or other materials should constitute at least a portion, if not the major segment, of artifacts that a child will encounter and interact with in the school.

Finally, the curriculum artifacts must be brought together into some kind of storage and retrieval system, which preserves the integrity of each artifact, but functions in such a way that materials would be almost instantaneously available. This seems to require some kind of curriculum system in which materials can be randomly stored and randomly retrieved according to a rational process built around the way children differ. In other words, we need a systematic way of organizing thousands of "pieces" of curriculum materials according to the variations among learners to enable those who use the system to "pull out" any one of thousands of artifacts according to a consideration of human realities and make it available to the learner quickly and conveniently.

The Need for a Curriculum System

One might infer from the discussion thus far that what is being suggested is a reinvention of the library, and in a way that is correct. The library is a powerful idea and an important concept, but the library is not a curriculum system in the sense outlined here, and it could not ever be. The library requires extensive space, and even with miniaturization of printed materials by means of microfiche, the storage and retrieval concept of the library is inadequate. The conceptualization of the Dewey Decimal System, for example, is generic to the subject matter of the books rather than the nature of the individual learner. Further, as a storage and retrieval system, the library system presumes nonrandom storage and retrieval. It is also very slow, and materials get lost too easily. Fortunately, systems are presently available that are small enough for a teacher to have in an office or classroom, will hold thousands of artifacts, permit random storage and retrieval, and enable teachers and learners to "take out" artifacts and handle or reproduce them. Furthermore, such systems are relatively simple to use. Before examining such hardware, however, let us think about the problem in terms of the existing situations in schools.

Consider a typical instructor's desk. As an object, a desk is generally about six feet long, three feet high, and three feet wide. Considering the space inside the desk and the usable space on top, somewhere between fifty and seventy cubic feet of space are available for the instructor's use. A typical instructor's desk often has every drawer filled with papers, and additional stacks of paper all over the top. It is not at all uncommon in such a situation for a given person to have that desk "loaded" with anywhere from 3,000 to 10,000 separate pieces of "stuff": letters, notes, pages of manuscript, books, examination papers, staplers, paper clips, globes, pencils, and the like. The most common artifacts present are usually separate sheets of paper on which information of all kinds is found. Furthermore, almost every sheet of paper is discrete—separate from the others—except for the books that may be there.

Our hypothetical instructor, of course, probably has some kind of rationale or system for keeping the papers in a more or less organized way. He might be meticulous and have every item neatly filed in a labeled folder, or he might simply have loose arrangements of materials here and there. Whatever the system, the odds are pretty good that if a secretary comes into his office and asks: "Can you tell me where the carbon copy of that letter we sent to Dr. Johnson is?" he will know. He may ponder the question awhile and look at the stacks and drawers full of paper, but in all probability he will be able to reach down into a particular pile of materials, leaf through them, and come up with what is requested in a moment or so.

Something along that line could be developed for teachers to use. The system ought not to depend on the casual reminiscings of the professional to determine where the particular items are stored. It is theoretically possible to design something about the size of a typical desk, having from 5,000 to 20,000 separate artifacts stored in a system conceptualized in terms of human variables—ability, motivation, personality, experience, difficulty, topical interest, and the like —and functioning according to the principles of random storage and random retrieval. The following section describes the general outlines of such a system.

Conceptual Basis for Curriculum System

Building a system for curriculum artifacts actually involves designing and implementing a storage and retrieval system for information. Curriculum artifacts will inevitably possess or reflect information or feelings: facts, concepts, pictures, charts, maps, sounds, diagrams, and the like. A library is an informational storage and retrieval system, but it is obviously too large for a teacher to have available for instant use. A textbook or file cabinet is also an information system, but neither is characterized by all the attributes stipulated in our criteria as characterizing a curriculum system in a school for tomorrow. The textbook contains too little information and is too rigidly sequenced; a file cabinet will hold more information, but we do not have the kinds of organizing constructs necessary to put material into the system in such a way that it can be instantaneously retrieved according to the characteristics of a given student.

Suppose we proceed abstractly and deductively in our deliberations and, instead of attempting to induce a system from the known variations among and between individuals, attempt to conceptualize a system simple enough but broad enough to encompass most of the variations that we might encounter in almost any school situation. If we start with a classification system accounting for two factors, one of which pertains to the nature of the individual and one of which pertains to the nature of the academic disciplines, we can imagine a simple system that looks something like this: 1 1
1 2
2 1
2 2

The first symbol in each pair of symbols refers to individual characteristics, while the second symbol in each pair refers to subject matter characteristics.

Such a system would allow us to generate four categories or codes for curriculum artifacts, and would be a start toward thinking about organizing curriculum materials in terms of individual differences. Obviously the differences accounted for in this system are severely limited in number, but they might be terribly important in any teaching-learning situation. Suppose, for instance, that the first symbol in each pair of symbols refers to sex: 1 refers to male and 2 refers to female. We might define our system in such a way that a 1 meant "high IQ" and a 2 meant "low IQ," or a 1 could mean "rigid personality" while a 2 could refer to "flexible personality." Those differences might be terribly important, but with the system being developed here, those would be the only differences that could be included in our considerations.

Proceeding with the same example, we could also categorize

subject matter areas in two groups. In that case, the second symbol of each pair of symbols might be used in such a way that 1 meant "arts and humanities" and 2 meant "sciences." Those would be very general distinctions, of course, but they suggest a way of thinking that could result in a simple classification system by which curriculum artifacts could be categorized according to *individual* and *subject matter* considerations. From the illustrations above, we might generate a system in which four kinds of curriculum artifacts could be included:

1 1   humanities material for bright students
1 2   science material for bright students
2 1   humanities material for dull students
2 2   science material for dull students

Other examples could be developed. The point is, by approaching the problem of developing a curriculum system in some kind of rational way, we can generate unique categories for curriculum materials that include individual and subject matter considerations simultaneously. A two-symbol classification system is obviously too limited, but it does suggest further possibilities.

Going to a four symbol system, for example, expands our potentialities for differentiation dramatically:

1 1 1 1	2 1 1 1	3 1 1 1	4 1 1 1
1 1 1 2	2 1 1 2	3 1 1 2	4 1 1 2
1 1 1 3	2 1 1 3	3 1 1 3	4 1 1 3
1 1 1 4	2 1 1 4	3 1 1 4	4 1 1 4
1 2 1 1	2 2 1 1	3 2 1 1	4 2 1 1
1 2 1 2	2 2 1 2	3 2 1 2	4 2 1 2
1 2 1 3	2 2 1 3	3 2 1 3	4 2 1 3
1 2 1 4	2 2 1 4	3 2 1 4	4 2 1 4
1 3 1 1	2 3 1 1	3 3 1 1	4 3 1 1
1 3 1 2	2 3 1 2	3 3 1 2	4 3 1 2
1 3 1 3	2 3 1 3	3 3 1 3	4 3 1 3
1 3 1 4	2 3 1 4	3 3 1 4	4 3 1 4
1 4 1 1	2 4 1 1	3 4 1 1	4 4 1 1
1 4 1 2	2 4 1 2	3 4 1 2	4 4 1 2
1 4 1 3	2 4 1 3	3 4 1 3	4 4 1 3
1 4 1 4	2 4 1 4	3 4 1 4	4 4 1 4

This portrayal of symbol combinations represents only one-fourth of the combinations possible using a four-symbol system. In the sets of symbols above the third symbol in each set is 1. All the other symbol combination possibilities have been varied to their limit, but obviously there are three additional sets that are theoretically possible. Consider the first symbol combination listed: 1 1 1 1. Obviously there could be a 1 1 2 1, 1 1 3 1, and a 1 1 4 1, but none of those sets of symbols appears anywhere. Using a system of four symbols, therefore, means we could have 256 different categories into which curriculum artifacts might be organized. Thus, any predetermined number of symbols in a classification system will generate a number of discrete categories equal to the number of symbols involved, taken to the same power of that number: 2^2, 3^3, 4^4, or 9^9, for example.

We need a system that will allow for sufficient differentiation between individuals and among subject matter areas to be helpful to persons interested in finding the right "fit" between learners and academic areas of inquiry. By proceeding this way we can obviously generate a classification system as large or as small as we desire. A two-symbol classification system would contain four discrete categories, whereas a seven-symbol system would contain 823,543 categories. However, the kind of logic implicit in this train of thought is actually restrictive. Ultimately it would result in "forcing a fit" to the individual or to the artifact. As powerful as such a classification system is, suppose we "back up" at this point in our thinking and begin again.

Suppose we start with the assumption that we simply do not know the number of individual characteristics that are important and must be considered in developing a curriculum system. That is, suppose we begin by assuming that many aspects of human existence affect learning, but we simply do not know at this time whether there are 4, or 34, or 296.

Furthermore, if we also proceed from the premise that each characteristic probably has a different number of gradations or discrete differences, then no "common" number of categories would be appropriate for all characteristics. That is, if sex is an important characteristic, only two differentiations may be necessary: male and female. On the other hand, personality or intelligence might require 15 or 120 distinctly different classifications to be maximally useful. Guilford's concept of the "structure of the intellect," for example, postulates 120 different aspects of human intelligence, and it might very well be appropriate to conceptualize a curriculum system in such a way that each of those variations could be accommodated within the system.

Following this train of thought, therefore, we could begin to conceptualize a curriculum system in which *characteristics of individuals* would be identified experimentally and experientially, and gradations or typologies would be ascertained for each of the characteristics identified. A single version of such a system might look something like this:

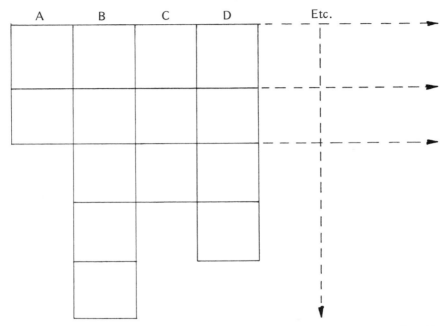

In the classification system outlined here, we have portrayed individual characteristic A as reflecting two "types," whereas characteristic B reflects five degrees or "types," as the case might be. Such a system would lend itself to further expansion as new individual characteristics are identified; it also lends itself to variations within characteristics, thus avoiding the forced fit required by the classification system set forth earlier.

To make this last point about forcing a fit more apparent, suppose we consider the six-symbol classification system suggested earlier and work it all the way through. Such a system would be workable, but it would impose severe restrictions on the user and the curriculum artifacts, even though it would provide for much more flexibility than conventional conceptions of curriculum. The following discussion is intended to show both the advantages and disadvantages of a fixed-number-of-symbols classification system. Ultimately we will argue that the fixed-number concept is too limiting and probably ought not to be employed, but because the power of the idea of a curriculum system can be dramatized along with the limitations of a fixed number system, it seems appropriate to explore the concept thoroughly.

Using a six-symbol system means, in effect, that there would be a total number of 46,656 unique categories possible (i.e., 6^6). If we further presume that the first three symbols of each set of symbols are to be applied to individual characteristics, and the last three symbols to subject matter characteristics, that would actually mean that we would have a six-symbol classification scheme which could be employed in a curriculum system which would reflect 46,656 unique categories into which curriculum artifacts might be stored for retrieval and use.

Let us further suppose that the first symbol of each set refers to *intellectual development,* the second symbol to *language development,* and the third symbol to *personality development.* In a theoretical sense, a classification system of six symbols that allocates the first three symbols for information about the individual would result in 216 differentiated "types," i.e., 6^3. If the 216 differentiated categories thus generated are thought of as 216 different "types" of learners, that means, in practical terms, that a six-symbol classification system, in which the first three symbols refer to individual characteristics, is capable of storing curriculum artifacts that differ in 216 ways among learners alone. If we further assume that the last three symbols of our six-symbol classification system apply to subject matter characteristics, we would also have 216 different categories of curriculum artifacts from the point of view of subject matter.

Taken together, such a conceptualization actually means that for each one of the 216 sets of three-symbol combinations applicable to a particular "type" of student, there are also 216 different categorizations of subject matter. Thus the total number of unique differentiations possible is 216 x 216, or 46,656 categories.

This discussion, which has been involved, has been undertaken in an attempt to help the reader comprehend how a rational system of differentiation among curriculum artifacts could be accomplished, keeping in mind certain developmental characteristics of the child and certain patternings of information within and among the subject matter fields. Though it sounds complex here, such a classification system would actually be very simple to understand and use day by day.

Without knowing exactly how such a curriculum system ought to be conceptualized and "loaded," i.e., how the artifacts ought to be put into the system, we do assume that a system should make fairly fine differentiations along both *human* and *discipline* lines. We recognize that the six-symbol conceptualization suggested here is inappropriate. There are a number of theoretical considerations, however, that suggest it would probably be a more useful and flexible approach for organizing and retrieving curriculum artifacts than is in use in schools today.

What is being outlined here as a curriculum system is actually nothing more than an elaborate system of categories. Curriculum artifacts would be categorized for storage and later retrieval, according to the known characteristics of individual learners and the known characteristics of the areas of knowledge. As such, the curriculum system would merely be a utilitarian concept and device. The whole purpose of the system would be to make it both possible and practical to match individual learner characteristics with subject matter characteristics quickly, conveniently, and accurately.

In other words the reader should keep in mind that our intentions are to focus sharply on curriculum artifacts and a curriculum system. Even when we are discussing such things as cognitive style or reading level, for example, we will be looking at those concepts in terms of their application to artifacts in a curriculum system. Assessing cognitive style is an evaluation problem. Working with a youngster in such a way that he encounters curriculum artifacts appropriate to that cognitive style is an instructional problem. Determining which curriculum artifacts would be most helpful to a youngster with a particular style of cognition would be a curriculum problem, and that will be our major focus here.

With that in mind, let us move on to an examination of at least some of the things that probably ought to be included in the conceptualization of a fixed-number-of-symbols curriculum system. The reader must keep in mind, of course, that we are attempting to describe a system that we know will be too limiting, but it is so much more flexible and precise than curriculum systems in today's schools that we can profit from an examination and understanding of a six-symbol classification system even if we decide to reject the concept later.

Developmental Characteristics of Learners

The word *development* implies a time line: changes in the individual organism over time. People change in many ways, and over time those changes might be described as "developmental" in nature. For example, it is not at all uncommon for educators to talk about such things as physical development, intellectual development, personality development, cognitive development, development of a value system, emotional development, and the like. Implicit in those phrases are the notions that certain factors that affect the developmental efforts lie within the individual organism, and certain factors are external to the organism.

For instance, governed by the information coded within his particular genetic structure, an individual develops along lines and in ways that can be ascertained, understood, and described. Not all of his development is narrowly prescribed by his genetic make-up, but the unique arrangement of his genes obviously directs an unfolding that has a remarkable impact on what he becomes. The life force within a human embryo, for example, engineers and controls its development so that it becomes a human being. And the "humanness" of that individual evolves, from the inside out. Profoundly affected by its interactions with its environment, the embryo, and then the child, moves steadily and surely in the direction of becoming, not a goat, a bird, or a stalk of corn, but a human being. The genetic gyroscope directs the human unfolding and growth that cause the tissues to form and the structures to develop that we recognize as "man." This developmental force is inherent in the nature of the unfolding tissue itself.

For example, both humans and monkeys procreate, but human beings talk and monkeys do not. We cannot account for speech unless we postulate the potential for speech as inherent in the human organism. Almost every human being that was ever born and lived for even a few years learned to talk. No monkey has ever achieved that feat. To say that children learn to talk by imitating others would be to miss the point. Monkeys imitate many human physical gestures and activities, but they never learn to talk. Furthermore, a moment's thought makes it obvious that even though children can hear the sounds adults make, they cannot see how the sounds are made at all.

Growth is the development and change that occurs within the individual as a function of his interaction with his environment. In some instances the organism withdraws, in some it accommodates, in some it assimilates, and in some it transforms. The nature of the interaction is in part a function of the environment and in part a function of the developmental aspects of the organism. No "either-or" explanation will suffice.

If we had to be limited to a six-symbol classification system, three kinds of human development seem particularly significant in terms of a curriculum system: *intellectual development, language development,* and *personality development.*

At this point in our discussion it now becomes apparent that the six-symbol coding device imposes a severe restraint on us as we work to conceptualize a meaningful curriculum system. For example, if we employ the following kind of classification logic:

1 intellectual
2 language
3 personality
4 broad field
5 disciplines
6 specialized areas

and accepted the fact that we would classify every curriculum artifact with a six-symbol classification number, it would still mean that for each symbol we would only be able to make any one of six distinctions possible for each of the factors under consideration. For example, if we were going to identify a curriculum artifact in relation to the phenomenon of intellectual development, we could define intellectual development in six, but only six, ways. In practical terms, that means we need to define the values of symbols 1 through 6 as points on a continuum, i.e., ordinal numbers, or categorical differences, i.e., nominal numbers. Either approach would probably be appropriate, and it might be possible to include some aspects of both, but it becomes increasingly obvious that even a system that allows for 216 "types" of different individuals is a very constraining system.

Every student of human intelligence and learning knows how varied and complex intellectual development is. Even so, if we put our minds to it, it might be possible to generate a typology of six different types of intellectual development that would be both qualitatively unique and yet quantitatively linear. There are difficulties and dangers in such an approach, but if it were done thoughtfully and on the basis of the best that we now know about the development of human intelligence, it might be an exceptionally useful system for classifying the curriculum artifacts in a curriculum system.

We might attempt to synthesize some of the major theoretical and empirical works in the area of human intelligence, arrange them on a six-point scale, and then include a fairly elaborate description and definition of each point on the scale. By describing in precise ways each point on the continuum in terms of the work of Piaget, Guilford, Spearman, and others, we might be able to set forth six fairly comprehensive and elaborate descriptions of intellectual development positioned along the scale in an ordinal way. Such a notion presumes at least two things: (1) the idea of a general or g factor in intelligence, and (2) the notion that there are a number of discernible positive correlations evident among the specific factors of intellect that have been identified and studied by various researchers in the field. That may not be an unreasonable supposition, but it does make it increasingly obvious that a six-symbol system is constraining. If we could encompass Piaget's "stages" of intellectual growth and Guilford's notion of "convergent thinking," "evaluation," and others, we might be able to set forth six reasonably discrete descriptions of intellectual development that would also reflect gradations or levels. We are not knowledgeable enough to pull that off, but we feel that it probably could be accomplished. If so, we would have made operational one symbol of our six-symbol set of classification numbers, as follows:

1 ☐ ☐ ☐ ☐ ☐
2 ☐ ☐ ☐ ☐ ☐
3 ☐ ☐ ☐ ☐ ☐
4 ☐ ☐ ☐ ☐ ☐
5 ☐ ☐ ☐ ☐ ☐
6 ☐ ☐ ☐ ☐ ☐

The second symbol in our six-symbol classification system refers to language development. In all probability, this should be an ordinal system of numbers, reflecting the readability level of the language used in the artifact primarily. If it were arithmetical rather than verbal or pictorial rather than verbal, estimates could be made of the difficulty level of the material. Rather than to use a single readability formula, it would probably be more appropriate to use several, or to use a number of criteria such as are normally employed in readability formulas (i.e., length of sentence, number of syllables per word, complexities of ideas being described, familiarity of words, etc.) to make more precise differentiations of curriculum artifacts to be coded and put into the system. Similar procedures might be employed if the artifacts involve spoken language, e.g., cassette recordings or films. In essence, then, our classification system would reflect these gradations of difficulty and complexity regarding the language of the artifacts involved:

☐	1	☐	☐	☐	☐
☐	2	☐	☐	☐	☐
☐	3	☐	☐	☐	☐
☐	4	☐	☐	☐	☐
☐	5	☐	☐	☐	☐
☐	6	☐	☐	☐	☐

The third aspect of individual development to be incorporated in the coding of artifacts for our curriculum system could be personality factors. As was suggested for the intellectual development realm, it might very well be possible to generate a set of six descriptions of personality "types" and arrange them on some kind of continuum reflecting psychological health, sense of adequacy, degree of self-actualization, or some such phenomena. Attempting to synthesize the work of personality theorists, such as Peck and Havighurst, Kohlberg, Rogers, Maslow, Combs and Syngg, and persons such as Rokeach, Fromm, and Erikson, might very well result in some fairly succinct statements or "types" of personalities that could conveniently be reflected on a scale from 1 to 6. Or, we might employ the typology suggested earlier in this chapter: altruist, hedonist, sentimentalist, reactionary, etc.

In other words, we feel that it might be possible to generate "types" of personality descriptions that would be both qualitatively and quantitatively different. If that could be done, we could make some tentative stipulations about the relationship of those personality qualities to curriculum artifacts. That would be especially difficult, we realize, since almost no work along those lines has been attempted. There is reason to believe, however, that it would be possible to categorize curriculum artifacts in terms of the ambiguity inherent in the materials, for example, or in terms of the potential source of threat or challenge to an ego structure, obfuscation or clarity of communication, consistency with or violation of community norms, or congruence or incongruence with conventional descriptions of reality. If so, it might prove both interesting and instructive to "try out" certain artifacts on certain personality "types" to see which materials are most effective in helping a particular individual learn.

Considering, even in this very general way, the variety of individual factors in relation to curriculum artifacts suggests a whole range of research hypotheses. For example, if a given youngster would be assessed as "high" on intellectual development (e.g., 2) and "low" on personality development (e.g., 5) but "average" on language development (e.g., 3), would complex but ambiguous curriculum materials be more effective in facilitating learning than simple, nonambiguous, and long but not involved materials? The reader can invent his own hypotheses. The point is, with such a curriculum system available and operational, a whole new concept of curriculum research might emerge and open up vast new understandings about the teaching-learning process. Because our present curriculum efforts and research processes tend to emphasize a single variable or simple arrangements of variables in what is admittedly a tremendously complex set of phenomena, we have not been very successful in making significant progress in our efforts to understand the complexities that are involved. The curriculum system outlined here might not allow for those complexities to be considered and manipulated as variables in research projects, either, but on the surface it seems that more of the complexities might be accounted for and seen in relationship to other factors than we have traditionally been able to include.

Characteristics of Subject Matter Fields

There are several ways in which the three columns of symbols referring to subject matter areas might be conceptualized. It might be appropriate to use some logical set of constructs for grouping academic disciplines into six general fields, for instance. If we used the general categories of

1 Life Sciences
2 Behavioral Sciences
3 Physical Sciences
4 Humanities
5 Communication
6 Mathematics and Philosophy

for the fourth column of symbols in our system, we could have a further breakdown of six subareas within each general area to be reflected in the fifth column of symbols. Thus in the life sciences we might find zoology, botany, entomology, physiology, anatomy, and allied medical fields. In the physical sciences we might find astronomy, geography, geology, chemistry, physics, and allied engineering fields. The same could be accomplished for each of the remaining areas of academic inquiry. We could employ the theoretical work of Phenix, King and Brownell, Bruner, and others to assist us in this endeavor.

If the final symbol in the system were used as a vocational or career-related factor, a six-category breakdown of vocational or career considerations could be built into the coding system, perhaps as follows:

1 Careers involving work primarily with people
2 Careers involving work primarily with objects and physical things
3 Careers involving work primarily with data and symbols
4 Careers involving work primarily with people and objects and things
5 Careers involving work primarily with people and data
6 Careers involving work primarily with data and objects

Again, this categorization may not be adequate. Further refinement would have to be done. Using the above categories for the purposes of illustration, however, we can invent all kinds of ways of looking at subject matter areas and vocational or career possibilities which might be particularly relevant and helpful to students in school. For instance, the category including Life Sciences, Entymology, and Careers Working Primarily with People and Data would be coded as follows:

☐ ☐ ☐   1 3 5

Materials in that category could include information pertinent to a person who might work as an accountant in a corporation manufacturing pesticides for farmers. If the first three symbols were 2, 4, and 6, the final coding of that category in the classification system would be 2 4 6 1 3 5. Here curriculum artifacts would be fairly high in terms of their intellectual potential, somewhat below average in reading level, appropriate for a rigid, insensitive, threatened person who might be interested in the life sciences area, particularly entomology, and who hoped for a career that would allow him to work with symbols and data rather than people or things.

In summary, we have outlined a way of thinking about curriculum materials that might be used to generate a curriculum system in which such materials could be stored and retrieved for students' use. The rationale for storing the materials in the system would include a consideration of three different kinds of developmental factors inherent in individual learners—intellectual development, language development, and personality development—and three different kinds of factors implicit in academic fields—broad subject matter areas, narrow academic fields, and vocational or career considerations.

There are many difficulties and many inadequacies involved in this way of thinking about curriculum, the most obvious of which are the restraints it imposes, but even such a restrictive system as this would enable school people to break out of the conventional conception of curriculum materials—i.e., big "pieces," rigidly sequenced, aimed at the group, limited in amount, distorted in validity, and the like—and think about developing a curriculum system rooted conceptually in what we know about individual differences and the nature of knowledge.

As we have stated several times during the course of this description, a fixed-number-of-symbols classification system is severely restraining, even when it allows for 216 different "types" of learners and 216 different classifications of areas of knowledge in a 46,656 category classification scheme. We have gone to some lengths here to attempt to underscore that point.

Children are different, and knowledge is almost infinitely varied. What we need is a curriculum system that will enable us to conceptualize the educationally important ways in which children differ. We also need to conceptualize the areas of knowledge in ways that are sufficiently discrete to enable teachers to use that information creatively in their search of the curriculum for appropriate artifacts for particular students, with particular characteristics, at a particular point in time.

Given our understanding of the problems and the possibilities involved, we feel it would be unwise to attempt to conceptualize and implement a curriculum system predicated on a fixed-number-of-symbols classification scheme. Our detailed discussion was intended to outline the power of the concept of a classification scheme for curriculum artifacts based on a consideration of individual learner characteristics and subject matter fields, but the discussion also dramatizes the fact that *any* such fixed-number-of-symbols classification system would be severely limiting. In actual practice there is no real necessity for such restraints.

A six-symbol system would be neat and "simple." It would be easy to understand and easy to use, but it would also require unnecessary "forcings" to make the learner or the artifacts fit into the system. We return to the point, therefore, that a classification system for curriculum artifacts, open-ended as to the number of individual characteristics that are important and open-ended regarding the classification of the areas of knowledge, would serve our purposes very well. Such a system would probably require the use of a computer to identify all of the possible combinations of characteristics, but such a system could still be relatively simple to understand and operate. In a school for tomorrow we need a conceptual system that will allow us to make reasonably fine distinctions among individuals and among the various areas of knowledge, and bring these two phenomena together in ways that will maximize young people's opportunities to learn precisely whatever it is that they need to learn.

What has been outlined, of course, would immediately require empirical verification of the usefulness of the categorizations within the classification system. That is, each artifact initially placed into the curriculum system would have to be coded regarding intellectual development, language development, personality development, and all of the other individual characteristics identified as useful for the curriculum system. Depending on the accuracy of the evaluation of a particular child by a given teacher and the accuracy of the original determinations of intellectual, language, personality, and other factors as related to the artifact, there might or might not be an adequate fit. Simple empirical checks could be incorporated in the system, and over time empirical verifications of the original coding or modification could be obtained. Likewise, inadequacies in the evaluation processes would probably become conspicuous over time allowing for new insights into the teaching process as well as new understandings about the nature of curriculum itself.

One final point before we move on. A school for tomorrow will not be organized or operated on the basis of grade levels as such, and the question arises, "How big should a curriculum system be?" We would like to suggest that there be six overlapping levels of curriculum systems, each spanning approximately eight years of growth. If the systems overlapped, but each included different artifacts, the series of curriculum systems would constitute a kind of "seamless curriculum," such as Shane[7] has recently advocated. In essence, the different systems arranged hierarchically in terms of age might look something like this:

Age 23–31 (post-graduate school years)
Age 19–27 (graduate school years)
Age 15–23 (undergraduate school years)
Age 11–19 (senior high school years)
Age 7–15 (middle school years)
Age 3–11 (elementary school years)

If each system contained 20,000 or more curriculum artifacts, a typical youngster would have direct access to 60,000 "pieces" of curriculum material during his public school years and that much more if he went on through college. That, plus the resources of a library, which would be available for use as it already is, should constitute an exceptionally rich set of resources for individual learners in a school for tomorrow.

The logistics of the system and the number of artifacts underscores one crucial point. Knowledge is increasing so rapidly, and so much is already known, that schools must find newer and more effective ways of helping teachers guide students through the maze of information in ways that are fascinating, encouraging, helpful, and fun.

It has been said that if what a youngster learns during twelve years of school were totaled up, it would amount to approximately one-billionth of all that is presently known. If that is true, the question immediately arises, "Which billionth would you absolutely insist that he learn?"

That is a terribly important question. Assume, for the moment, that every person in the United States learned a different billionth of the world's knowledge. If that hypothetical situation could be realized (and it would mean that no two people in the entire United States would be able to communicate, because everybody would know something different from everybody else), all of their knowledge together would still represent only about 20 percent of all that is presently known. And considering the fact that we are currently producing somewhere between 900,000 and 2,100,000 articles every year in technical journals alone,[8] that figure rises every year. Obviously, curriculum workers must rethink their conceptualizations of what curriculum is and what it might be.

Notes

1. Max Ways, "How to Think About the Environment," *Fortune,* February 1970, pp. 99-100.

2. Much of this section is drawn directly from James K. Duncan and Jack R. Frymier, "Exploration in the Systematic Study of Curriculum," *Theory Into Practice* 6 (October 1967): 180-199.

3. The paradigm set forth here is arbitrary in differentiating [   ] from O, and it would be equally reasonable (and probably more accurate) to think of a continuum as the basis for portraying the environment with which the individual interacts. Using the example referred to here, we might think of a library as a part of a larger social system, e.g., the city government, down through the book or a single paragraph, say, to perhaps a particular picture or word. Such a conceptualization might be more accurate, but it would also be much more difficult to describe and to manipulate theoretically or empirically. We recognize the inadequacies of the dichotomous distinction between [   ] and O, but we feel it is a useful beginning and may be elaborated or modified later as more sophisticated conceptualizations or observational devices are developed.

4. Arthur W. Combs and Donald Syngg, *Individual Behavior,* rev. ed. (New York: Harper & Bros., 1957).

5. Jack R. Frymier, *Fostering Educational Change* (Columbus: Charles E. Merrill Publishing Co., 1969), chap. 4.

6. In other words, the extent to which an artifact is perceived by a learner presumes a continuum, one end of which reflects perception and the other end of which reflects nonperception. Dichotomous distinctions will be made, but such categorization is arbitrary

and for purposes of discussion only. It is hoped that the categorization process will enable the reader to conceptualize the phenomenon of perception in ways that will lend themselves to empirical manipulation.

7. Harold Shane, "The Educational Significance of the Future," mimeographed (Bloomington, Ind.: Indiana University, 1972), pp. 8-9.

8. Charles P. Bourne, *Methods of Information Handling* (New York: John Wiley & Sons, 1963), p. 2.

4
Instruction

Instruction in a school for tomorrow may well be different in emphasis rather than in kind. But what balance of student and teacher roles of initiator and responder will be needed if we are to foster the development of rationally autonomous individuals? What new patterns of instructional arrangements would we need? What standards will we invoke to guide our choosing?

John Hough
Hanford Salmon

It is natural for people to want sure solutions to complex problems. A more realistic stance, however, is to provide people with a way of thinking about complex problems so that they can develop solutions that are congruent with the human and material resources that define their unique social situations. Instruction in schools of tomorrow will be no less complex than instruction in today's schools, because instruction is and always will be, in part at least, a complex social activity. This chapter will present a number of thoughts about instruction that may be useful in conceptualizing and solving instructional problems that will surely exist in any conception of a school for tomorrow.

We will not presume to specify what instruction in a school for tomorrow should look like. That must be decided on the basis of the unique human and material resources available in particular situations. What we will do is to present and explore some ideas about instruction that we think are useful.

As we explore these ideas, it may be helpful to think about a specific school. Reading this chapter with a school in mind should provide a specific context for assessing the credibility and potential feasibility of applying some of the ideas explored here. In other words, we suggest reading this chapter with a particular mind set:

that is, "Do these ideas suggest instructional innovations that could be implemented in a specific school, given *reasonable* imagination, dedication, and effort on the part of the professional staff, the students, and the community?"

It is often helpful to start a discussion by making clear what will and what will not follow. In this chapter we will not indulge in specific predictions of or prescriptions for radical changes in American education. First of all, we do not think that rapid, revolutionary changes are very likely. Rather we see evolutionary changes in the years ahead. Secondly, we are not convinced that specific predictions and prescriptions are needed. Too often such prescriptions simply cannot be followed, given the circumstances that define a unique school situation.

In writing this chapter we were guided by several assumptions, and much of what we say later will follow from these assumptions.

1. We assume that professional educators, students, and parents already know "better" about instructing than the instruction that typically exists in schools today. We need to find the resources and develop the competencies and the will to *do* many things that we already know should be done.

2. We assume that a school for tomorrow will continue to be influenced by a changing world. Some of the factors that influence instruction and that will continue to change are personal goals and values, social goals and values, and the means of attaining personal and social goals.

3. We assume that the autonomous individual, or self-directed person, is created, not born. Many factors influence whether a person will develop into an autonomous individual, and one of those factors can be the instruction that is a part of schooling.

One thing seems clear: if autonomous individuals are to be created, many schools must shift the balance of the instructional roles of initiator and responder. Descriptively, in most of today's schools teachers are the primary initiators of objectives, instructional contact with students, and evaluation of student learning. Exceptions can be found in some classrooms, and more broadly in some experimental schools, but they are rather rare.

A school for tomorrow could be organized so that students are more often the initiators. Students could take a larger role in

developing objectives, planning and implementing instructional procedures, and performing evaluations. Though one might envision
teachers almost totally delegating such responsibilities to students,
the few examples that we have of experimental schools built on that
pattern give little hope that such a movement will gain general
acceptance. It seems more realistic to advocate a more balanced
sharing of teaching responsibilities by teachers and students. Whether
such a conception of education should be implemented in selected
classrooms of a school or in a whole school all at once, we are not
prepared to say. One thing, however, seems certain: shared responsibility will require revised expectations and the learning and use of
new behaviors by both teachers and students.

In this chapter, we will explore some of the implications of
sharing the teaching responsibility with students and changing teacher and student expectations and behaviors. We will do this largely in
the context of classroom instruction. In doing so, we do not deny
that many important educational experiences do and should occur
outside the formal educational setting. The home and the community are in many ways fertile educational environments, but we
are concerned here with instruction in the context of formal schooling.

Instruction has been defined as the arrangement and use of
human and material resources for the purpose of facilitating learning.
Thus instruction is the means by which curriculum is implemented as
actors use artifacts, operations, knowledge, motor skills, and feelings
to facilitate learning. If we are able to think of actors as including
both teachers and students interacting in a more balanced condition
of initiation and response, we should be able to create an image of a
very complex and dynamic social situation in which the actors will
need a great deal of instructional support in order to share the
responsibilities for instruction in a balanced way consistent with the
potential development of both teachers and students.

The balance in the role of initiator and responder to which we
refer would represent a substantial but attainable innovation in many
classrooms. We should not, however, delude ourselves. The problems
relating to the support of instructional innovations have been found
to be numerous and pervasive. Support may take the form of
inservice education or emanate from supervisory and administrative
services. In addition, one of the most powerful sources of support
can be other teachers and students who are also trying innovative

instructional practices. Having the support of one's administrators and supervisors is fine, but it is comforting to know that one's peers are also trying new approaches to instruction and experiencing the excitement of success and the frustration of failure. A supportive collegial climate of instructional innovation is not likely to be one in which innovations are either encapsulated, rejected, or co-opted by the administration. In such a climate innovations are more likely to persist.

The use of analogy may help illustrate this condition. Recent developments in the field of medical science have shown us that the body, as a system, eventually encapsulates or rejects transplanted organs unless a great deal of special care is provided. Special techniques are now used to regulate the body system so that it supports, rather than rejects or encapsulates, the transplanted organ. If we relate a school system to the body system and an instructional innovation to a transplanted organ, we can see the need to provide systemic, organizational support in order to maintain "transplanted," instructional innovations. Desire to innovate is not enough. Desire coupled with inservice education that teaches one how to innovate including *doing* what one knows, is not enough. Some very promising instructional innovations have been thrown out, successfully isolated, or co-opted, because the innovators and innovations were not given adequate systemic support.

In other words, not only must a school mobilize for *change* in terms of instructional innovation, it must also carefully mobilize and plan for the *maintenance* of that change in the face of the natural tendency of teachers, students, and other professional personnel in the school to resist and/or expel it. No matter how carefully a change is planned, if the mechanisms for sustained innovation are not created simultaneously, the change will not be lasting and significant. More will be said about this in chapters 6 and 7.

Types of Learnings

Before we begin a systematic discussion of instruction and how it can be carried out to optimize learning and encourage the development of autonomous individuals, let us take a closer look at the intended product of instruction, i.e., learning and the maintenance of prior learnings.

When considering instruction, we are concerned with what is learned, or learnings, *and* with the characteristics of the learner.

Later, we will propose that most learners may learn some things best by using one type of instructional strategy. In this case the type of content learned may be paramount in determining the instructional strategy used. We will also propose that different students may learn the same content best by using different instructional strategies that are more congruent with their unique capabilities and motivation. In such cases the nature of the learner may be paramount in determining the instructional strategy to be used.

There are many ways of conceptualizing learnings. One way is to think of learnings as including knowledge learnings; motor skill learnings; feeling state learnings; and the application of these three types in convergent, divergent, and judgmental situations.

Convergent applications involve situations in which knowledge, motor skills, or feelings are used in a highly structured context in which the parameters that govern behavior are substantially structured by the situation. The applicational behavior may be considered correct by definition, custom, or empirical verification. Examples of convergent behaviors can be found in all subject fields. In mathematics, for example, the convergent application of knowledge of the processes of subtraction, multiplication, and estimation of the magnitude of the trial divisor is needed in the solution of long division problems. This is an example of convergent application of knowledge, because answers to long division problems may be considered correct or incorrect.

Divergent applications involve situations in which knowledge, motor skills, or feelings are used in a less structured context. Divergent behaviors cannot be really considered right or wrong. Rather, they are considered to be reasonable or unreasonable, appropriate or inappropriate. Once again, examples can be found in all subject fields. One that is familiar to most of us is the discrepant event situation characteristic of certain types of inquiry learning. Thus, a student might apply knowledge of economics, geography, and social behavior to the hypothetical question, "What would the recreational industry of New England be like if the average yearly temperature of the world were to increase by fifteen degrees fahrenheit?" This is an example of divergent application of knowledge because there is no single answer but a range of *reasonable* answers.

Judgmental applications of knowledge, motor skills, and feelings are evaluative in nature. The evaluative situation may be tightly bound (convergent) or more open (divergent). An example of convergent judgmental application of motor skills can be found in learning to parallel-park an automobile in a manner that meets the criteria specified in a driving test. An example of a divergent judgmental application of feelings may be found in making judgments regarding appropriate use of color and texture in the works of several painters, all of whom intended to create the feeling or mood of sadness in their work.

Thus, we may classify learnings (and also objectives, in the case where learnings are intended and specified as objectives) as depicted in figure 4-1.[1] We must be careful to remember, however, that when we emphasize one of the twelve types of learnings, we are indicating *primary* interest in that type of learning (or objective). As was previously stated, most learnings are mixed, so that when one learns to use a drill press, for example, though the apparent primary learning may be skill in using the drill press, feelings and knowledge are usually being learned concurrently.

Figure 4-1. Classification system for learnings and objectives

LEVELS OF LEARNINGS	DOMAINS OF LEARNINGS		
	Cognitive	Motor	Affective
Basic Type of Learning	Acquisition of knowledge	Acquisition of skills	Acquisition of and awareness of feelings
Convergent Application	Use of knowledge in convergent situations	Use of skills in convergent situations	Use of feelings in convergent situations
Divergent Application	Use of knowledge in divergent situations	Use of skills in divergent situations	Use of feelings in divergent situations
Judgmental Application	Use of knowledge in judgmental situations	Use of skills in judgmental situations	Use of feelings in judgmental situations

If, as we have asserted, a school for tomorrow should increase its potential to provide educational experiences that will encourage responsible autonomous student behavior, then the learnings that take place in such a school should not be determined largely by teachers. We do not believe, however, that all students would be able to determine all of their own educational objectives or that responsible, autonomous behavior would be encouraged in all cases. Rather, we propose an individualized approach that would extend this heavy responsibility to students when they are ready *and* willing to accept it. This will surely require substantial inservice education of many, if not most, teachers to enable them to share their historical responsibility wisely and help the traditionally dependent student learn to plan his educational program wisely. Certainly, organizational support for such an instructional evolution must be pervasive, understanding, and skillful, or the program will collapse for lack of an adequate foundation. American education does *not* need a rebirth of well-meaning permissiveness founded in abdication of responsibility.

Variables that Influence Learning

In considering the critical variables that determine whether a student is ready or not ready to learn (relatively speaking, of course) we will consider only two variables: *motivation* and *capability*. This may seem an overly simplistic approach. Perhaps it seems so because it is so conceptually simple. Much, of course, depends on our definitions of motivation and capability.

Motivation: Intrinsic and Extrinsic

We define intrinsic motivation in terms of three additive variables: (1) a person's ability to define a goal or objective toward which he wishes to work; (2) the person's ability to see what, for the moment at least, is a relatively clear path to the attainment of that goal or objective; and (3) the internal condition that causes a person to engage in and persist in a task even though the goal and the path to goal attainment may not, at the moment, be clear. The following direct quotation of a parent points out, not only that the concept of intrinsic motivation is well understood by "laymen," but also that laymen may have insights and intense feelings about the relationships between curriculum content and student intrinsic motivation that seem to have eluded many "professional" educators.

You could never motivate John in school at all. That does not mean that you cannot motivate John. But because he cannot be motivated in terms of the curriculum of the school, to automatically be just pronounced dunce of the year I think is a little unfair. And I think it hasn't just happened to John, but it has happened to lots of kids . . . more times than people want to recognize.

I mean you've got math, social studies, English, spelling, and so on . . . that's it . . . I mean that's what they've got to offer, and if you can't be motivated, you know, you're some kind of thing from outer space . . . you don't belong . . . you don't fit in . . . you're out in left field. But that doesn't mean that child isn't motivated. They just haven't found what he's motivated in.

You only have so many goals that you give them to motivate themselves toward. And if they can't motivate themselves toward those goals, the hell with them. When you talk about a relatively clear path to the attainment of that goal, well, you put a horse racing class in there and you've got a straight A student! But our school system will never recognize that . . . never . . . never. That kid could go out and raise a million dollars raising horses and the school system is always going to see him as a bum . . . an unmotivated bum that couldn't do anything else and he got lucky because he was able to make a living raising horses. But, if he had been a straight A student, *and* motivated and had graduated in the top of his class and did well, they would say they had something to do with it. It scares me because I can't help thinking that there must be so many other kids going through the same thing.

Extrinsic motivation also involves three additive variables: (1) a person's ability to understand and accept the objectives that another person sets for him; (2) the person's ability to see what, for the moment at least, is a relatively clear path to the attainment of those objectives; and (3) the internalized effect of external stimuli, such as praise or correction, that causes a person to persist at a task even though the objective and the path to the attainment of the objective may not, at the moment, be clear.

We hold that the condition of intrinsic motivation is, in general, more conducive to developing responsible autonomous behavior than the condition of extrinsic motivation. Yet, at the same time we recognize that for most people at certain states of their education, the condition of extrinsic motivation, i.e., the acceptance and achievement of objectives proposed by others, is a precondition to developing intrinsic motivation.

Nothing succeeds like success. Continued success of the right kind can lead to achievement of competencies that enable a person to define his own goals and succeed in their attainment. The result is often an enhanced and more realistic conception of self and others, which in turn enables one to make more discriminating choices about when to accept and work toward the attainment of goals suggested by others and when to be "one's own man."

Thus, we may envision two interacting continua of intrinsic and extrinsic motivation. We all reside somewhere on those two continua at any given point in time, and our intrinsic and extrinsic states of motivation largely determine the instructional strategy that, at that moment, will lead us most efficiently and effectively to the attainment of the objective or objectives toward which we work.

Perhaps an example will help clarify our conception of motivation and how it applies to teachers and students. Suppose a high school student wants to be a writer. In comparison with other aspiring writers of his experience and maturity, he considers himself to be quite good. He sees the path toward the attainment of his goal fairly clearly. He must write, read the works of others, and read commentaries on the works of others. He accepts these tasks as necessary for achieving his goal. He writes and reads considerably, and he feels that his work is improving and that he is developing a style he can call his own. As the months pass, he becomes increasingly satisfied with his work, and that feeling of satisfaction drives him on toward his goal. He continues reading and writing prolifically. Finally, he dares to send several of his manuscripts to publishers, but they are all rejected.

His English teacher, though no writer herself, knows a good deal about writing and writers and something about the publication world. In talking with the student, she encourages him but tells him she can see at least two areas where his writing needs improvement: his poetic images often lack vividness and are a bit trite, and the dialogues in his short stories seem at times to be stiff and unconvincing. Somewhat reluctantly, he agrees with her and asks for help. She suggests that he postpone the writing of any further poems or short stories and spend some time reading and analyzing the works of a few selected poets, with particular emphasis on how those poets have used imagery. In addition, she suggests that he spend time listening to conversations between people and then writing down those conversations as if they were part of a story. She also offers to arrange for him to get criticism of his work from a writer who is an English instructor at a nearby college. He agrees to follow her suggestions, and after several months of selective reading and practicing writing poetic images and short examples of dialogues, he begins to feel that he is improving. His English teacher reads and criticizes his exercises and gives him a good deal of encouragement. Finally he has several meetings with the college English instructor, who confirms the high school teacher's judgments, gives the student some specific feedback on the exercises he has been doing over the last few months, and suggests that he now rewrite several of his poems and short stories. This he does. With encouragement from the college English instructor, he submits several of his poems to a local literary society that publishes an informal journal several times a year. One of his poems is accepted for publication, and he begins to feel a bit better about himself as a writer. He returns to writing new works and continues reworking many of his previous writings. He even begins to entertain the possibility of taking some college courses in literature and writing, something that he had previously rejected as a restricting waste of time.

In this example, we have illustrated aspects of both intrinsic and extrinsic motivation. The student's long-range goal remained the same. His English teacher did not tamper with that goal, but she did suggest several specific objectives for the student to work toward. She arranged for human and material resources that would facilitate the student's attainment of those objectives and reinforced the student's behavior through encouragement. She actually did very little to influence the student's intrinsic motivation because it was already there. The student did not have to define his general goal, though he did accept and work toward the attainment of several objectives proposed, not by himself, but by a person who for him was a "significant other."

Our example, though real, has been a positive caricature used to illustrate our conception of motivation. But what about those students whose goals are unclear or who are unable to see school-related objectives as being related to the attainment of their goals, such as the student whose parent's comments were quoted above? Our conception of motivation leads us to an obvious, though perhaps oversimplified, answer. Help such students define and clarify their goals and open up the curriculum as much as possible to include objectives that students can see as being related to the achievement of their goals. Shift the balance a bit so that students can more often be initiators of what they see as worthwhile to learn. The word *curriculum* is derived from the Latin word meaning to run a race. Why not allow that race to be a "horse race," at least in part, if raising horses is the student's goal?

The alternative to what we have suggested is one that we have all experienced as teachers and as students: that is, gently or harshly trying to convince students to accept our objectives (to run *our* race, which they often see as being unrelated to their goals) and using extrinsic motivational techniques to keep students working toward the attainment of those objectives. We have had much experience with the implications of choosing this alternative; in many cases we have increased student dependence and/or student alienation. We are not suggesting a return to the "what shall we do today?" era, but a wise and human implementation of what we already know; in the long run, people typically expend more energy and feel greater satisfaction when working on tasks for which *they* see a reason (tasks that lead to a goal they see as their goal) than when they are forced or manipulated into performing tasks for which they see little personal payoff. We also suggest that self-direction in learning is more likely to develop from instructional situations in which students work on tasks that lead to the attainment of *their* perceived goals than from instructional situations in which students work on tasks that they perceive as being unrelated to their goals. This is nothing new. Many of us already know this; what we need to learn is how to do it.

Capability

Now let us turn our attention to the second learner characteristic that determines whether or not a student is ready to learn: capability. There are many factors, in addition to motivation, that determine whether a student is capable of learning at a given point in time. Some of these factors are physical, intellectual, and social development; inherited capacity to learn; prior experiences and learning; self-concept; and physical and psychological condition. All of these factors (with the possible exception of inherited capacity) can be modified at a given point in time, but collectively they represent a given condition of capability over which the teacher often has little real control. Teachers do have some control, however, over defining, or helping students define, objectives that are attainable and challenging. It is that simple. It is not simple, however, to arrange instructional situations that are congruent, not only with the student's objectives, but also with his learning rate and style with respect to specific types of learnings.

Thus, as we think about instruction, in addition to thinking about the types of learnings or objectives that we hope to facilitate, we must also consider the characteristics of the learner that largely determine whether or not he will be able to learn. Though these factors are numerous and complex, they may be grouped under one of two classifications: (1) level of motivation and (2) learning capability.

When we talk about capability, we emphasize that we are not in any way suggesting a return to the anachronistic notion that students ought to be pigeonholed on the basis of standardized intelligence and psychological examinations and programmed through their educational experiences on that basis. Our concept of capability is very flexible and fluid, varying from day to day and from task to task; it requires careful and highly sophisticated diagnostic ability from those who would facilitate the learning of others.

Parental insights about the concept of capability are often quite profound, as we can see from the comments of a parent whose "child" will be twenty when he graduates from high school:

> I'm sure there are some kids who are just hanging around trying to get through with a minimum of effort, but there are a few who *really* want to get through but they have had problems, they have had psychological hang-ups, but they really *do* want to get through. But they are not treated any differently than a ten-year-old in grade school.

Instructional Strategies and Instructional Behavior

If several students are sufficiently motivated and capable of a specific learning (achieving a specific objective), will the same instructional strategy be equally effective for all those students? If a student is sufficiently motivated and capable of achieving certain objectives, will the same instructional strategy be equally effective in facilitating the achievement of the different types of objectives (i.e., cognitive, motor, and affective, at the levels of convergent, divergent, and evaluative application)? The answers to questions like these would yield information that would be invaluable in selecting instructional strategies to facilitate optimum learning for students with different levels of motivation and different capabilities.

What is an instructional strategy? In our view it is a distinct pattern of teacher and student verbal and nonverbal behaviors that include both actions, e.g., initiation and solicitation, and reactions, e.g., response, clarification, and appraisal. As these behaviors are used in instructional settings, they form four distinctively different patterns, called "strategies." As far as we can ascertain, there are only four basic instructional strategies and eleven basic instructional behaviors. Three of these strategies may be further divided according to the source of the initiation of instructional communication, i.e., teacher or student. Therefore, we will discuss seven strategies in which a large number of subtle variations are possible. These subtle variations are extremely important, because the variations in behavior used within strategies reflect the uniqueness of instruction.

Before proceeding with a discussion of these eleven behaviors and seven instructional strategies, it may be helpful to point out the distinction between strategies and methods. When we use the term *strategies* we are referring to direct, interactive, group, and independent communication patterns. The term *methods* we reserve for such instructional innovations as tutorial peer teaching, computer-assisted instruction, independent study, simulation, trust walks, inquiry training, marathon "think-ins," programmed instruction, and sensitivity training.

The instructional strategies that we will discuss are applicable to any of these methodological innovations or to such organizational or curricular innovations as black studies, modular scheduling, open classrooms, rationality education, open-ended curriculum, mini-courses, storefront schools, and humanistic curriculum. The strategies are not synonyms for them, however. They describe the instructional communication that occurs within these various methodological, organizational, and curricular innovations. The strategies also describe what occurred between Mark Hopkins at one end of a log and a student at the other end and, as far as we know, every other instructional situation that involves actors, artifacts, and operations.

Instructional Behaviors

Earlier in this chapter we stated that a greater instructional balance in the role of initiator and responder would be one way of facilitating greater student autonomy and self-direction in learning. In considering the following description of instructional behaviors and strategies, the reader should think of his pet methodological, organizational, or curricular innovations and ask himself which instructional strategy or strategies, involving which instructional behaviors, would be most congruent with those innovations. And, further, he should ask himself, "If I wanted to foster development of student autonomy and self-direction, what behavioral variations within the four basic strategies would I use?" To put it more directly, "How would I behave? How would students behave? What would we *do*?"

Instructional behaviors are observable human behaviors defining the source and direction of the communications that constitute instructional strategies. Although one could define behaviors differently—and there are those who have—the eleven behaviors defined and illustrated below are sufficient for later discussion of instructional strategies.[2]

Clarification

Clarification is a responsive behavior. It is the process of (1) helping the person who has emitted a behavior become more aware of his own behavior or understand its meaning or implication, or (2) helping the person responding to the behavior, or some other person observing it, understand its meaning or implication.

An example will help illustrate these two types of clarification. A fourth-grade class has been discussing how climatic conditions often determine a people's way of life, such as the food that they eat and their means of providing shelter. The teacher asks a question: "If an Eskimo were hunting seals along the coast of the Arctic Ocean for several days and needed shelter, what might he build his shelter from?" A student responds, "He would build an igloo, because there wouldn't be anything else." The teacher could respond by saying, "What do you mean when you say he would build an igloo, because there wouldn't be anything else?" Or he could say, "Do you mean that he would build an igloo, because there would be ice and snow to build one from, but there wouldn't be trees that far north to cut down and use for a temporary shelter?" In the first instance, the teacher forces the clarification of meaning back on the student by asking the student what he means. In the second instance, he seeks clarification for himself and possibly other students.

Clarifying behaviors often solicit responses from others in the process of seeking clarification. When the primary purpose of the solicitation is that of seeking clarification, the solicitation is considered a clarification, not solicitation.

Response to Solicitation

Responding to a solicitation is by definition a responsive behavior. The response to solicitation typically takes the form of either a direct answer to a question or a response to a direction. The response may involve the use of knowledge, motor skills, or feeling states. The key to the conceptual understanding of the nature of this behavior lies in recognizing that the person to whom the solicitation is directed responds to the solicitation, that is, he answers the question or follows the direction. It is not necessary that the question be answered correctly or that the direction be followed to the satisfaction of the person who gave the direction. It is important only that a legitimate response to the solicitation be made with the intent of answering the question or following the direction.

Several examples will illustrate the behavior of responding to solicitation. When a teacher responds to a student's question, "What page is the map on?" by saying, "Page 423, in the appendix," he has responded to a student solicitation. In like manner, when a student responds to another student's question, "Who wants to keep notes on our discussion today?" by saying, "I will; I guess it's my turn," the second student has responded to the first student's solicitation.

Responses to solicitations can be responses to directions as well as questions. The response can take the form of motor behavior, such as demonstrating physical skills, as well as of verbal responses. For example, the student behavior emitted as a result of the teacher direction, "All right, now try that dance step again," is a student response to a teacher's solicitation in the form of a direction. Students who raise their hands in response to the direction, "Everyone who feels as Jim does, raise your hand," are responding to a solicitation regarding feeling state.

The behavior "response to solicitation" encompasses all behaviors of teachers and students that are legitimate responses to questions or directions. The responses can be verbal or nonverbal. They can also be responses to requests for clarification such as, "Can you tell me a little more about that? I don't think I understand exactly what you mean."

On the other hand, if a student asks a question and the teacher "responds" by asking for clarification, the teacher "response" is considered clarification rather than response to solicitation. This can be illustrated in the following teacher and student interaction: "Miss Brown, why does the light go on when I turn on the switch?" "Well, Betty, think for a moment about the parts of a switch that we were just talking about, and how they work." In this case, the response is considered clarification rather than response to solicitation, because the teacher did not answer the student's question, nor did she intend to.

Initiation of Information

This behavior includes all instances in which information is initiated by either teacher or students. The information may be either opinion or fact and may deal with knowledge, motor skills, or feeling states. The lecture and the student-initiated idea are typical examples of this kind of behavior in schools.

The information may be initiated either verbally or nonverbally, e.g., by means of demonstration or by visual or verbal symbols involving, for example, the use of chalkboards or felt boards. Information given by means of other audiovisual aids would also be classified under this category of behavior.

However, if the information is given as a result of a request for clarification or a solicitation, it is considered a response rather than initiation of information. The reason for this, of course, is that the information was not initiated; it was solicited by a question or request for information.

Solicitation

Soliciting behaviors typically take the form of a question or direction. The solicitation may be for expression of knowledge or feeling states, or for performance of skills, and it may emanate from teacher or students as they deal with either substantive or managerial issues. The key to the conceptual understanding of this category of behavior lies in the recognition of the essential nature of a solicitation. It is an invitation to another person to say or do something. It typically takes the form of a question or direction but does not ask for clarification. It is necessary only that the solicitation be intended to call out a response from another person; whether the person responds or whether the response is correct or appropriate is not at issue.

Typical examples of solicitations are the questions, "What are your feelings on the matter?" and, "How might you verify that hypothesis?" Examples of solicitations in the form of directions are: "Miss Brown, could you come here and help me a minute?" or, "Tom, you bring in the nature specimens for our report tomorrow."

Corrective Feedback

Corrective feedback is referred to as an "appraisal behavior" and includes a variety of behaviors used to indicate the incorrectness or inappropriateness of behavior. It is restricted to responses to statements or behaviors that can be considered incorrect or inappropriate by commonly accepted custom or convention or by some form of empirical verification.

When a teacher or student uses corrective feedback, he is not saying that he does not like another person's answer or behavior, but that the statement or behavior is wrong or inappropriate by definition or convention or because it can be empirically verified as being incorrect. In other words, the person goes beyond his own judgment and opinion to some other source of authority to establish the correctness or incorrectness of another's behavior. The person giving corrective feedback is simply acting as a transmitter of some other authority within the culture; he is not giving personal criticism or correction.

The following is an example of corrective feedback by a teacher: When asked, "What is the square root of sixteen?" the student answers, "Three." The teacher says, "No, the square root of sixteen is not three. The square root of sixteen is four. Three is the square root of nine." Corrective feedback is also used by students. Some examples are the student's comment to the teacher, "You spelled 'receive' wrong on the board," or a student's comment to another student, "That isn't what Ella said. She said that we should debate the idea, not argue over it."

Confirmation

Confirmation includes behaviors designed to indicate to another person that his behavior has been correct. Such behaviors are restricted to responses that can be considered correct according to commonly accepted definition, custom, convention, or empirical verification. Whereas corrective feedback indicates the incorrectness of the response, confirmation indicates the correctness of the behavior.

Included under this behavior are statements confirming that the other person has been correct by simply repeating what the other person has said. Suppose the teacher asks, "What does a falling barometer indicate?" and the student says, "It indicates a change in weather and sometimes a storm." If the teacher says, "Yes, a falling barometer does sometimes indicate that a storm is coming," this is an example of giving confirmation. If the teacher's comment is, "That's right," this is also considered confirmation.

Confirmation is used by both teachers and students. For example, the student's comment to the teacher, "Your summary of our decision was complete," or a student's comment to another student, "Yes, I think the answer to that problem is right," are both illustrations of confirmation emitted by students.

Confirmation can be both verbal and nonverbal (e.g., shaking the head), and can deal with issues involving knowledge and motor skill performance. It must be possible to substantiate the confirmation by fact or commonly accepted convention or definition. Such statements as, "Good," or "That's great!" are considered confirmation behaviors if the student's response is correct by definition, convention, or fact.

Acceptance

The behavior of acceptance is often subtle in its overt manifestation in classrooms. The key to recognizing this behavior lies in understanding that acceptance contains no explicit value judgment when expressed to another person. The explicit behavior that is communicated is, "I heard what you said, and I think I understand what you meant," or "I observed your behavior, and I think I understand how you feel." The implicit and sometimes explicit message expressed concurrently is, "and I acknowledge your right to believe that," "behave that way," or "feel that way." The acceptance behavior does not, however, express a condition of correctness, approval, or disapproval.

Whether found in verbal or nonverbal behavior, acceptance is characterized by a state of unconditional regard for another person. Though the person expressing acceptance may hold other beliefs on the subject, feel that he would have behaved differently in the same situation, or have different feelings, he expresses to the other person that there is room enough in his world for other views on matters, other ways of doing things, and other feelings.

Perhaps an example will help explain the nature of this behavior. A student has just expressed his belief that young men who go to Canada to avoid being drafted in the Vietnam war are escaping from their responsibility to their country. Another student responds, "I think I understand why you feel that way, but it seems to me that they should have the right to go to Canada to express their protest if they wish. I think that is a responsible way of protesting against something they feel is wrong in their country." The first student responds, "Well, I guess we both feel strongly about the issue, though we seem to hold different viewpoints. I guess this is another example of where we will respect the rights of others to hold different beliefs." The student's acceptance simply says that he accepts the other student's right to hold a different point of view. It contains no implication that either should change his point of view.

Positive Personal Judgment

This behavior involves positive value behaviors of praise, reward, or encouragement. Also included are behaviors that indicate agreement with others when behavior cannot be considered correct or appropriate by definition, custom, convention, or empirically verified fact: for example, when a teacher agrees with a student's opinion.

Whenever a person's statement implies to another that he likes what that person is doing or that what the other person has done is very good, such behaviors are classified as positive personal judgment. If a student is asked to give his interpretation of a poem, and the teacher says, "Good, that is an excellent interpretation," this statement is a form of giving praise. An example of value-oriented encouragement is, "You all did very well today, and I am really proud of you. I want you to keep up the good work."

The important distinction between confirmation and positive personal judgment is that confirmation simply indicates the correctness or appropriateness of behavior, but positive personal judgment indicates *personal* approval.

Negative Personal Judgment

This behavior includes negative value statements that criticize or reject ideas, feelings, or behaviors and cannot be supported by convention, definition, custom, or empirical verification. The person simply indicates that he does not like what the other has done or said; he does not justify his criticism by commonly accepted definition, custom, convention, or empirically verified fact. When a teacher asks a student for his opinion and then follows that statement with, "No, that is not right," he is rejecting a student's opinion without reference to commonly accepted definition, custom, convention, or empirically verified fact. He is simply saying that he does not like or agree with what the student has said. Also included would be such teacher statements as, "Be quiet. You're making too much noise, and you know I don't like that," or "Does anyone like the way Billy has been behaving today?" In this last example, the statement is in question form, but the real intent of the statement is to criticize Billy for his behavior, so the question is considered negative personal judgment.

Denying the feelings of others, sarcasm, and jokes at the

expense of others are also examples of this behavior. Jokes and sarcasm are often subtle and may be difficult to identify. For example, suppose a class is responding quite well to the teacher's questions, a number of hands are raised, and the teacher says, "Oh, I see we are all responding today, even Tommy." If there is clear indication that the teacher's statement is one of sarcasm or a joke at the expense of Tommy, this is a negative personal judgment.

The key for identifying these behaviors very often is found in expressions of the likes or dislikes made directly through statements of opinion or through such subtle behaviors as sarcasm, denial of feelings, or jokes at the expense of others. These statements are often designed to criticize, modify, or terminate the verbal or nonverbal behavior of others. Negative personal judgment can be expressed verbally or nonverbally through gestures.

Silent Covert Activity

This behavior includes periods of silence in the classroom when it is the expectation that someone, students or teacher, is thinking. Such silence may be the result of teacher directions to think about something, brief periods of silence following questions, and clarification, etc. When the expectation is that during this silence someone is formulating a response to a question, developing a hypothesis, or thinking through a process, these periods of silence are considered silent covert activity.

Silent Overt Activity

This behavior includes nonverbal, observable, overt acts that are associated with instructional tasks. For example, if the teacher asks the students to read silently a short section in their textbooks, the time during which they are reading is considered silent overt activity. This behavior is also illustrated by students working quietly at tasks in learning carrels, manipulating materials in the process of setting up a science experiment, getting materials or books out of their desks, writing, drawing, typing, or performing skills in a physical education class.

Instructional Strategies

Direct Communication Strategies

Instructional strategies are defined by the type, source, and pattern of instructional behaviors. The first of the seven instructional strategies we will discuss are the direct communication strategies. In the *teacher initiated, direct communication strategy,* the flow of communication is from the teacher (T) to the student (S).

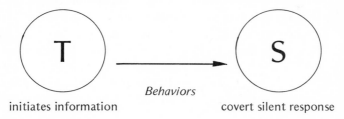

initiates information   covert silent response

The observable and persistently used behavior of the teacher is that of initiation of information, and of the student, covert silent response.

Closely related to the teacher initiated, direct communication strategy is the *student initiated, direct communication strategy.* In this strategy the flow of communication is from one student to another, or from the student to the teacher, and the observable and persistently used behaviors are those of student initiation of information and covert silent response.

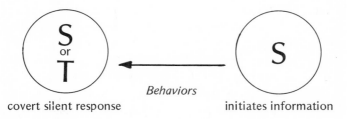

covert silent response   initiates information

Though the direct communication strategies often involve a number of people in one setting, e.g., a television lecture and demonstration with a number of students watching it or a student giving a report to the class, one should not assume a condition of mass communication in the sense that the same message is being communicated to all listeners. Indeed, the success of the so-called mass media is related to the idea that listeners and viewers with widely ranging backgrounds, capabilities, and motivations have different responses to the message that is being communicated. The successful use of the direct communication strategies seems to be enhanced when at least two conditions are met: (1) the message being communicated is perceived by the listener to be useful, and (2) the communication is clear and coherent. Clarity and coherence are often enhanced when the communicator makes appropriate use of figure-ground relationships by focusing attention on the major points being communicated and, in addition, makes appropriate use of concrete and abstract and personal and impersonal examples. In addition, direct communication is enhanced when the communicator accurately reads subtle cues from his listener such as, "I don't understand," or "I think you're wrong, and I wish I could tell you so," and then asks for feedback that will lead to a clearer message or encourages the listener to find out if he really disagrees. Finally, though the direct communication strategy is commonly used, it is also commonly abused by attempts to achieve ends for which it is not well designed and by poor execution of direct communication principles.

With respect to fostering the development of autonomous, self-directed learners, the direct communication strategies are a two-edged sword. On one hand, their use can create and perpetuate a condition of learner dependence. On the other hand, when used appropriately, they are consistent with the development of self-direction. For example, one characteristic of the self-directed learner is that he realizes he does not have all the information he needs to achieve his objective and knows the appropriate source from which to get that information. When that source is another student or the teacher, and the learner asks for information, he has chosen to involve himself in a direct communication instructional strategy as a receiver of information. Such a student soon learns that others can help and that they can be a very flexible learning resource, because they are human.

Interactive Strategies

The second set of strategies are the interactive strategies. In the *teacher initiated, interactive strategy,* the flow of communication is controlled by the teacher and directed to the student. The teacher solicits, and the student responds. These are the primary behaviors. In addition, the behavior of clarification is sometimes used by the student, and the response used by the teacher. However, the reverse is more common: that is, the teacher asks for clarification and the student responds. This strategy is also typically characterized by the use of appraisal behaviors. The teacher may tell the student that he is right or wrong, that he agrees or disagrees with the student, or that he accepts the student's comments or behavior. In any event, the communication is reciprocal, though the teacher is directing the communication.

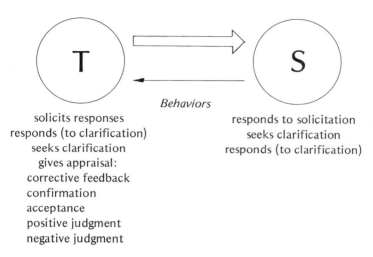

solicits responses
responds (to clarification)
seeks clarification
gives appraisal:
corrective feedback
confirmation
acceptance
positive judgment
negative judgment

responds to solicitation
seeks clarification
responds (to clarification)

In the *student initiated, interactive strategy,* the student largely controls the reciprocal flow of communication, whether the student is acting as teacher, or a certified teacher is playing that role. In either case, the characteristic purpose and behavior patterns of the student initiated interacting strategies are quite different from the characteristic behavior and purposes of the teacher initiated form.

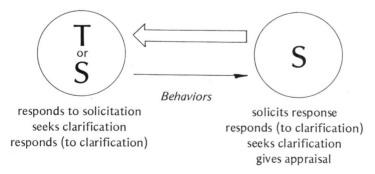

responds to solicitation
seeks clarification
responds (to clarification)

solicits response
responds (to clarification)
seeks clarification
gives appraisal

The successful use of the interactive strategies seems to depend on three factors: (1) alertness and sensitivity to both the explicit and implicit meanings embedded in the communication; (2) the soliciting of responses (e.g., asking of questions) that can be supplied; and (3) the careful sequencing of solicitations to serve such purposes as: (a) shaping behavior, (b) drawing out knowledge from which conclusions or hypotheses can be formed, and (c) diagnosing the point at which learning difficulties occur. When appraisal behaviors are used in this strategy, care must be taken to use these behaviors in ways that encourage interaction rather than prematurely terminating it. For example, when the strategy is used to elicit a variety of points of view, for the teacher or another student to imply that the point of view expressed by a particular student is "right" or "wrong" is likely either to reduce the number of points of view expressed by students, or to channel the points of view to conform with the one that is considered "right." Both negative and positive personal judgment behaviors, when given in response to answers that can be considered right or wrong, can cause unwanted results, depending on how they are used. It is one thing to tell a student that he's wrong and help him understand why. It is another thing to do so in such a way that he does not want to venture another answer and get "slapped down" again. The same thing is true with respect to positive personal judgment. Many times students will not answer questions because they do not want the teacher to smother them with praise in front of their peers.

As with the direct communication strategies, the interactive strategies are potentially a two-edged sword with respect to fostering student autonomy and self-direction. The interactive strategies can be used to create extreme dependence on the teacher or other students, or they can be used as instructional techniques that place the student in an excellent position to direct and be responsible for his own learning. The person who asks questions of others to gain knowledge and clarify his own thinking without developing a dependent relationship with that person is well on the road to becoming an autonomous person.

Group Strategies

The third set of strategies are the group strategies. What often passes for a group strategy is, in fact, nothing more than a complex example of the interactive strategies. Real group strategies are, however, quite different from interactive strategies. Interactive strategies involve reciprocal communication between two people at a time, the purpose of which is usually to facilitate the learning of one member of a diad. Group strategies, on the other hand, involve multidirectional communication that is designed to foster learning or achieve a particular end for members of a group. Group strategies are guided by a common goal, and they function in a group context. Though two members of the group may engage in reciprocal communication, they do so, not just to further their own ends, but to further the ends of the group.

There are two basic types of group strategies. The *teacher-student group strategy* involves the teacher in a special teacher role as a special type of group member. The types of behaviors used are indicated in the strategy model below. The teacher plays the primary role of moving the group discussion toward the *group* goal, through the use of clarifying and accepting behaviors. Students, on the other hand, make use of a wide range of behaviors, because it is they who structure the problem solution, and provide input, and draw from others the knowledge necessary to solve the problem or achieve the group goal.

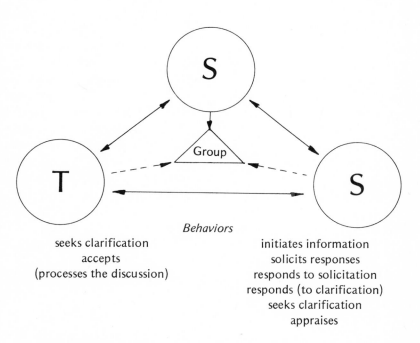

Behaviors

seeks clarification
accepts
(processes the discussion)

initiates information
solicits responses
responds to solicitation
responds (to clarification)
seeks clarification
appraises

Further discussion of the teacher's unique position in this strategy may be helpful here. Most teachers, regardless of their desire, cannot participate in classroom group discussions as the students' peer. This is a function of a long history of teacher and student expectations regarding the role of the teacher and the traditional purpose of instruction, i.e., to facilitate *student* learning. In the rare cases when the teacher is able to enter group discussion as a peer, teacher behavior then appropriately becomes indistinguishable from student behavior. The behaviors used in this type of group setting closely resemble those used in the *student-student group strategy,* in which students structure their own purposes for the activity and engage in group discussion to achieve their stated ends. Between the teacher-student and the student-student strategies is the situation in which the teacher structures the task and then "turns the group loose" to achieve the tasks.

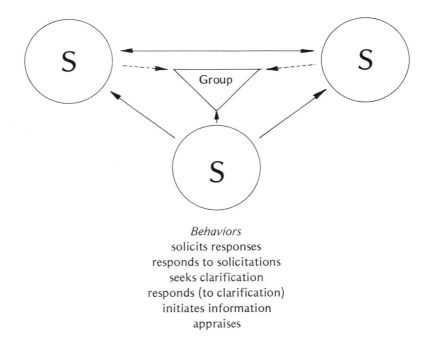

Behaviors
solicits responses
responds to solicitations
seeks clarification
responds (to clarification)
initiates information
appraises

The key to the successful use of the group strategies is the creation of what we will call "group life." By this we mean nothing more than that the group, as perceived by its members, becomes an entity that group members think of as something very real. We call "group life" that which happens to individuals in real group settings that transcends their individuality. When the condition of creating a group life has been achieved, then in a very real sense it is the group that does the instructing. The teacher's role typically becomes one of facilitating the activities of the group as *its own* vehicle for instruction.

This type of instructional strategy has great potential for fostering student autonomy and self-direction. It also provides rich situations in which students learn the fine balance between supporting others and accepting support from others as they work toward developing an identity and toward the attainment of their own goals as well as the goals of the other group members. Like the previous two strategies, however, the group strategies have a double cutting edge. Groups can foster group member dependence and can successfully assimilate one's individuality. When the group becomes the master to be served, it can destroy not only one's identity, but one's autonomy.

Independent Strategy

The last of the four types of instructional strategies is the *student independent strategy*. In this strategy, the student works independently with his own ideas and/or with instructional materials that he manipulates to facilitate his own independent learning. The observable behaviors are silent overt behavior, such as manipulation of a microscope, and silent covert behavior, such as reflective thinking.

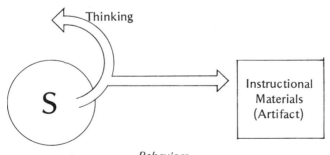

Behaviors
silent covert or overt behavior

The key to the successful execution of this instructional strategy seems to lie in the application of two principles: (1) the resources needed to achieve the objective must be within the "reach" of the student, and (2) the degree to which the instructional environment is structured should be appropriate for the task. The degree of structure and teacher support provided for students in this strategy varies not only from one activity to another but from one student to another. Some independent activities are quite fully structured by the teacher and/or the instructional environment, e.g., use of certain types of computer-assisted instruction and language laboratories. In some activities the main responsibility for structure resides with the student, such as in student-designed projects and experiments. At either extreme the successful use of this strategy seems to depend, in part, on student ability to perform the task independently and student motivation (clarity of objective and perceived relationship between the available resources and the attainment of the objective).

Consider by contrast the following incident. An eighth-grade girl was ill a good portion of the fall semester. Although her friends carried homework to her from time to time and her parents had made arrangements with the school through the guidance counselor to keep homework assignments generally up to date, her parents felt that she should go to each of her teachers when she finally went back to school to find out if there was any additional work she ought to do in order to catch up completely. Most of the teachers were very cooperative in providing the additional information the student requested in order to conduct a kind of independent study and have a feeling of satisfaction that she had completed the work expected of her. When she went to her art teacher, however, the teacher responded to her request with the devasting putdown, "If you could do it at home, they wouldn't need me." Obviously, this kind of response, which indicates no desire to remove obstructions to independent learning, creates in the student a sense of dependence on the teacher.

The successful use of the independent strategy puts a very different responsibility on the teacher. Once the independent activity is set in motion, the teacher must be careful to intervene only when the independent activity has broken down and is no longer serving an instructional purpose. The teacher might enter the situation as a diagnostician to determine what is blocking progress, help alleviate that block, and then get out as quickly as possible to preserve the independence of the student. Typical teacher entry behaviors, therefore, are those designed to seek clarification of the learning difficulty. Once into the situation, response, initiation, solicitation, and appraisal behaviors are used judiciously to remove the block to further productive independent instruction. When carried out in its most effective form, the independent strategy has great potential for fostering student self-directed behavior and learning. When the teacher is "too available" or intrudes without good reason, this strategy can generate conditions of dependence between teacher and student.

The admonition that a teacher should not be "too available" or intrude without good reason should not be misinterpreted or exaggerated to mean that the teacher should never intervene unless invited to do so by the student. It should go without saying that the teacher must also utilize effective entry behaviors to assess progress and to detect trouble of which the student may not be aware. In other words, the teacher should not rely entirely on a student request for help as the sole clue to the breakdown of the independent activity mechanism. Further, it should be emphasized that when we use the word *teacher,* we include students who are helping other students to learn.

The variations on these four basic types of instructional strategies will be as numerous as the ingenuity and wisdom of the teachers and students involved. Some teachers will find some strategies more compatible with their professional and personal talents than other strategies. Some students will find some strategies more compatible with their learning styles than other strategies. Some subject fields will have objectives that lend themselves to the use of some strategies rather than to others. This is reasonable, desirable, and to be expected. One of the most important functions of instructional support is to help both teachers and students use their individual talents in the most effective ways. Instructional individualization and professional talent differentiation are two means of achieving the effective use of human talents.

From an instructional point of view, however, what is neither reasonable nor desirable is the use of the wrong strategy with the wrong student or the wrong objective. Within the context of facilitating student autonomy and self-direction, if students and teachers together sought to answer the question, "What are the most effective instructional strategies for facilitating different types of learnings with our motivational and capability levels?" then the balance and variety of instructional behaviors and strategies used in schools would be rather substantially altered. Such a change would represent an instructional innovation of substantial magnitude, and its success as such would depend in large measure on carefully planned inservice education for both teachers and students and a great deal of sustained organizational support.

The reader might be led to the hasty and inaccurate conclusion that the preceding strategies involve only intellectual and essentially passive behavior on the part of learners. Nothing could be further from reality. All of these strategies may also be active, emotional, and physical. The following comment of a parent concerning her children speaks to this point.

I can remember talking with Mrs. S about Jack, I can remember talking with Mrs. H about Peter and my feeling about Dan. Now Peter was a good student, Jack and Dan were lousy students, but they had one thing in common. *These kids hated being cooped up in that classroom.* That sitting there, day in and day out, was almost beyond anything they could endure. Right now, if Dan is home for a week with nothing physical to do, he darn near drives me up the wall. It is a physical thing that is a *need* much more in some children than in others. Some kids can sit quietly and be happy. Some kids have got to be going . . . doing something with their bodies. Putting them in the classroom and having them sit there all day long is more than they can stand.

And you know what the trouble is? Educators . . . like intellectual talk, and reading, . . . and they simply cannot understand that *other people don't.* They have got to be doing something. You can tell them about something all day long, some can read about it in a book and enjoy it but there are others who have got to get out there and *do* it with their own bodies. You can't just tell them how to do it. They have got to do it. Some can read about archeological expeditions, and others have got to go out there and do it. Dig up things, physically, with their own hands. And that's the two different types of people.

Model for Generating and Answering Instructional Questions

Let us now return to an earlier statement about the relationship between instructional strategies and behaviors, levels and types of objectives, and human motivation and capability.

We can join the three variables that we have been discussing thus far in this chapter: (1) types and levels of learnings (objectives), (2) levels of student motivation and capability, and (3) types of instructional behavior and strategies. In joining them we can create a three-dimensional model that may be useful in helping conceptualize (and ultimately operationalize) instructional situations that facilitate self-direction in learning. Figure 4-2 presents a three-dimensional model that puts objectives, learner variables, and instructional strategies into a very large number of potential interactions. For example, the heavily outlined section of the larger cube represents the question, "Without respect to capability, is the use of some form of group strategy an equally efficient and effective means of helping students, with varying levels of intrinsic and extrinsic motivation, learn to be aware of and to express their feelings?"

Figure 4-2. A model for generating instructional hypotheses

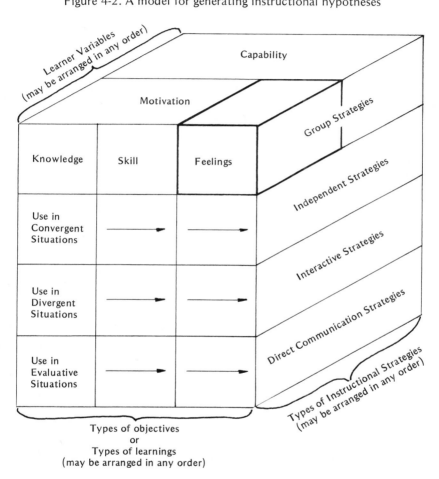

By slightly modifying the small section in figure 4-2, the following question may be represented: "Is the use of some form of group strategy equally effective in helping students of high and low intrinsic motivation learn to become more aware of and better able to express feelings, without regard to the student's capability?"

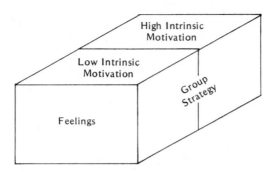

One additional example of how the model in figure 4-2 may generate instructional questions will have to suffice (*remember that the describers on any face of the cube may be rearranged without doing violence to the model*). "Are all four instructional strategies equally effective in helping students, of varying levels of verbal ability and intrinsic motivation, learn to use knowledge in divergent situations?" (See diagram on opposite page.)

Suppose that, when seven teachers asked such a question in one school, in six out of seven cases they found that students with high intrinsic motivation generally learned to apply knowledge in divergent situations better as a result of instruction using an independent strategy (regardless of their verbal ability), and that students with low intrinsic motivation generally learned the same thing better as a result of instruction using an interactive strategy (regardless of their verbal ability). Would such knowledge influence instruction? Would such knowledge influence instructional decisions if, as a result of inservice education, the decision maker felt competent in (1) measuring motivation and verbal ability, (2) classifying objectives and learnings, and (3) using the interactive and independent strategies?

Evidence for Answering Instructional Questions

The reader might be somewhat reluctant to be influenced by such knowledge without knowing more about the nature of the evidence gathered by the seven teacher colleagues. Evidence that learning has taken place may be found by observing (1) changes in *products* of student behavior, (2) changes in student *behavior,* or (3) changes in student *disposition* to behave in particular ways.

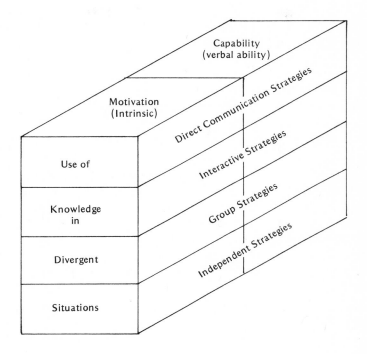

For example, let us assume that one objective a student accepts is to learn how to group objects within a set of objects so that the groups are characterized by having common elements. When presented with ten objects, the student cannot perform the operation at first, but following instruction involving a mixed interactive and independent strategy, the student can create two groups of objects with common elements, each of which has distinctively different characteristics from the other. We may infer that the student learned to group objects according to common characteristics by observing evidence in the form of the *product* of his behavior, that is, the arrangement of objects on his desk.

With respect to learning to use clarifying behaviors in group discussions, a director of inservice education may gather some evidence about a teacher's change in the use of clarifying *behavior* by observing and comparing the teacher's use of clarifying behavior before and after three inservice training sessions involving the use of mixed direct communication and group strategies.

The disposition to behave in new ways is evidence of yet another type of learning. In this case, what is being learned is not a behavior as such (the behavior may have already been learned) but the disposition to use prior learning in situations where the student was previously not disposed to use that learning. An example of this type of learning may be found in the disposition to use a dictionary when writing compositions. One might infer change in disposition to use a dictionary by observing the products of student behavior, e.g., the number of misspelled words in a composition, but this would be risky. The student might simply have learned to apply the i before e except after c rule, and thus significantly reduced the number of misspelled words in his compositions. Better evidence of change might be gathered by direct observation of student behavior while writing class compositions or the student's own report that the reduction of spelling errors and increase in his use of descriptive adjectives is a result of "writing with a dictionary by his side."

There are, of course, a number of intended and unintended learnings that occur as a result of instruction but are not measured. Some of these are among the more important learnings acquired in school, but teachers never become aware of them, because (1) they fail to evoke the behaviors in either formal or informal testing situations, (2) there is no really convenient way to evoke the behaviors in the artificial context of the classroom and/or the influence of the learning on behavior does not become apparent until months or even years later, or (3) the teacher misinterprets student behavior or products and never engages in a reality check with the student to clear up the misinterpretation. The feedback is distorted.

In talking about obtaining evidence that learning has occurred, we have been talking more about measurement and evaluation than about instruction. In describing various types of learnings and objectives we have been talking about curriculum. But teaching is an activity that involves curriculum, instructional, and measurement and evaluation functions. Furthermore, these functions merge in the active phase of teaching, so that it may be quite difficult, for example, to distinguish curriculum from instruction in the active phase of teaching.

Curriculum Decisions and Fostering Autonomous, Self-Directed Learners

In determining what shall be learned, teachers may function in ways that both facilitate and inhibit student self-direction. When teachers make all or most of the important decisions regarding what students will learn, it is quite likely that their behavior is not conducive to helping students learn self-direction. When they delegate this responsibility and do nothing to help students learn to formulate their objectives in responsible ways, they are likely to create the conditions of a self-fulfilling prophecy that "students really aren't capable of determining what they should learn."

We propose that if teachers behave in either extreme, they will surely "inherit the wind" of a rapidly changing world that has passed them by, and/or they will have ducked their professional responsibility. Furthermore, they will not do much, except by negative example, to help students learn responsible self-direction.

How much freedom should the student have to determine the outcomes of his own education? This question seems simple, but it involves philosophical, psychological, sociological, and political issues. We cannot deal with all of these issues here, but we can at least point out how issues in such diverse realms bear on the question. In the philosophical realm we are concerned with the relationship between the individual and his society. Is the individual student a free agent in the educational process, or is his education sponsored and controlled by society for its own benefit? In the psychological realm, does a person develop more fully and more effectively if he sets his own goals and guides his own destiny? Is he likely to be more highly motivated toward ends of his own choosing? Sociologically, pockets of poverty, bigotry, and ignorance affect the whole fabric of society. Who decides what is "good" for the children and the society in such situations—the children and parents of the local community or the society in general as represented by its educators? Politically, do the people serve the national or regional interest as a first priority, or does the state serve the interest of the individual and groups of individuals as a first priority? These are all basically questions of how much freedom people should have in our society and especially in our schools.

The original question was deceptively simple, but its solution is

a complex and crucial consideration in education and in the formulation of curriculum and objectives. The actual resolution resides ultimately with individual teachers and their students. It is one of those
professional decisions that must be made by every teacher. Therefore, the question is not an academic one. National policy, regional
mores, ethnic identity, and school policies all affect the solution, but
there is a point at which the decision about the formulation of
objectives must be made. In this context a teacher can rephrase the
question: "How much freedom should *my* students have in determining the outcomes of their own education?"

We cannot answer the question for individual teachers, but we
can provide a way of helping teachers conceptualize an answer for
themselves. If one considers the full range of educational objectives
held by both students and teachers in the classroom, one might
diagrammatically represent the students, the teachers, the objectives
of education held by teachers and students, and the influence of
students and teachers on each other in the process of determining
objectives. Let us diagram that space in figure 4-3.[3]

Figure 4-3

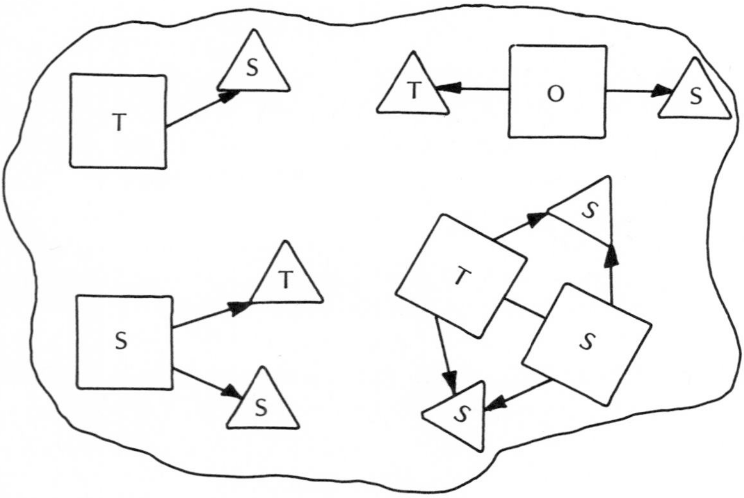

The fact that the figure is closed suggests only that all the educational objectives under consideration by both student and teacher
can be bounded: that is, some space can include all of them and

exclude those that are not under consideration. The irregular form of the diagram simply suggests that the objectives under consideration change with time and that the objectives belong to quite diverse people, both students and teachers.

To establish any substantive order in a classroom where there are many and diverse objectives requires that some structure be provided to interrelate the objectives and help to establish some priority. It is one of the primary functions of the teacher to determine or share in determining the outcomes of instruction. In figure 4-3, six symbols are used: T stands for teacher; S stands for student; O stands for objective; ☐ represents the primary source of influence in determining what the objectives will be; ⟶ stands for the direction of that influence; △ stands for the person or persons who are the object of the influence.

In condition ☐T☐ ⟶ △S the teacher represents the primary source of influence in determining curriculum and objectives, and the teacher exercises his influence on the student in an attempt to get the student to accept his objective. The success of this condition depends on the teacher's ability to influence the student. Typically, teachers use reason, sanctions, or personal identification to achieve influence. If the student accepts the objective, he does so because (1) the teacher convinces the student that the objective is reasonable, (2) the student desires the positive condition associated with yielding to the teacher's influence or wants to avoid the negative condition associated with failing to yield to the teacher's influence, or (3) the student wants to please the teacher.

In condition △T △S ⟶ ☐S☐ the situation is reversed. Here a student is depicted in the process of influencing the teacher and other students with respect to what the curriculum or objectives should be. The same three techniques of reason, sanctions, or identification are employed as the means of exercising influence.

In condition ☐T☐ ⇄S ⇄S ☐S☐ the teacher and students are engaged in a condition of negotiation. There is a condition of open discussion in which each party tries to influence the other. The same techniques of reason, sanctions, and identification are often operative. There is, however, a give and take, a search for mutual understanding. Often there is compromise, but ultimately there is agreement on the objectives.

Condition $\triangle \leftarrow \boxed{O} \rightarrow \triangle{S}$ represents a situation in which the reasonableness and relevance of the instructional objective is obvious to both teacher and student. Either the teacher or the student may have proposed the objective, but there is no need to influence the other party to accept the objective. The source of influence emanates from the obvious reasonableness and relevance of the objective as perceived by both teacher and student.

What will be required in a school for tomorrow is the ability to walk a tightrope of sharing with students not only curricular but also instructional and measurement and evaluation responsibilities. Successfully accomplishing a balance of teacher and student participation in the teaching act depends in part on (1) changes in motivation of teachers and students, (2) the optimum use of teacher and student competencies, and (3) a great deal of organizational support involving new conceptions of inservice education. Yet, attending to the above three factors will not in itself insure the kind of school for tomorrow that we have outlined.

There will be those who will, with real justification, ask for evidence that such changes (1) make positive differences in student learning, (2) make the school's curriculum more responsive to dynamic social changes, and (3) facilitate greater student autonomy and self-direction. What these people are asking for is accountability. *In part,* accountability may anchor itself in evidence that instruction is serving its purpose more adequately. We have already made reference to the risks that one takes in inferring instructional effectiveness from evidence of student learning, but we repeat that with all of its risks, we cannot afford to duck the issue. Humane and wise analysis of data regarding student learning is *one* source for standards that can be used to hold teachers and students accountable for their behavior.

We further assert that as teachers and students gather better and better evidence regarding instructional effectiveness and learning, both will become more capable of diagnosing each other's instructional and learning problems and that, in the long run, both teachers and students will end up being the winners. Such a notion of professional and student accountability will not become a reality just because some or even many teachers and students in a school desire that it happen. The process of making curricular and instructional decisions, implementing those decisions, and then evaluating the effectiveness of instruction, involves much knowledge, and the development of new attitudes about teaching. We maintain that one way of developing dynamic and effective instruction in a school for tomorrow is to support teachers and students who want to try. Finally, we believe that the model for asking and answering instructional questions may provide many teachers with the conceptual organizer needed to become students of their own teaching, and for students to become students of their own learning.

Notes

1. Adapted from John Hough and James Duncan, *Teaching: Description and Analysis* (Reading, Mass.: Addison Wesley Publishing Co., 1970) p. 63.

2. Adapted from Hough and Duncan, *op. cit.,* pp. 120-128.

3. From Hough and Duncan, *op. cit.,* p. 97.

5
Evaluation

A school in which every child is treated always as an end in himself, not as a means to other ends, requires a different conception of measurement and evaluation. But what kind of measurement and evaluation system will we need to provide students, teachers, and support personnel with the information they need to make wise choices based on chosen rational standards.

John Schneider
Jennings O. Johnson
James K. Duncan

Introduction

"If we could first know where we are, and whither we are tending, we could better judge what to do, and how to do it." So said Abraham Lincoln over 100 years ago. This statement is equally true now, and it is certainly appropriate to this chapter on evaluation. What will a school of tomorrow be like? What will we measure? What will we evaluate? Who will make the evaluation? Some schools of tomorrow are undoubtedly with us today, yet whatever is tomorrow will be different from today. In like manner, understandings about the intent and use of evaluation processes are with us today, but the instruments, their use, and the skills of the practitioner must change. The emphasis given to evaluation in all its dimensions and the confidence placed in the evaluator will correspondingly change. However, a brief review of the conventional wisdom about evaluation will help us, since our particular view is set in that context.

Evaluation has many dimensions. As a term, it is used in both scientific and nonscientific senses, often interchangeably with measurement. It is possible to distinguish between measurement and evaluation, but doing so may be only an academic exercise and may serve no useful purpose. From our perspective, measurement is part

of evaluation but not all of it. Evaluation also includes the exercise
of judgment, or choice.

Tyler suggests that evaluation may be used in at least four ways:
to appraise the achievement of individual students; to diagnose the
learning problems of an individual student or an entire class in order
to provide information that will be helpful in planning subsequent
teaching; to appraise the educational effectiveness of a curriculum or
part of a curriculum, of instructional materials and procedures, and
of administrative and organizational arrangements; and to assess the
educational progress of large populations in order to provide the
public with dependable information about educational problems and
needs and guide our efforts to develop sound policy regarding education.[1]

Wilhelms and Diederich state that evaluation must perform five
tasks, namely, facilitate self-evaluation, encompass all the objectives,
facilitate teaching and learning, generate records appropriate to various uses, and facilitate decision-making on curriculum and educational policy.[2] All these purposes are important and, it is hoped,
ongoing processes in the school. We intend to focus evaluation on the
individual student while recognizing that curriculum concerns, organizational concerns, record-keeping concerns, and so on are important to what happens with a particular student at a particular time
and in a particular place. In this chapter we know "whither we are
tending." Evaluation is to serve a primary end of schooling: the end
of rational autonomy.

Educational Evaluation in a Different Perspective

To say that the focus for evaluation efforts will be the individual student seems innocuous enough at first glance, but if we push
the matter a little, it turns out that a complete reordering of our
typical views on educational evaluation seems required. Somehow we
have to start at a different place, with a different point of view, and
work toward a different destination. As authors, we are aware that
the case for reordering can be made logically, but it is neither very
convincing nor very illuminating. It hinges on the single point that
there are some very marked differences in the way different individuals view human experience. If the evaluator looks at human experience from a succession of individual human perspectives, the result is
kaleidoscopic. The variety of patterns—and patterns they are—seems

infinite. An educational experience is variegated beyond belief when viewed from different individual perspectives. Most of us know what we think the school program looks like, and therefore what it is, but it simply does not look like that to anybody else. This is the gist of the logical argument. The variance in the evaluator's data appears to increase beyond all reasonable or manageable proportions and the measures of central tendency seem to wash out, robbing us of a fundamental parametric anchor. The old, reliable, normal distribution curve becomes humpier, bumpier, increasingly skewed, and finally discontinuous.

The logic is simple. When you come at the world from the mean and work the variances out from there, things hang together pretty well. We've been doing that for a long time. We have been basically conservative processors of information. We have dropped an anchor (e.g., an IQ mean of 100) and tied our diverse observations to it. When you come at the world from the variances, things seem to fly apart. If you focus your evaluation efforts on the individual, you will be working from independent unanchored observations and seeking anchors to which they can be tied.

The reader may not be as thoroughly conditioned as we are to this matter of working from anchors or standards to order the diverse data derived from educational observations. Intelligence quotient—100 plus or minus—grading scales A to F, percentiles, and stanines are in the blood of most educators. In every instance, the anchor is down before the observation is made. Such thinking and feeling is so pervasive in education that there is little or no likelihood of conducting evaluation from an individual point of view unless we can predispose ourselves to set our standards *during* our observations or *after* our observations are completed. We know that standards or criteria for judgment inhere in evaluation. We cannot do without them if we are to focus our evaluation on the individual student. We need to come at the problem in a variety of different ways if we are to shed any light on what all of this means for educators and evaluators. We shall work by analogy, fully conscious of the pitfalls involved in such an approach to improving understanding.

In a school of tomorrow, efforts will be directed toward enhancing rational, autonomous individuals. Evaluation efforts that tell us how third-graders are performing or what proportion of student families receive government support will not do. We need to know about Celeste, Saul, and every other individual. It is much easier to be "right" about group assessments than it is to be right about individual assessments. As a matter of fact, if we seek to enhance individual autonomy rather than to provide a system in which individual autonomy may be enhanced, we are coming at the whole matter of educational evaluation from a new point of view. (The same conceptual tools of evaluation still apply. The changes come because the phenomenal world we are dealing with looks different to us.) The educator's task becomes more like that of the doctor, the architect, or the custom tailor, and less like that of the producer of automobiles or prefabricated houses.

We may get a better sense of the differences involved here if we begin to think of having a custom tailor. Each client brings to the tailor a set of ideas about clothes, styles, and colors and a unique physique with its own set of measurements. The client consults with the tailor, examining fabrics, deciding color, being measured, and, in general, deciding what he wants and how it will be made. This is very different from going into a clothing store and looking through the racks at the available clothes for something in about the right size. The clerk may be helpful, and alterations are possible, but the chances are slim that the resulting purchase will be anything like tailor-made.

In general, schools are more like clothing stores than tailor shops, and teachers are more like sales clerks than tailors. They tend to think of something on the "racks" that might suit the "customer" rather than finding out what the customer wants and needs and creating it according to mutually determined specifications.

The longer one works in schools, the more difficult it is to grasp this idea, and even if one can see the difference, it does not seem to make much difference. One would probably get a pretty good and durable set of clothes, whether ready-to-wear or tailor-made, but the differences turn out to be considerably more significant in education, in terms of both means and ends.

Let us have a try at the same idea using medical analogies. (We are aware that drawing such analogies is difficult, because medicine so often involves diagnosing disorders, and we will not push the analogies too far.) Suppose the reader goes to the doctor because lately he has been having severe headaches, occasional dizzy spells, and intermittent stages of deep depression. Assume he relates these symptoms to the doctor, who turns directly to his "Physicians' Desk Reference" (a listing and description of available drugs) and says,

"Let's see now, we have a number of drugs that might be suitable for you. I think drug X is the best. Let's try that one, OK?"

If our doctors worked in such a manner, we would be disappointed and disillusioned. We would not expect a doctor to think in terms of providing us with one of an available variety of ready-made cures. We do not mind his using ready-made cures, but we expect that he will carefully tailor them to our needs and the nature of our disorder.

Many educators tend to think in terms of providing students with one of an available variety of ready-made educational experiences. They get a quick view of the students "symptoms," turn to the "Teachers' Desk Reference," select one of a variety of educational experiences, and prescribe it for the student. This is the clothing store analogy all over again: "What do I have on the racks that would be suitable for this customer?"

As educators, some of us have been doing this longer than others, but all of us have been taking essentially this approach. Some teachers have more to choose from on their "racks" than others; some teachers have a more comprehensive "Teachers' Desk Reference" than others; and some teachers work harder at helping the student select what he wants and at making alterations. But the fact is that education is rarely, if ever, tailor-made for the student. One major difficulty is that we know the "stock available in our store" better than we do the "customer." He "walks in off the street," and we do our best to fit him with what we have.

Let us think a little about how we expect to be treated in a hospital. The doctor, of course, guides the admission. He has an in-depth knowledge of the patient's condition and needs. These are communicated to the hospital. They take the patient as he is, no matter what his condition, and do their best to arrange a hospital environment and experience that will improve his individual well-being. The patient is admitted, treated, and discharged on a highly individualized basis. Schools are not like this, although in some ways they approach it.

Let us now mix our metaphors and risk the attendant confusion. We often think of a school in somewhat the same way we think of a factory. The products of a school are its students. We produce a number of high-quality models who go on to college, and a good number of utility models who will hold reasonably good jobs and be contributing members of society. Aside from a number that we reject along the way, the rest will be low-cost models that we hope will be capable of surviving in society.

Most of us find our view of the school falling somewhere between our view of a hospital and our view of a factory. Let us look more closely at the conditions in the typical factory and the conditions in the typical hospital. In the factory we find (1) control of all raw materials in product formation, (2) standardized treatment, (3) control of all forces bearing on product development, (4) control of end product, and (5) if necessary, rejection and disposal of end product. In a hospital, we find (1) very limited control of raw materials (patients), (2) variable treatment, (3) limited control of forces bearing on "product development," (4) limited control of end product, and (5) rejection and disposal of end product only if all efforts fail. Which conditions are more nearly characteristic of the school? Should schools be modeling themselves more in the image of the hospital or the factory?

The consideration of these two different institutional models has helped us raise provocative questions about our own views of schools and suggested some new perspectives. For example, questions about quality with respect to the hospital refer to the health *services* rendered. Questions about quality with respect to the factory refer to the *products* produced. We know the factory has control of the end product: factories are oriented to product control. We know the hospital can control the quality of its services: hospitals are oriented to the control of services. As a matter of fact, they are organized in terms of services: nursing services, surgical services, orthopedic services, psychiatric services, and so forth. Are schools organized in terms of services or in terms of products? Do they provide "fourth-grade services" or are they engaged in producing "fourth-grade products"? Do our present evaluation practices help more in the control of "products" or in the control of "services"?

It is somewhat confusing to mix the factory and the hospital metaphors and then relate them to the school in this way, but the fact is that many educators deal with education in the context of just such a *mixed metaphor*. Some of the difficulties in education may stem from just this sort of confused thinking. We do not know whether the school is an "educational hospital" or an "educational factory." And, of course, it really is neither, but we are not sure whether we should judge a school in terms of its end products, its services, or both. We do believe that a school that focuses evaluation efforts on the individual student probably has to work at evaluation in ways that are much more like those of a hospital than those of a factory. Maybe we can illustrate this belief.

Assume we are helping admit patients to a hospital. The first is a little boy with rather severe burns on his face and arms. The second is a middle-aged man who appears to have had a mild heart attack. The third is a young man whose jaw has been broken and who needs oral surgery. The fourth is a maternity case. The fifth is also a maternity case but is anticipating multiple births. The sixth is being admitted for observation because of gastrointestinal disorders. And so on. Obviously, all of these are people with a host of "normal" functions that seem to be unimpaired. They can all see and hear; all are ambulatory; and none of them has stopped eating. They are, then, very much alike, but from the hospital viewpoint, they are very different. We know that the organization of services to attend to their needs will have to be individualized in particular ways.

Our "clients" are school children. Do we admit "clients" to schools who are much alike, but in some critically important ways quite different? What does it mean when we answer "no" to this question? If our answer is "Yes, they are different in some critically important ways," what would we say if we were asked to specify these critical differences? How would we answer the serious questioner who asked, "How do you plan to organize your education services to provide for the well-being of this young person or that?"

These questions get pretty sticky, don't they? Are we pushing the school-hospital analogy too hard? We think not. It cannot be denied that there are very marked differences between hospitals and schools and the medical and teaching professions. But, the fundamental facts in both cases are that these institutions are expected to work at improving the human condition by providing certain professional services. Maybe health services are easier to "deliver" than educational services. Maybe hospitals have more resources than schools. Maybe institutions that are primarily concerned with treating disorders can take a different point of view toward their clients. None of these "explanations" (or maybe rationalizations?) seems very convincing to us. Even the explanation rooted in the idea that schools must deal with all the children of all the people all the time simply says to us that the scope of the problem is vastly enlarged while its nature remains the same.

We have attempted to demonstrate that in a school for

tomorrow the program of evaluation must start in a different place, work from a wide variety of different points of view, and proceed to different destinations. Evaluation starts with individual students, and, as a result, the world of the school and human educational experience looks entirely different. Although we use many of the same tested tools and procedures of evaluation as we always have, the data are different. The variability has increased. The central tendencies are still there (where would we be without them!), but they are elusive. We can find them, but until we do, the whole picture of educational experience is bound to appear chaotic.

We think the purposes of educational evaluation will shift toward facilitating the delivery of educational services and away from providing information about the quality of educational "products." Such a shift in the purposes of evaluation will not constitute a complete reversal of educational evaluation policies, but will be great enough to make dramatic differences in the evaluator's view of educational experience and the nature of his judgments.

We hope we have said enough to make our point about this new perspective. We also hope that it does not appear to be an *ideological* matter, because we do not think it is. The stubborn fact is that if you look at educational experience from individualized viewpoints, the stuff evaluators deal with increases fantastically in its diversity.

Observation and Data in Evaluation

Efforts to evaluate begin with some internal organization of the thoughts, feelings, and beliefs of the evaluator. Evaluation is rooted, then, in what the evaluator knows, feels, and believes. The diving judge at the Olympic Games, the clinical psychologist, the doctor, and the teacher come to the evaluation situation with a great deal "built into them." No matter how open they are, they know what they are looking for and are prepared to "see," or to experience through observation, something others might be unable to experience. When observation is conducted for the purpose of evaluating, there is a perceptual reaching out by the evaluator—an attempt to discover in the phenomenal world something he believes to be there.

The kind of processes the evaluator uses also make a difference. The processes of observation predispose us to discover certain kinds of things. Standardized objective tests produce a different kind of information from informal interviews or direct observation. Competent evaluators use a wide variety of formal and informal techniques. A wide range of objective and subjective considerations are entailed in these observational processes. The competent evaluator knows that the observational processes he uses have an impact and leave their mark on the data and that the data can be interpreted only as one understands the impact the processes have had.

To help us review observation as one of the fundamental processes in evaluation, let us consider each of these elements: the observer and his intentions, the observational processes, and the reactive effects induced by observation. True, there is interaction among the observer, his processes of observation, and the observed, but we can be mindful of that as we proceed.

One fundamental problem in observations that are intended to serve the purposes of evaluation can be summed up in the question, "Are the resulting data useful?" This is a functional form of the reliability-validity questions. Because reliability and validity are, in practice, inextricably related, we can deal with them together. What disposes observations to validity or invalidity or to reliability or unreliability?

The Observer

A human observation is a transaction between an observer who knows, feels, and believes and a real world situation including all that is "out there." The observer initiates, guides, and interprets the transaction. The act is a perceptual one in which the meanings that arise are in some way a result of what the observer brings into the act. "Perception is not immaculate." Observation produces a view of Lisa, for example, that says she is not only some of what she is but some of what I think her to be. Whatever my "theory" is about Lisa, no matter how minimal I take it to be, it becomes incorporated into my understanding of Lisa as I observe her. It is probably a fact, if all other things are equal, that the more observations I make of Lisa, the more my view of her will conform to what she actually is. The reliability and validity of the data arising from observations are enhanced by increasing the number of observations. Yet I can never entirely rid the data of what I think about her and what I have thought about her. My "theories" about her will still make a difference—I hope a valuable one. We are all aware of how difficult it is for some bad boys ever to be seen as good and some good boys ever to be seen as bad. The reliability and validity of my understanding of a child are a function of the "theory" I hold with regard to that child.

Observers are capable of distinguishing which observations produce descriptive and which evaluative data. Lisa has brown eyes. Lisa is pretty. Any observer needs to be capable of making such distinctions. Both descriptive and evaluative data belong in educational evaluation; but unless they are distinguishable, we run the very grave risk of talking ourselves into something that is not so. Description and evaluation can sometimes become abysmally difficult to sort out, but let us try now to do some sorting.

We need to make a distinction between data that are wholly descriptive and data that are primarily evaluative. The distinction will rest on an understanding of intention or purpose. The evaluator observes in some context and these contexts make demands on him. When the context defines for the evaluator how suggestions and actions should be understood, we can say the evaluator has intention or purpose. When the context does not define how suggestions and actions should be understood, we can say the evaluator is without intention or purpose.

Data arising from situations in which the evaluator observes with intention or purpose are, in our terms, evaluative data. The act of evaluating is an act of judging or an act of appraising that includes a best estimate of value. Because the observation is performed in a context that defines how the situation is to be understood—that is, the evaluator has intention—there are explicit or implicit criteria to serve as a basis for judgment.

We define descriptive data as data arising in contexts that do not define how suggestions and actions should be understood. Intent or purpose is not defined by the context of the situation. The observer "sees" for the sake of "seeing" not for the sake of appraising. As a descriptive account goes beyond what *is* to express meanings associated with values, the account becomes increasingly evaluative.

The acts of human evaluators range over a continuum from those that produce almost wholly descriptive data to those having a wealth of evaluative data. As the context increasingly demands that meanings associated with values appear in the data, the occurrence of judgments in the data increases and the data become increasingly evaluative in nature.

In our sense of the term, human observation is a form of human experience. A knowing, feeling, believing observer brings himself to a transactive relationship with a real world situation, and things happen to him. He probably began the transaction with some kind of intentions. Maybe he wanted to know what Betsy was like, or whether Mike understood the differentiation process in the calculus, or what he should be doing to help Myrna feel better about herself. Regardless of what the goal of the observation was—and we are aware that there are an infinite variety of such ends—we need a way to talk about the kinds of ends we seek. We need a functional way to talk about them that will be useful to educators. We can borrow a tried and true one from science. It is a rough and ready sort of system without a lot of subtleties, but it makes rudimentary good sense when applied.

Data for What Purposes?

Educational evaluators gather and use data for different purposes. These purposes can be generally classified as (1) to describe, (2) to explain, (3) to generate alternative courses of action, and (4) to determine and control a course of action. When data are gathered for the first three purposes, we are engaged in what we shall call diagnosis. We shall examine this idea in much more detail later. Diagnosis very often leads to prescription, the fourth purpose.

The data gathered by students, teachers, and evaluators serve different purposes. We are not always intending to diagnose or prescribe when we gather data. We are like the scientists in that we need a strong data base from which to work. We need to know descriptively what the educational world is like. We need to understand that world and the people in it. And we need this kind of information and understanding even if we do not propose to use it to determine courses of action. Data are gathered by students, teachers, and evaluators to describe, explain, predict possibilities, diagnose, prescribe, and control educational experiences. Because these kinds of data have different uses and may be collected for different purposes, we need to be consciously aware of the distinctions among them and some of the bases for judging their quality.

We sometimes think of data as hierarchical. That is, the type of data that provides a basis for control is the highest form and the type that describes is the lowest form. We would rather *not* do this here. Instead, we hold that data intended to describe are good if they describe well, and data intended to provide a basis for control are good if they provide a sure basis for control. In short, data serve many ends and their quality can be ascertained only by a consideration of the ends they are intended to serve.

What does all this mean for the use of data in educational evaluation? We seek and gather data sometimes because they are useful to us in a descriptive sense. We need to know about a child. We need substantive experiential inputs that tell us what the child is like. If a teacher or administrator asks "What is Enrico like?" we should be able to give a full, rich, descriptive and nonjudgmental accounting of what he is like. But the demands on evaluators go beyond this. The descriptive account may reveal that Enrico withdraws from other children during free time activities. Why does he do this? We are now being asked to explain, to render a judgment about the reasons for Enrico's behavior. The fact that he withdraws from other children is in our descriptive data. If the context of the situation demands that we discover why he withdraws, we must go beyond descriptive data to evaluative data. Our intention must be to explain why.

As we go beyond the data used to describe, our intention in gathering the data changes. We may ask that the data be good enough to explain, to predict, or to control situations. The amount and quality of the judgment required in the data tend to increase as we move from data used to explain to data used to control. The data become increasingly evaluative in nature. But data intended to explain, predict, or control are of a different order. We put different requirements on data intended to serve different purposes.

School people gather data intended to help them predict how Johnny will fare in a certain educational setting. We would also like to know why he will fare the way we have predicted, but that is not absolutely necessary. If a good evaluator says Johnny will work well with Mrs. Simon, the test of the quality of such evaluative data lies in whether Johnny does work well with Mrs. Simon. We may be a little disturbed if, when the evaluator is asked why, he says "I don't know, but I feel very sure he will." He is predicting outcomes, not explaining them. He is using the "crystal ball" of his experience with Johnny and Mrs. Simon and his better intuitive judgments. In the day-to-day running of education and schools, these probably make up the greatest bulk of the evaluative judgments made. It would be great if we could fully describe Johnny and neatly explain why he and Mrs. Simon would work well together. And, we probably should constantly work toward that, but the fact of the matter is we must act educationally on our predictive judgments whether or not we can explain. Human experience does not wait for explanations. It proceeds much more often without them.

You may have surmised that when data are used in this fashion, a great deal of intuition and inference is involved. Are we to trust it? Looking ahead to figure 5-1 (page 186), we note that, as the level of inference goes up, we can expect our credibility in the judgment to go down. When data are used for prediction, it is the "track record" of the predictor that establishes the credibility of the judgment. How often he is right is the criterion, not how well he can explain why he is right. But let us not forget that there is a criterion here. We are urged to freewheel it, to respond intuitively, even to avoid explaining. It is our position that such advice is irresponsible unless we are held accountable for the success of our predictions. How often were we right and how often wrong? We all know teachers who consistently exhibit good judgment, and we all know others who do not.

Lastly, we seek data to be used in the control of educational experiences for children. The kinds of data here need to be pretty "hard" in the sense that they are unequivocal. This is the prescription-management level. We will "force" the educational experience on the child. We must be right and right for the right reasons. Like the doctor administering drugs or performing surgery, the margins of error are very slim. In education, we must call for valid and reliable explanations of the prescription from an evaluator whose judgment we can trust. His "track record" in predicting outcomes should be good. And we may want a confirming or consultative judgment.

Hopefully, this sorting of kinds of evaluative data in terms of their uses will prove helpful. Evaluators are called on to describe, to explain, to predict, and to give the assurances we need to warrant controlling educational experience. If the purpose is diagnosis and prescription, we may use the data to describe, explain, and produce alternative courses of action. The kinds of data are different and so are their qualities. We need to be aware of these facts and more importantly to recognize the bases on which we judge the data's qualities. Data are good because they serve an educational purpose and serve it well. Data are substantive tools used by evaluators to help them make judgments.

Observational Processes in Diagnosis

A tremendous variety of tests, scales, inventories, sociometric devices, projective techniques, etc. has been used to gather data about students. The validity and reliability of these instruments can be readily estimated by technical means. However, educational evaluation rests heavily on informal observational procedures and some form of intuitive monitoring. It is a matter of looking carefully to see what is going on rather than bringing some refined instrument to bear. This will become increasingly the case as evaluation is used to support the development of autonomous individuals.

As we move toward increasingly informal observations and increased reliance on intuitive judgments, we make it increasingly possible for the biases of observers to influence the data. And the biases of some teachers and some evaluators are pernicious as we all know. Although we tend to think of some biases as serving good outcomes and some as serving bad outcomes, in our view *unidentified* personal biases in evaluation data serve no useful end. Yet we are aware that there is personal bias in the outcome of all observation. Our approach to this problem in evaluation can be clarified by defining what we mean by the terms *objective* and *subjective.*

The reliability and validity of the data obtained through observation ultimately depend on how the subjectivity of the observer is handled. Every observer is biased. Every observation results in a subjective processing of sense experience in which the bias of the observer may have its impact on the data. The root question we ask about data arising from observation is: What would be common to all observers similarly situated and what can we attribute only to the idiosyncracies of the individual observer? The data that are idiosyncratic represent the biases of the observer. The data that are common to all observers are classified as objective. Both kinds of data have their uses, but they must be distinguished.

We distinguish the two kinds by invoking a concern for intersubjective agreement. We ask of the data arising from the observations of two or more observers, what in these data that reflect your subjective experiences is common to all observers? In this way we come to classify data as objective because of the evidence of intersubjective agreements. Kaplan's summary of this notion is an apt one: "Do you see what I see?"

Obviously all of our data will not be objective in this sense. We will have data that we must recognize as more or less objective. Hence we will suggest that the data of evaluation be recognized as moving from highly subjective kinds to increasingly objective kinds. In any case, the reliability and validity of the data are important whether they are subjective or objective. Because informal observational processes and intuitive judgments are more open to invalidity and unreliability, we need to pay particular attention to validity and reliability of observations in such instances.

The precepts we should follow to enhance the reliability and validity of informal observational processes may have been driven out of consciousness by our extended concern for the more technical aspects of validity and reliability as they relate to formal testing. We do know, for example, that the more direct the transaction between the observer and the observed, the more reliable and valid the data. An "eyewitness" account is better than a secondhand account. Our evaluation processes should be characterized by much direct observation. We need to be close to those observed, and our data need to be flooded with eyewitness accounts. Bombarded as we are with technical approaches to reliability and validity, we may find we do not really trust these informal eyewitness accounts. But the law does, and we know historians bank heavily on primary sources to support their interpretations.

There is one peculiarly significant aspect of the principle calling for direct observation that we sometimes overlook. For example, if I want to know how a person feels, the most direct approach is to ask him. He alone can witness his actual feelings. (If I try to observe his feelings directly, I am limited to drawing inferences from some external behavioral cues that are manifest to me.) Much of the data educational evaluation seeks comes from the human experiences of others, and they alone are the true "eyewitnesses" to those experiences. This suggests a liberal use of formal and informal interviews. We need to exercise caution here. It is the reliability and validity of the resulting data that are important, not directness of observation per se. Direct observation may produce reactive effects in those being observed and thus completely destroy the validity and reliability of the data. We should prize directness of observation only as it enhances the reliability and validity of the data obtained.

Observational processes tend to systematize data. We cannot observe without categorizing, classifying, or relating the bits of the data. We are conservative and conceptually-organized processors of information, and we tend to be impressed by well-organized data. They look good, and they must be reliable if they are that precise and well-ordered. This, of course, is nonsense; data are not reliable because they seem well-ordered. They are reliable because they portray some real situation accurately. We do need order in the data to be able to manipulate, analyze, and think about them, but we can struggle for order at the expense of reliability and especially at the expense of validity. Our maxim here might be to seek "good" data, and if they were meant to have order they will and if not they will not, but we will be able at least to trust them.

All observations take place in some spatiotemporal setting. The reliability and validity of the resulting data cannot be understood apart from that context. Sound evaluation data cannot be either ahistorical or provincial. Every student lives in a space-time context. Every observation must account in some way for the effects of that context on the resulting data. It is so easy for evaluators to become provincial or ahistorical and fail to recognize context effects. Meanings, especially meanings of evaluative data, derive much of their validity and reliability from the context in which they were derived.

In a school of tomorrow, the fundamental principles are probably going to be more useful as guides than are the technical skills associated with, for example, statistical tests of reliability and validity. We have spoken about the kinds of data and kinds of observational processes. We have reviewed some of the more fundamental considerations and some observation indicators (when these processes indicate data). We pointed out earlier that observation produced reactive effects in the observed and we also said we would be mindful of the fact that the reliability and validity of observations are affected by the interactions among the observer, his processes, and the observed. Let us turn to the reactive effects now.

Reactive Effects

Probably the classic illustration of reactive effects is to be found in Western Electric studies conducted at a plant in Hawthorne, New York. The experimental treatment effects were completely masked by the reactive effects of the subjects, and the phenomenon came to be called the Hawthorne Effect. It is only one kind of reactive effect, but probably a very important one. There are others. If we ask a person how he feels, the very act of asking may change how he feels. People sometimes take on roles when they are being observed. For example, some people literally try to meet what they believe are the observer's expectations. In other instances, attempts at observation may strongly encourage the observed to keep his own secrets. Obviously, the general observational climate should encourage open and frank disclosure. We guess most educators are highly sensitive to the need for this. It is also a matter of interpersonal rapport between the observer and the observed. Another direct way to identify and sort out the reactive effects in observation is to use a variety of observational techniques. Some techniques are more reactive than others. Some techniques produce systematic reactions not produced by others. We suggest that just as one observer is not enough, neither is one observational technique. We need to be able to distinguish what is really going on from what is going on because we are observing.

Interaction in Observation

Imagine the untrained person administering and interpreting a Rorschach or an X ray. How much faith could we have in the reliability and validity of the resulting data? We are all sensitive to this problem when the instrumentation is unique and rather specialized, but when it comes to the use of more common tools, the interview for example, we may wholly disregard the problem. Anybody can interview. But can anyone? The evidence clearly suggests that interviewing requires skills. An interview schedule in the hands of one interviewer may result in data of excellent quality and in the hands of another, in data that are virtually useless. The act of observation is a transaction involving the observer, the observed, and the processes of observation. The resulting data are only as good as the functional quality of these interrelationships will allow. Interviewers who establish rapport with their subjects get one kind of data, and those who do not get another. It may be that we have for too long relied on data that were distorted because of the conditions under which they were gathered and interpreted. No effective evaluation can proceed on the basis of invalid and unreliable data. The maxim here is simply that the observer needs to be the master of his techniques. The test of this mastery lies in the assurances he can give that the results of his observation are reliable, valid, and suitable as bases for helping to determine educational courses of action.

Judging

If our values enter into the data arising from our observations, what can we do about it? If we are convinced that George is dumb when, in fact, he may not be, how can we correct or compensate for that view? First, we can recognize that we have *judged* George as dumb and that this was our value judgment, no matter how firmly we might be convinced that the descriptive data supported that contention. If we can see that we have made a judgment, we will realize that it is our judgment, not George's behavior, that we are talking about. Others can then take a look at George and his behavior to see if they confirm or deny what we have claimed.

There are two other considerations we should mention. One is the matter of prejudice. We are making a distinction here between making a faulty judgment, as in the case of George, and coming to the observation with a prejudgment already made. This latter situation is sometimes aptly described by the expression "My mind is made up, don't confuse me with the facts." Little can be done about such situations—and they do occur—aside from encouraging people with a variety of prejudices to judge the same situation.

The second consideration has to do with the matter of drawing inferences from observable cues. We shall deal much more fully with that matter later in this chapter, but let us point out here that the levels of inference, or the degree to which inferences are used to generate meaning from facts, vary widely. We might suggest here that the relationship between our confidence in a judgment and the level of inference involved in making the judgment probably should be graphically portrayed as in figure 5-1. Degrees of confidence in judgments are probabilistic, and the degree of our certainty is a function

Figure 5-1.

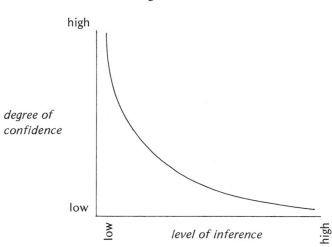

of the amount of inference involved in arriving at the judgment. But more about this later.

Data Analyses in a Future Tense

The methods of data analysis are so common to our everyday experience that we might be hard pressed to identify them. We classify and name, we measure and assign order or magnitude, we group together and average, we subdivide and partition, we relate this to that, we test the data from our experience against models, and we ask if our data confirm our theory or maybe if our theory predicts our data. There is nothing mystical about these methods. They simply are our very human way of dealing with our experience. It is true that there are refined technical ways and means of dealing with data arising from human experience, and there are marked differences in the technical skills different people have for analyzing data. At root, though, we are all stuck with the fact that there is a limited number of methods open to us.

We can and do classify the data arising in our experience. We put them in "pigeonholes" and label the pigeonholes. How else could we get "a handle on" the animal kingdom, educational objectives, personality types, occupational opportunities, or even human aspirations? Sometimes our pigeonholes are the equivalent of unrelated boxes, and sometimes there is a carefully worked-out and ordered relationship among the boxes. In any event, we know that good classification requires that there be enough boxes to classify all the data we wish to classify and that it be clear to us *and to others* which data go into which box and why. A classification system needs to be inclusive and the categories within the system need to be mutually exclusive. And, of course, the classification has to serve some useful educational purpose.

The data used in classifying have to be of a quality sometimes called "nominal," meaning that we can attach names to the data. If we correctly characterize a person as honest, or sensitive, or malevolent, we have provided a tremendous amount of information at the nominal level.

We classify data arising from our experience by ordering them: for example, this came first, and that came second, or Gerry seems more capable as a quarterback than Norm. An intuitive idea is involved here: namely, that we can order phenomena from first to last, highest to lowest, or greatest to least, and this implies some quantitative or qualitative continuum. The data we can put on such a continuum are sometimes referred to as ordinal data. If our ordering is a "true" one, we can make some very significant comparisons. We can tell who has more of something, and who has less. Ultimately, this kind of information can help us decide where to put our resources to facilitate the educational well-being of great numbers of children. It is the nature of the continuum that is crucial, not the fact that we can order the phenomena. Ordering phenomena helps us make a kind of comparative sense out of what we have found, but the real sense lies at deeper levels.

We also have data that, in our everyday sense, are truly measured. Michael is six feet, two inches tall. Mary earns an average weekly salary of $65. Raleigh has a measured IQ of 120 on the Lorge Thorndike Intelligence Test. (We will be speaking of error in measurement in the next section.)

Maybe our long experience with arithmetic, money, or measures of space and time inclines us to think that if data are to be really good, they must be of this kind. But again, what makes them meaningful is the continuum on which they have been ordered. Mary's family has an annual income of $4,000 and Celeste's family has an annual income of $24,000. It is useful to be able to say that Celeste's family has an income exactly six times the size of the income of Mary's family. But is that the point? Hardly.

We can, then, analyze data by *classifying, ordering,* or *measuring* in its stricter sense. These are means by which we refine our interpretations of data. Nonetheless, we should recognize that the meanings we get from the data arise from a much deeper level of understanding. The operations of categorizing, comparing, adding, or subtracting simply sharpen these more basic meanings.

Many data analyses rely on certain descriptive statistical notions. We speak of an average or a median. These are measures of central tendency. Taking all the variations in the data into account, how can we best describe the data with one descriptor? We are seeking to overcome the diversities in the data and find an efficient way of describing what the data "say" on the average. This is useful. For example, there are variations in a child's performance from day to day. Is he doing well or not so well? We answer this, of course, by seeking a good description of his average performance. In a school of tomorrow, such an application of "central tendency thinking" appears to be useful because the focus is on the individual. "Central tendency thinking," which masks individuality, may not be so useful.

Variability is the root of the human condition. Variable data are tough data to process. It is difficult for us to make sense out of variability, but it can be handled. We have measures of variability such as range and standard deviation. We work with variability in data when we work with percentiles or stanines. These are measures of dispersion or variability based on group characteristics, and they help us deal with variability. However, the systematic treatment of variability requires clinical or statistical skills that most of us do not have. In a school of tomorrow, data will be prized because they are variable, and we will need people with specialized talents to help us.

Sources of Error

We can always be sure that some of the error in our interpretation of events is caused by our sampling the events. If we observe a student's behavior, we observe only some of it. We see him at certain times and under certain conditions; he is doing some things that are characteristic of him and not others. We are all aware of the day-to-day variability in student performance and characteristics. Data gathered at any given time on a student may either underestimate or overestimate his potential, his performance, or the degree to which he holds a given characteristic.

The moral here is that the more observations made, the less the error. The more samples we have of a given population of events, the surer we can be that the accumulated data on the samples represent the population. For example, Larry's batting average over the games of a season is a better measure of his batting performance than his average in any one game in which he may go 0 for 4 or 4 for 4.

Errors emanate from our measurement or observational efforts. Perhaps the test we gave was not a good one, or the testing conditions prevented optimal performance. We are conscious of these pitfalls in all forms of testing, but we are sometimes unconscious of the fact that these same kinds of errors occur in *any* observation. In some cases the observation tool is the evaluator acting as an observer. He, too, is liable to err, because the conditions under which his observation takes place affect the quality of his observation.

Error inheres in measurement and observation; there is no way to get away from it. We can work to refine our instruments and our skills of observation, but some error will still be there. The statisticians give us good advice. Every measurement has an "error band" associated with it, and we should report the error band along with the measurement. Louisa's IQ probably falls somewhere between 97 and 107. There is a difference between true IQs (if there could ever be such) of 97 and 107. We need to keep our appraisal of Louisa's IQ open to the possibility of such difference.

Even when we are not measuring, we can do the same thing, and our data can reflect the notion of an error band. Dean shows a moderately strong to strong self-concept. Manuel shows average to good qualities of imagination in his creative writing efforts.

Other sources of error may appear that are not typical. For example, there are recording errors and errors stemming from analyses of data. Computers occasionally take good substantive data and convert them to nonsense because of program errors. Sometimes events occur that badly distort the characteristic behavior of a person. Eternal vigilance should be directed toward ferreting out the error and ridding the data of it as well as eliminating the source of such errors whenever possible. The importance of high-quality records skillfully kept needs emphasis. The data in them are data about people. If nothing else, they should be as true to those they represent as possible.

Data Interpretation

The most crucial, most widely used, and least understood activity in evaluation is interpretation. We all have "cognitive maps," or theories, in our minds that incorporate what we know, feel, and believe about a given situation. There are patterns of information that arise from our observations and reported data. We even allow for error. How do these relate? What does our theory say about the information patterns? "I don't believe it," or "I am confirmed by the data," or "What goes on here?"? And what do the data say to our theory? "There are some things you don't know," or "You were right," or "Did you really think you were adequately accounting for the empirical facts?"? Of course, the heart of interpretation in educational evaluation lies here. In the dialogue between ourselves and the real world that takes place in observation, we are trying to bring about some better order and understanding. We know something; the real world "knows" more; we are trying to ferret out the secrets. Interpretation in educational evaluation is good, if the dialogue is good, and the real world is not recalcitrant.

We can make some suggestions that may be helpful here. The more good information and understanding we bring to the observation, the better the dialogue is likely to be. The more aware we are and the better we understand our own feelings, the better the dialogue will be. Finally, a sound dialogue of this sort is complex and fragile; it cannot be pressured or hurried.

Data, Inference, and Credibility

The tried and true canons of evaluation apply as never before in this newer perspective on individual evaluation. The data are richer, more subjective, and more complex. The inferences we draw from the data are still inferences that affect the lives of people; they must be sound.

We will provide a way of looking at evaluation in the next section of this chapter. We will order evaluation data along two continuums: one ranging from the increasingly objective to the increasingly subjective and the other ranging from the wholly descriptive to the wholly evaluative. The means for assuring the quality of the inferences we make from data that differ vastly in kind and quality are the means we have always used. Nevertheless, we must recognize that when dealing with subjective-evaluative data, the problems of assuring high-quality inferences are subtle and often complex.

In the past we have avoided using data of some kinds because the problem of defending the credibility of our judgments seemed beyond our capacities. In this new model we will have to come to grips with that problem. The model includes data that we would not have included before. But the new model has the advantage of telling us what kind of data we have and hence alerting us to the problems of inference associated with the data. If we can bring to bear the principles we have developed, we will be able to answer with some degree of assurance the questions "What is going on with Manuel?" and "What should we be doing about it?"

Evaluation-Diagnostic Model for a School of Tomorrow

Assumptions

As a foundation or cornerstone for evaluation in tomorrow's school, we might make five assumptions:

1. There is a difference between the goals of evaluation and the functions evaluation may accept. As educators, we may well agree that the goal of evaluation is to decide the worth of something, while the functions performed in evaluation are those involved in diagnosis and prescription with the intent of realizing the goals that we value.

2. In our view, judging an individual's performance against another performance by the same individual has high priority for informal, individualized evaluation. The congruence between the performance and the objective is useful, if we emphasize what we expect in the student's performance as the criterion and apply refinement and readjustment in an ongoing sense, rather than assessing terminal events only.

3. Evaluation broadly encompasses both judgment and description. Most authorities tend to agree with this viewpoint. We agree with Urmson when he states, "At some stage we must say firmly that to describe is to describe, to grade is to grade, and to express one's feelings is to express one's feelings, and that none of these is reducible to either of the others, nor can any of them be reduced to or defined in terms of anything else."[3]

4. Our image of a teacher or a student is an image of a choosing person, one who makes a decision on the basis of the forces he feels and the information he receives. We have all been in situations where the alternatives were contradictory and unclear. We probably desired more information to make a decision. We often make choices based on our own experience, and we consider information from ourselves and other sources.

5. A new view of evaluation requires making increased and compelling use of data. Gathering, analyzing, organizing, classifying, ordering, and measuring data must end in serving our unique educational purposes well.

Diagnostic Antecedents

We know that ultimately the worth of an educational process or procedure must be decided. First, we must address ourselves to the diagnostic function of evaluation. The intention to observe diagnostically seems to clarify the meaning of evaluation and brings the individual student—his past, present, and expected performance—into sharper focus.

Essentially, the nature of diagnosis is observation. We cannot avoid the subjectivity inherent in observation. Additionally, personal value commitments, perceived norms, priorities, feelings, substantive test scores, and so on are information bits. Using intersubjectivity criteria, information bits are informative and valuable.

The process of diagnosis makes intensive use of information bits to produce adequate descriptions. Compiling data gives us the occasion to search for explanations in and among the situations described. Proposing alternative courses of action and testing them at a conceptual level assesses the potentials of the alternative courses of action; this may be termed *secondary* decision making. Decisions made relative to selecting courses of action are *primary* decisions, because they are prescriptive.

In a school for tomorrow, we envision an increase in the diagnostic capabilities of the teacher and the self-evaluation abilities of the student. It appears that evaluation in tomorrow's school may well have the following "what" and "how" dimensions: The "what" to evaluate is growth, and the "how" is the use of teacher and student subjective approaches augmented by objective methods. These subjective approaches may take the form of diagnostic observation: gathering data and making decisions in order to assist student selection of alternate learning activities.

Diagnosis is at the same time mysterious and comprehensible; it is hidden and yet exposed. We all engage in it on differing levels of sophistication and understanding; it is a common activity in many service-oriented professions.

For example, let us contrast the diagnostic behavior of a teacher and a veterinarian, using the same activity "constant."

Activity	*Teacher*	*Veterinarian*
Diagnostic observation	Third grade student seems reluctant to read; cannot sound and understand many words and phrases encountered in reading text and library books; observes student reading in other subject matter areas.	The dog in this case has a very good appetite, drinks lots of water and passes quite a bit of urine (all of these are different behavior patterns noted by owner), and loses weight gradually.
Gathering data	Discusses problem with child; determines specific reading skills needed; formally and informally assesses word vocabulary, phonetic usage, and comprehension; consults results of informal and formal	Considers malabsorption and age of animal; tries to pin down most likely differentials (causes that could be attributed to the symptoms). Determines the specific gravity of the urine, and

	achievement tests. Determines lack of ability to use phonetic reading skills.	blood sugar and glucose tolerance levels; measures insulin level. Determines an insulin deficiency—regulatory mechanisms not working.
Making decisions	Arranges data on phonetic skill related to word recognition needs, social interest, and motivation of student and determines consonant blends and vowel constructions. Reviews instructional materials and methods that could be used. Reflects on availability, priority, and sequence for alternate instructional approaches.	Arranges data and tests and determines insulin deficiency, a specific form of diabetes (clinical). Reviews treatment procedures (in this case, increasing insulin levels) through injections or oral prescriptions.
Prescribing	Obtains instructional materials; instructs, guides, facilitates, provides feedback, teaches.	Specifies and administers insulin; adjusts dosage on the basis of body weight and amount of calorie intake.
Measure	Child learns or does not learn (increases knowledge and usage of reading skills).	Symptoms disappear or do not disappear, or other symptoms appear.

Diagnostic behavior can extend beyond this typical "service" contrast. We may borrow Galloway and Mulhern's term, *self-service*. Self-diagnosis, in terms of evaluating expected learnings for mature students and in terms of evaluating necessary, facilitating strategies for teachers, may help us in understanding and applying diagnostic technique and prescription.

We conceived an exploratory model (figure 5-2) to give substance to the "whats" and the "hows." The model's purpose is to make credible and useful the subjective, intuitive elements that so frequently occur as hidden evaluation in school. Basically, the evaluation diagnostic model is an attempt to spell out such concerns as (1) categorizing phenomena as a kind of data, (2) recognizing the kinds of information, (3) systematizing our intentions *and* our observations to yield better-quality information in order that our judgments may become more valid and reliable than previously, and (4) realizing that the evaluation process is a human activity of diagnosis.

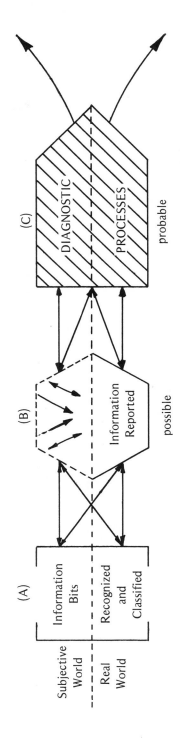

Figure 5-2. Evaluation-Diagnostic Model for a School of Tomorrow

Part A of the Model: Information Bits Recognized and
Classified

At first, we may wish to classify and begin to sort out the kinds
of information or data we have received, should receive, or are receiving. We propose four kinds of data.

1. Subjective descriptive data. Resulting from awareness
through the senses, this kind of data reflects feelings and emotional
awareness to assist knowing, learning about, and categorizing phenomena for purposes other than decision making.

2. Subjective evaluative data. This form of data uses standards,
feelings, and emotional awareness to assist knowing, learning about,
and categorizing phenomena. This information seems to be received
without the conscious use of reasoning as an influence on the decisions we need to make.

To clarify the difference between subjective descriptive and subjective evaluative data, suppose that a preschool girl had a great need
for attention and affection in the classroom to the point of being
rude to other children and teachers. Bits of information described as
subjective descriptive data were: The teacher learned that the child's
parents were separated; she seldom saw her father; she made up
stories about her father; the mother seemed cool and unaffectionate
toward her; the teacher recognized her normal need for attention;
her behavior became docile when she saw her mother observing from
the doorway; the mother seemed greatly embarrassed by her
daughter's acting-out behavior.

The teacher decided a poor relationship existed between mother
and child. This is *subjective evaluative data.*

3. Objective descriptive data. This kind of data assigns symbols
to empirical phenomena according to an accepted rule for the purpose of categorizing the information.

4. Objective evaluative data. This form of data is derived from a
logical reasoning process of noting and recording phenomena by
using criteria to categorize reality happenings in order that decisions
may be made.

The following example may help to clarify the difference between objective descriptive and objective evaluative data. The teacher
observed that a junior high school boy reading at his appropriate

level had strong phonetic and structural analysis skills measured on daily reading performance, scored at the sixty-seventh percentile, but seemed somewhat weaker in comprehension, scoring at the forty-third percentile. In probing the child's understanding of reading selections, the teacher found he could answer factual recall questions well, but failed when asked opinion questions. The student participated in discussions of his reading strengths and weaknesses. After a wide-range reading achievement test was given, results demonstrated low scores in critical reading areas. These results were presented to the student. These bits of information may be described as *objective descriptive data.*

Considering the objective descriptive data of the boy's reading problem, it was decided to have the student work intensively in a special program consisting of a series of instructional materials providing immediate feedback to the student. This information may be termed *objective evaluative data.* Obviously, description frequently moves to judgment in observing phenomena, and one kind of information is often part of and built on knowledge of the other.

In the real world, of course, it is not that simple to bring order to the many bits of information we observe and encounter. Perhaps it will help to visualize this data mixture on a matrix (figure 5-3).

Part B: Reporting and Categorizing Information

A strong argument can now be advanced for organization of the data. One real contribution may be to formalize somewhat the ways and means of organizing data into meaningful units.

A process that strengthens the teacher's or student's diagnostic capability and minimizes error should include a category system to assist in collecting, organizing, and reporting information pertinent to an educational diagnosis. In categorizing and relating bits of information we need to consider the individual contextual parameters of both teacher and student. The frame of reference may be influenced by the way a person integrates *what should be* and *what is* (feeling states and factual perception). Monitoring the real world, we use our model (figure 5-4) of what should be as a standard to which we can compare what actually is. When a discrepancy occurs between the real world and our ideal world, we know about it. Thus, discrepancies can furnish us with relevant information. We may also wish to consider relationships, the connective points between the individual

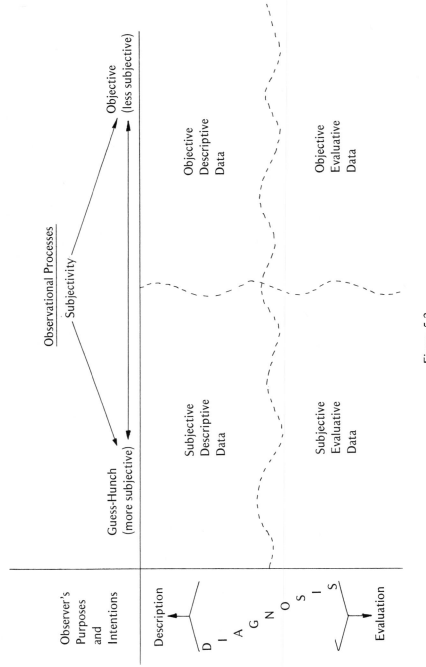

Figure 5-3.

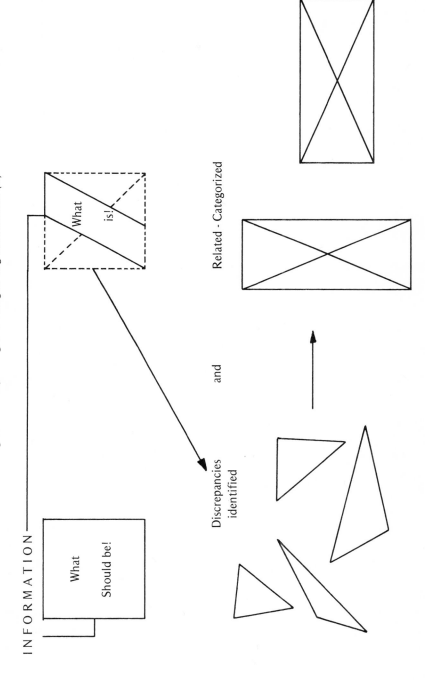

Figure 5-4. Reporting and Categorizing Information (B)

INFORMATION

What
Should be!

What
is!

Discrepancies
identified

and

Related - Categorized

characteristics, the spatiotemporal dimension of what was, what is, and what should be.

Discrepancies and relationships result from considering selected learner and teacher characteristics, learning environments, and subject content (curriculum). "What should be" information and "what is" information may be sorted out by discovering the variances or discrepancies, then relating and categorizing the relevant information. (See figure 5-4.)

Part C: Diagnostic Processes

We may consider what we have been doing in parts A and B and now add C (figure 5-5) as *diagnostic* processes: partly observation, partly cognitive, partly notation, partly analytic, and partly intuitive.

Recognizing data and classifying it, discovering discrepancies or variances and reporting them are precursors and parts of diagnosis. An intention to diagnose can be determined in A. Parts A, B, and C are linked purposefully. We consider some sectors of the diagnostic process *possible* and some *probable*. Keep these qualifiers in mind while contemplating the diagnostic process portion of the evaluation model.

Summary of Diagnostic Processes

1.0 Descriptive Information from Individual Student, Gathered and Organized (PRESENT)

As indicated in part A, information bits are recognized and classified. If questions of objectivity arise, and in an effort to reduce error, the evaluator may wish to consult descriptive information compiled by others and ask the question, "Do you see what I see?"

2.0 Descriptive Information from Similar Individuals in Similar Situations (PAST)

Organized information about the behavioral characteristics of individuals from past experiences, including learning environments and curriculum, could be consulted by the evaluator in delineating information about the individual under consideration. This information could consist of any or all of the *products of description* and any or all of the *products of judgment*. (see Appendix 1) This information, to be most useful, should probably have been compiled by the same person who requests the information later. Greater objectivity may be arrived at by

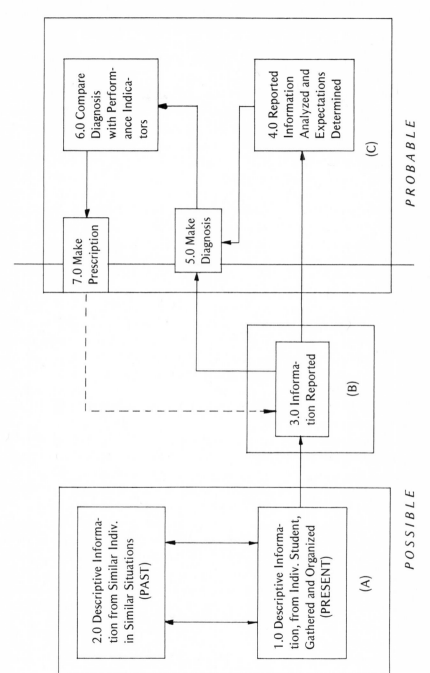

Figure 5-5. Diagnostic Processes (C)

intersubjectively analyzing descriptive information collected by
others about the same person in the past and present.

3.0 Information Reported

This is a cutaway point for present thinking about the realistic
and possible use of this process. It is assumed that part A of the
evaluation process—clarifying the antecedents of description and
evaluation and getting involved in more logical alignment of
objective/subjective, anecdotal, and actual inputs in the fitting of
information bits together—and part B—dealing with variances and
considering relationships—will promote lower-risk probabilistic
decision making in diagnosing learning strengths and weaknesses.
Consulting the reported information should make diagnosis and
prescription possible. However, at this time, it is only *probable*
that the technique described on the probable side of figure 5-5
could be employed.

4.0 Reported Information Analyzed and Expectations Determined

A performance criterion or standard for each behavioral characteristic learning environment and curriculum listed could be compared with the implications derived from discrepancies and
relationships (see Appendix 2). This comparison, a judgment
product, could be derived as an expectation with the student's
learning expectation for that specific characteristic expressed as a
strength or weakness.

5.0 Make Diagnosis

A diagnosis may consist of a consideration of the expected individual student performance, in light of immediate need and feedback, arranged in order of priority according to intentions
originally a part of the need for student diagnosis.

6.0 Compare Diagnosis with Performance Indicators

Stake has postulated the use of performance indicators that
could make the diagnostic method a logical outgrowth of the use
of learning expectancies.

Diagnostic tools generally do not prescribe which treatments are most appropriate among those available to us. We need a large catalogue of performance indicators which underlie learning strengths and weaknesses within and
across subject-matter domains. The important characteristic of such indicators is neither that they correlate highly with terminal performance nor
that they are logically integral to that process. Rather, it is critical that they
provide bases for selecting from among competing instructional treatments.[4]

7.0 Make Prescription

Feasible alternate learning experiences derived from performance indicators may be suggested by teacher and/or student. Constraints and requirements, such as the content and process to be learned, instructional methodology, organization, facilities, costs, and time, may be given as adjustments for reality. Descriptive and evaluative feedback from the learning context and experiences themselves may be used to modify or revise the behavioral characteristic environmental and curriculum information, requiring reanalysis of the information.

Characteristics of the Model

Many of us have heard modern critics of education depict teachers as so insensitive to students that learning is impaired. Less often teachers are accounted for who are sensitive to children's diverse learning needs. While many behavioral cues are evident, it is not at all clear how and why some teachers are as "tuned in" to students as others seem to be "tuned out." Do we frequently judge and decide with incomplete knowledge, imprecise measurements, and uneducated guessing?

Using the model, we may develop new yardsticks for correlating information and performance expectations. The performance yardsticks should be performance expectations for rational, autonomous individuals. An autonomous performance brings some of its own criteria and provides some information about growth. However, we must have some established major criterion against which we and the individual place his performance. In bowling, for example, the system of handicaps enables bowlers of various abilities to play on the same team, maintain individual participation and, importantly, feel success and accomplishment.

If autonomous individual growth is to be assessed as a service to the individual, we must ultimately face the challenge of clarifying and understanding the intuitive monitoring by teachers, students, administrators, and community.

Informal Data Sources and Judgment Criteria. Generally, observers gather data about others both directly and indirectly depending on how well we "know" the other. Our style of data gathering follows inclinations forged by experiences, perceptions, and values. Data gathering seems to be a mix of internal and external perceptions. Our information collecting is limited by the degree to which and the way in which we receive information from the external world (other people, objects, and events) and the internal world (our thoughts, feelings, beliefs, and impulses).

The four kinds of data described in the model are used by most observers in making educational decisions affecting students. Information for evaluative decision making and information for description often come via intuitive, empirical, or logical routes. Theoretically, these data criteria have been suggested: relevance, significance, scope, reliability, validity, credibility, and pervasiveness.[5]

The subjective nature of much of the evaluation necessary in a school of tomorrow cannot be ignored; the observer who gathers, describes, and analyzes information for probabilistic judgment should realize that all human experience has subjective elements and that no pure objective experience exists.

We agree with Kaplan when he states, "behavioral science observation involves special circumstances such as performance in an environment. In science, observation is a search for what is hidden, not because it is hidden, but because its exposure will facilitate . . . relationships."[6] Introspective data can meet the test of inter-subjectivity; what you experience is not *your* experience alone. When agreement is reached on an external perception, we need additional evidence; each of us will find it in our own perspective. Thus, the model calls for the intuiting of controls.

In explaining a model, Selye states: "we must first recognize units of classification. Further understanding requires the establishment of connections between recognized units of nature. The more connections, the better we understand what smaller units exist in the unit and of what larger systems is it in turn one unit."[7]

Sensitivity as a Diagnostic Element

The voices of Jackson and Silberman remind us that our most pressing educational problem is learning how to create and maintain a humane environment in our schools.[8] We seek ways that teachers in a school of tomorrow can more effectively use their *human* skills in facilitating meaningful evaluative interaction with learners.

Maria Montessori indicated that the role of the teacher should include the observation of the child's internal personality as demonstrated through outward behavior.[9] Madame Montessori did not operationalize this concept, but many of her writings and contemporary interpretations stress that the teacher's major function is *sensitivity* to children's behavior through accurate, quiet, and extended observation.

The informal evaluation of others is an experience in which we all participate. But, like badly tuned radios, we do not receive all the tonal shadings and nuances, and static may distort the communication. Can we become more attentive to the whole person—finely tuned, if you will—and listen as if inside the other? To become supersensitive is to become a fully tuned receiver of communication.

Maslow recognizes that man no longer has instincts in the powerful, inner voice and animal sense; only instinct remnants are left. These inner voices are now weak, subtle, delicate, and easily drowned out.[10] If we can listen to these voices in ourselves, we may listen to them in others, thereby communicating with others in a deeper sense.

Aiken describes how sensitivity relates to communication through this analogy:

If a piano wire of given length, thickness and material is stretched to a certain tension, it will vibrate in response to another identical wire that is vibrating. If I as an individual or as a member of a group have some commonality of experiences with another individual, I can vibrate in respect to that commonality—and in turn transmit it.[11]

Summary

We drew many concepts and ideas in this section from the work and thinking of Robert Stake who acknowledges that human judgment should be treated as relevant data. "People at all levels of expertise make most decisions intuitively. It may be true that some things will always be done better intuitively."[12]

There is much to recommend quantifying evaluation methods and viewing them in the shadow of educational diagnosis. We described the unique information processing that could contribute to diagnostic decision making and alternate, prescriptive treatment selection.

An educational diagnosis may be performed by the teacher, by the student, by the teacher with student assistance, or by the student with teacher assistance. A diagnosis would additionally depend on the ability, age, maturity, and instructional subject matter of the students in a learning situation. We are confident that the teacher of tomorrow will be able to rationalize the intuitive, informal information about students that is received, both solicited and un-solicited, and, using a classification system, logically arrange the bits of data that will facilitate diagnosis of identified learning needs.

The use of an iteration procedure conceptualizing a hidden in-formal mental process may be especially meaningful to some of us. We must begin probing the depth of the actual and anecdotal founda-tions of the personal, interactive teacher-student activity.

The authors believe that reporting descriptive and judgmental information can be accomplished within the realm of possibility today. Computer-assisted data storage and retrieval for complex data needs or simple paper and pencil check sheets and profiles for narrow diagnostic needs have already been developed. A recent (1969) Title III Project, Personalized Education Prescriptions, in Bucks County, Pennsylvania, analyzed the kinds of data necessary to determine kinds of student behavior necessary to diagnose and appraise learning style in order to modify teaching methods. After pupil data was brought together, it was clear from project evaluations that the Pupil Description Worksheet focused teacher and school efforts in helping the student.

What we have proposed in this evaluation-diagnostic model seems to invite a comparison of the astronomer and the evaluator-diagnostician in tomorrow's school.

Through search, scanning, and repeated observation, the astron-omer soon acquires a "feel" for the heavens, and a cognitive map of its particulars: sizes, shapes, relations, movements, and so on. Although at any one time he may not be able to reproduce all of its particulars, his map is of enormous service in locating where he is, allowing him to scan a specific area without losing touch with other areas, and, of course, helping him immediately sense any new and different object. A similar "feel" and "map" is acquired by the teacher and the student through direct and repeated contact with each other, teacher observation of a wide variety of student behavior and nonbehavior, and active teacher-student communication. In time, and as figure and ground separate, the diagnostician-evaluator becomes sensitive to what is and is not happening, makes observa-tions, attempts to diagnose or construct a conception of what phenomenon has occurred, and finally prescribes courses of action.

As a beginning, teachers need to be trained to become more sensitive, perceptual, diagnostic observers of young people, recogniz-ing their own and others' intentions and limitations and seeing new relationships and discrepancies in expanded categories of data. Without being overly optimistic, if the teachers and students of the schools of tomorrow can begin today by organizing and reporting description and evaluation information, the *probable* aspects of the complete process described in the model may become *possible*.

Evaluation in the School Context: Some Practical Possibilities

The practical problems associated with applying this new perspective on evaluation and implementing the model we have proposed are not as difficult as we first imagined. Let us look at what is required and see what demands are being made on us. Then we can propose some ways in which these demands can be met.

The kinds of data we will gather and the intentions we have with respect to its use are fundamental considerations here. We are suggesting a substantial increase in the amount of subjectivity in the data to be gathered. We have always gathered subjective data but we have, for the most part, not been very rigorous in our handling of this data. We are suggesting that descriptive as well as evaluative data be gathered and that the two be distinguished. Overall, we have suggested that the amount of data gathered and used be increased substantially and that considerably more attention be paid to the reliability and validity of the data and of our uses of the data.

Increasing the Amount of Information

Probably the major untapped sources of information about students are the students themselves. We have relied almost solely on the professionals in the school to provide working data about students. The student knows a great deal about himself, particularly in the descriptive sense, but also in the evaluative sense. In a school for tomorrow we look for more student initiative and a less punitive climate. If this is the case, students can be expected to be major contributors to the data about themselves.

Self-understanding is a major goal in the education of autonomous individuals. As we move more of the responsibility for understanding the self away from the teacher and the professional evaluator and toward the student, we increase the likelihood of the student's becoming autonomous. Attractive as this suggestion may appear on its surface, we must be careful not to read more into it than should be there. The capacity to describe and evaluate the self is a *learned* capacity. Students will need direction, guidance, and support if they are to take over some of the work of evaluation. And, as in any other endeavor, some will be more capable than others.

There is a high degree of ego-involvement in efforts to describe and evaluate the self. This, of course, has significant effects on the reliability and validity of the data gathered. Data generated about the self have that first-person, "eyewitness account" quality, which is in many ways so desirable in the records of human experience. At the same time the account is self-oriented, and systematic personal biases will have powerful effects on the data. When students do contribute significant amounts of descriptive and evaluative data to our information banks, we need to use a variety of means to be sure the data are valid and reliable.

We believe a program of evaluation that shifts responsibility for evaluation increasingly into student hands and is developmental in nature could work very well in a school for tomorrow. It would serve the goals of the school. We have no reason to believe that students cannot learn to be skilled in self-evaluation. Certain conditions should prevail regarding the uses of the data gathered, but we shall pay some attention to that later.

There is a tacit recognition here that unless teachers are provided with more time and opportunity, they will be unable to increase the amount of information available for use in understanding students. Where they are provided time and opportunity they can well be asked to make more observations, and we should probably think of the data arising from such observations as being the best for our purposes. But we cannot rely on teachers to provide more data. The use of paraprofessionals is another matter.

There are many keen, sensitive, and observant adults who are capable of maintaining excellent relationships with children. Although some training in the techniques and methods of observation is very desirable, even the untrained aide could help in gathering useful information. We believe that paraprofessionals could make a very significant contribution here, and we would argue for the careful selection and training of people to fill such roles.

In institutions where diagnosis and individualized treatment are standard practice (e.g., hospitals and rehabilitation centers) a very complete diagnostic work-up is required at the time of admission. In our experience school admissions are not so characterized. It seems to us that a comprehensive diagnostic work-up for entering students would be most helpful to the staff in a school for tomorrow. Much of this data might be derived from the self-report of the student and his parents, but trained paraprofessionals could gather more through interview, testing, and background records.

The investigations conducted by caseworkers in rehabilitation centers, for example, are highly focused. The intent, of course, is to provide enough information about the client to begin some kinds of therapeutic efforts immediately. It seems to us that a similar condition ought to prevail in a school for tomorrow. Both the student and the professional staff working with him ought to have some clear idea about where to begin and how to proceed. Our point here is that the data gathered at admission will not be useful unless it is highly individualized and reflects the unique potentials for learning that the student brings to the school.

Drawing again from the experience of caseworkers and institutions that perform diagnostic and treatment functions, it is clear that problem cases get considerably more attention than do cases in which the evidence clearly indicates the appropriate course of action. This would suggest, if we follow their lead, that the bank of information on students having the greatest difficulties would be the most extensive. We also know from casework experience that the more difficult the case, the higher the level of expertise that is drawn into the effort to diagnose properly. This suggests that the efforts put into diagnosing and determining courses of treatment might be very different for different students. Ultimately, the information available on the students having the greatest difficulties might far exceed the information available on students with lesser difficulties.

It seems to us that it is *practical* to talk of substantially increasing the amount of information available to students and professional staff for diagnosing and prescribing learning experiences. By judicious use and development of students as sources of data, we can increase the amount of information available and help our students become more autonomous. By carefully selecting and training paraprofessionals, we add perceptive human eyes and ears to a staff of teachers who are typically overworked. Lastly, by adopting the approach of the professionals regularly engaged in diagnostic and treatment functions, we can increase the information gathered as the student comes into his program and deploy our evaluative expertise in ways that reflect the difficulties associated with providing proper learning experiences for different students.

Increasing the Flow of Good Information

Where information can be and is used for punitive purposes, we can be sure that secrets will be kept. A school for tomorrow needs to avoid such conditions whenever possible. If students or parents have a feeling that the information will be used to help rather than hurt, they will be much more candid and much more apt to "tell it like it is." But it is not easy to establish such conditions. Some people may be convinced if we say that the information is to be used to help, but the ultimate test for most people is whether they know that we actually use the information to help. The kind of trusting climate called for here has to be developed. We know it will not spring up because it was mandated. We have all experienced situations in which we did not feel free to reveal ourselves to others. In a school for tomorrow the elimination of such feelings will be a critical and perennial institutional objective.

In such an institutional climate we should find less need to keep information confidential. Students especially should know what the data say about them. Professional staff should have free access to information about students and should feel more free to use the information gathered by others. Where information is of good quality and is used to help rather than hurt, few teachers would refuse to use past records of students. For all of this there will be a need for confidentiality in some matters. We feel it is particularly important to rethink the idea of the confidentiality of records, with particular regard to the access students should have to their own records.

It may be that the professional staff will need to rethink their own role with respect to the use of information. The authors are aware that teachers and school people sometimes use information about students in unhelpful ways. In some instances professional staff may actually build a case against a particular student. This, of course, is unconscionable. Evidence that such a thing is happening is a sure sign that there are difficulties in the institutional climate that are restricting the free flow of information.

Guidance counselors refer sometimes to what they call "curbstone counseling." The expression rather picturesquely describes a dimension of evaluation in a school for tomorrow that we feel may be very important. The essence of the idea is that professional staff feel free at any time and at any place to talk with a student or, perhaps better, to listen to a student. In order for this to happen with any regularity, both students and staff need to have a great deal of mobility. The staff needs to be available to students. We have noted earlier that teachers may already have more than enough to do, but whatever means can be found to free them from routine and tightly structured activities should be used. If this new time can be redirected into increased informal contacts with students, we believe it will pay dividends. Here, too, the paraprofessionals trained as observers can be especially helpful.

There are a number of ways in which a school for tomorrow can increase the flow of good information. We believe that a school for tomorrow should establish this as a basic objective for the institution itself. The suggestions for organizing and administering a school for tomorrow lean very heavily on information and its availability. If a school takes such an approach and resolves to use the information to help individual students, we believe there will be a tremendous increase in the capacity of the professional staff to provide the kind of intelligent, individualized attention necessary to the development of autonomous individuals.

Reliability and Validity of Information

There is a tendency these days to worship information for its own sake. The more we know the better. But a lot of information serves no useful purpose and some information is actually harmful, because it is not true. Schools face difficulties on both of these counts. In a school for tomorrow we will need to work hard at insuring that the information we have is meaningful and can be trusted. In other words, the information must be as valid and reliable as we can get it.

In the early part of this chapter we pointed out what is involved in so gathering and interpreting data that they might be increasingly reliable and valid. We need not review those considerations here. But the matter is too vitally important to be left there. Faulty information has a way of confounding schoolmen's efforts under the best of circumstances.

Therefore, it seems wise to recommend that a school for tomorrow consider developing a new professional staff position. One in such a position would have direct responsibility for helping the professional staff improve the quality of the information gathered and used by staff and students. We are not referring here to the kind of services rendered by those who gather data (i.e., guidance counselors, clinical psychologists, or directors of research). We are, rather, proposing that very useful services could be rendered by one who understood what constitutes information of good quality and how to gather and use it.

Simply increasing the amount of information about students will not do. The information has to be reliable and valid. Validity and reliability of information are philosophical and technical matters of the greatest importance. It is conceivable that a professional staff might rise to this challenge unaided. We tend to believe they need the guidance and support of a person especially trained and skilled in these matters. The information to be gathered and used is information about people. It is to be used in their behalf. It is to be used to develop rational, autonomous individuals. It will guide intentional courses of human action. There should be no compromise on questions about the quality of that information.

Appendix 1. Further Definition of Terms

Products of Description

Units are relatively segregated or circumscribed items of information having a thing character. A unit has properties, each unit with a unique combination of properties.

Classes are recognized sets of information grouped by virtue of common properties.

Relations are a recognized connection between two items of information based on variables or points of contact that apply to them.

Implications are expectancies, anticipations, and predictions; where one item of information leads naturally to another.

Performance Criterion is a statement that describes in observable and measurable terms the performance of the student for each behavioral characteristic.

Expectation is the degree to which the individual student performance meets the predetermined performance criterion.

Products of Judgment

Classification	Prescription
Expectation	Discrepancy
Diagnosis	Relationship

Appendix 2. Information-Analysis Form

Selected behavioral characteristics, learning environments, curriculum	DISCREPANCIES				RELATIONSHIPS			
	Units	Classes	Relations	Implications →	(Performance criterion compared with implications yields) Individual Expectations	Implications ↓	Relations	Classes	Units

Notes

1. Ralph W. Tyler, "The Objectives and Plans for a National Assessment of Educational Progress," *Journal of Educational Measurement* 3 (Spring 1966): 1.

2. Fred T. Wilhelms and Paul B. Diederich, *Evaluation as Feedback and Guide* (Washington, D.C.: ASCD, 1967), p. 234.

3. J. D. Urmson, "On Grading," in *Philosophical Essays on Teaching,* ed., B. Bandman and R. S. Guttchen (Philadelphia: Lippincott, 1969), pp. 194-217.

4. Robert Stake, "Language, Rationality and Assessment," in *Improving Educational Assessment and Inventory of Measures of Affective Behavior* (Washington, D.C.: ASCD, 1969), p. 385.

5. Daniel Stufflebeam, *Educational Evaluation and Decision-Making* (Itasca, Ill.: F. E. Peacock Publishers, 1971).

6. Abraham Kaplan, *The Conduct of Inquiry* (San Francisco, Calif.: Chandler Publishing Co., 1964), p. 127.

7. Hans Selye, *From Dream to Discovery: On Being a Scientist* (Toronto: McGraw-Hill, 1964), p. 274.

8. Charles Silberman, *Crisis in the Classroom* (New York: Random House, Vintage Books, 1970), p. 373.

9. Maria Montessori, *Spontaneous Activity in Education* (New York: Schocken Books, 1965).

10. Abraham H. Maslow, *Toward a Psychology of Being,* 2d. ed. (New York: Van Nostrand Reinhold Co., 1968), p. 192.

11. Warren R. Aiken, "Lasers," *A.R.E. Journal,* May 1971, p. 102.

12. Robert Stake, "Objectives, Priorities, and Other Judgment Data," *Journal of Educational Research* 40, no. 2 (April 1970): 185.

Bibliography

Adams, William R. "Studies of Teaching in the Diagnostic Process." In *The Diagnostic Process.* Proceedings of a conference held at the University of Michigan, May 1963.

Aiken, Warren R. "Lasers." *A.R.E. Journal,* May 1971.

Feinstein, Alvan R. *Clinical Judgment.* Baltimore, Md.: Williams and Wilkins Co., 1967.

Gerbner, George. "A Theory of Communication and Its Implications for Teaching." In *Teaching: Vantage Points for Study,* ed., Ronald T. Hyman. New York: Lippincott, 1968.

Goodlad, John I. "Diagnosis and Prescription in Educational Practice." *Education Digest,* May 1966.

Kaplan, Abraham. *The Conduct of Inquiry.* San Francisco, Calif.: Chandler Publishing, 1964.

Lee, Doris May. "Teaching and Evaluation." In *Evaluation as Feedback and Guide, ASCD 1967 Yearbook.* Washington, D.C.: NEA.

Maslow, Abraham H. *Toward a Psychology of Being.* 2d ed. New York: Van Nostrand Reinhold Co., Insight Book, 1968.

Miller, Donald R. "An Analytical Framework for Public Education and Educational Management." Sacramento, Calif.: Operation PEP, Statewide Preparation for Educational Planners, 1969.

Montessori, Maria. *Spontaneous Activity in Education.* New York: Schocken Books, 1965.

Selye, Hans. *From Dream to Discovery: On Being a Scientist.* Toronto: McGraw-Hill Book Co., 1964.

Silberman, Charles. *Crisis in the Classroom.* New York: Random House, Vintage Books, 1970.

Stake, Robert E. "Objectives, Priorities, and Other Judgment Data." *Journal of Educational Research* 40, no. 2 (April 1970).

———. "Language, Rationality and Assessment." In *Improving Educational Assessment and Inventory of Measures of Affective Behavior.* Washington, D.C.: ASCD, 1969.

Webb, Eugene J., et al. *Unobtrusive Measures: Nonreactive Research in the Social Sciences.* Chicago: Rand McNally & Co., 1966.

Urmson, J. D. "On Grading." In *Philosophical Essays on Teaching.* Ed., B. Bandman and R. S. Guttchen. Philadelphia: Lippincott, 1969, pp. 194-217.

Part 3
Choosing and Defining
Professional Means to Support
a School for Tomorrow

6
Organization

What will be needed in a school for tomorrow is not only the courage to do what we believe we should do, but also the organizational support to help us do so in a climate where success is hoped for and failure is cherished for what we can learn from it. How can such a school be organized to provide students and teachers with the organizational support they need to feel free to venture, to do, and to expect success?

Donald Anderson
Lloyd Duvall

Introduction

Before attempting to describe an organizational pattern for a school for tomorrow, a few definitions and disclaimers are in order. An important distinction exists between *a* school for tomorrow and *the* school for tomorrow. Using the article *the* would imply that the authors possessed the intelligence to design the ultimate school for tomorrow and that they were able to reach consensus on this design. Since neither of these conditions exists, this chapter will focus on *a* school for tomorrow.

School organizations typically have been based on a traditional hierarchical authority structure. While this characteristic of the bureaucracy will not disappear, organizations in schools of the future will reflect a great variety of patterns and much differentiation.[1] For this reason we will not suggest a specific organizational design or pattern; rather we will describe a model within a general theoretical framework, that of information systems.

Organizing schools generally is defined as the process of establishing policies, programs, and procedures for achieving school objectives, coordinating school personnel and other resources, measuring and correcting activities, and facilitating communication—both within the school and between the school and its environment. For the purposes of this chapter, organizing will not focus on goal setting or organizational change and development. An earlier chapter on goal setting and policy formulation deals with these vital organizational concerns. The emphasis here will be on the acquisition and cataloging of all kinds of resources and on improving their use.

To speak of organizing a school for tomorrow, a school built on the premise that individuals rather than groups are the chief building block, may seem contradictory. A contradiction does exist if the emphasis of organizing is strictly on coordinating, or putting the pieces together. Typically the process of organizing schools concentrates on grouping students. We will attempt to abandon or at least minimize this notion. The focus will be on organizing the resources to be used by individuals, particularly individual students.

A school is defined as a delivery system established to provide educational services to clients in a given attendance area. A school is not as large as a school district or as small as a classroom unit. In traditional organizational schemes, a school would resemble most nearly an organization at the school building level.

The general framework to be used for describing a school and its organization is one of systems. A system is a "set of objects together with the relationships between the objects and their attributes."[2] It is "an organized assemblage of interrelated components designed to function as a whole to achieve a predetermined objective."[3] A common model used in describing a system is as follows:

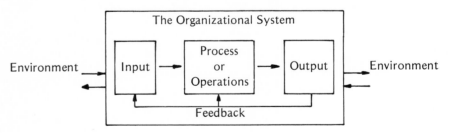

The model draws attention to (1) the relationship between the input into the system, the transformation of energies within the system, and the resulting product or output and (2) the relationship between the system and its environment. The system concept implies interdependency with respect to a common output or outcome.

Many objects or elements of the system interact in production of the output. The concept also implies activities that are repeated and relatively enduring. For purposes of analysis, systems can be broken down into subsystems. A school, for example, might be divided into an instructional system, a guidance system, a transportation system, etc.

Input, output, and *feedback* are terms that have found their way into the vocabularies of many practitioners and students of social systems. Two other concepts associated with systems are not so commonly used or understood. The degree to which a system is receptive to inputs from the surrounding environment is a measure of the system's *openness.* Systems that are not receptive are considered to be closed; systems that are receptive are classified as open. Schools, especially as they are governed by and accountable to their "publics" in the United States, are greatly affected by the community and the state, their environment. Clearly American schools can be classified toward the open end of the open-closed system continuum.

Yet another systems concept applies here, that of *equifinality.* In physical systems, there is a direct cause and effect relationship between the initial conditions and the final state, between input and output. In biological and social systems, such relationships are not so definite; the many and complex variables are more difficult to identify, much less to control. The concept of equifinality in systems means that final results may be achieved with different inputs or initial conditions and in different ways. A social system like a school can accomplish its objectives with varying inputs and with varying internal activities. This concept reinforces the position that no single illustration of organizational inputs and patterns can meet the objectives of a school for tomorrow.

In the remainder of this chapter, we shall outline the basic premise underlying a school for tomorrow and describe a theoretical framework for organizing a school for tomorrow. We will attempt to establish the congruence of the basic premise and the organizational framework chosen, an organization based on information systems. Beyond this theoretical discussion, we shall identify components of the system, propose an operational model, describe personal relationships within the system, and illustrate the system's operation.

An Information Processing System

Basic Assumption

Fundamental to understanding a school for tomorrow as an information processing system is an assumption that permeates the rationale on which the school is based. That assumption is that schools exist for the betterment of individual students. In current practice, most schools are organized around the notion that individuals are members of groups, and groups form the basic operational units of the school. Individual identities, then, are subsumed in the identity of the group. This is not to say that groups are unimportant, but in a school for tomorrow the focus will be on the individuals who comprise the groups. The basic instructional unit will be the individual student, not a teacher to whom a group of students is assigned.

Information Systems

"Any organism is held together by the possession of means for the acquisition, use, retention, and transmission of information."[4] This short statement by the "father of cybernetics" defines the nature and purpose of information. In an organizational setting, information is the material of administrative and managerial operations. Without information no person can make decisions, monitor operations, evaluate progress, or deploy resources. In general terms, then, information is a critical element in organizational operations.

Before examining the characteristics of information systems, it will be helpful to establish a clear understanding of a number of words and concepts that will be used throughout. The term, *information system*, contains two complex terms that entail a number of concepts. *System* was defined earlier. *Information*, although in common usage in the language, is ordinarily not very clearly defined. We define it as "communication of knowledge."[5] Implicit in this definition is the concept of movement. Communication requires exchange of information. Information, therefore, is knowledge in a dynamic state capable of being transferred, communicated, and used.

Data, on the other hand, are bits of knowledge that are static and, in isolation, meaningless. Data represent facts that are accumulated and stored for some future use. Such an accumulation of data, a data bank, can be a simple file drawer, a computer disc or tape, or even a person's memory. Data form the raw material for information formation. Information is built from data that have been studied, analyzed, and placed in some configuration that makes them useful. In terse form, information is useful data; data are potentially useful bits of knowledge.

Developing an Information System. An information system is created when a mechanism is established for collecting data, transforming them into information, providing information to users, and providing feedback. Such a mechanism does not evolve from some magical mix of data surrounding a given problem. Rather, information systems result from a process, followed sequentially, focused on a specific problem or problems, and designed for use by identifiable persons.

A basic problem in developing an information system arises from the fact that not all information is of equal usefulness to all users. This suggests that information has inherent characteristics that make it more or less important to users. Four of the most important of these characteristics are (1) value, (2) validity, (3) cost, and (4) timeliness.

1. A primary *value* of information is in what might be called procedural advantage. The degree to which information can assist in making organizational procedures more effective is a measure of the value of the information itself. Another type of value is perceived value. This value exists in the perceptions of the user. That is, the user must see value, worth, and opportunity in information or he is not likely to use it, regardless of its potential. This value then is a value perceived by the user rather than an absolute or even relative value. A third value is the worth of the information in actual dollar amounts. The value that develops from the user's choosing a less expensive process or approach represents a value figure for the information acted on by the user.

2. Information *validity* is the characteristic that reflects the confidence one can place in the information. Perhaps it is obvious that validity and value are closely related. In fact they cannot be separated. However, they are separate characteristics that can be of great assistance when used in tandem. The relationship between value and validity can be shown in the following diagram. In the diagram, information represented by the figure (1) is worth receiving but the confidence level is very low because it is obviously untrue; the information labeled (2) is true—the user can have confidence that it is

	Valuable	Not Valuable
Valid	X Teaching Proficiencies	(2) All teaching candidates breathe.
Not Valid	(1) All teaching candidates are geniuses.	(3) All teaching candidates are dead.

accurate—but it is of little use; and the information labeled (3) is neither useful nor truthful. Only the information in the square marked X is valid and valuable; obviously it is the information that should be used.

3. To produce information in any quantity involves a *cost*. Machines, material, and personnel necessary to develop information are costly in any organization. Therefore, information has costs that are directly attributable to its collection, production, and flow.

Cost is a critical factor in the life of any organization. If cost is important, and if information has an associated cost, it follows that information cost can become too costly. Cost, then, must be related to value to help determine the point at which it becomes too costly. True cost can be determined only when it is compared with value.

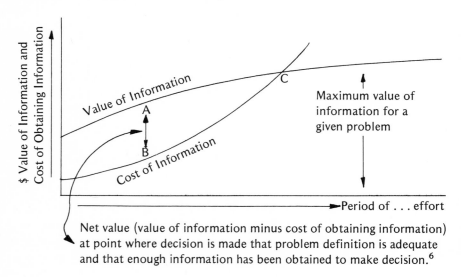

Net value (value of information minus cost of obtaining information) at point where decision is made that problem definition is adequate and that enough information has been obtained to make decision.[6]

In the diagram, line AB represents the greatest net value of the information, the most information realized for the lowest cost. At point C, there is no net value to the information because the cost of information acquisition equals information value.

4. Information *timeliness,* like validity and cost, is related to value. "Information is of value only if it can be received quickly enough."[7] If information is received by a user after a decision has been made, the information has only historical value at best. The value of information is greatest when it is most needed. This very pragmatic consideration is crucial in any information system. Without the time dimension, true information ceases to exist, information loses validity, and cost versus value becomes intolerable.

Steps in System Development. It was stated earlier that information is the very "stuff" of organizational operations. But, due to the hierarchical nature of organization and the specialized functions of persons in an organization, all users do not need the same information. Information is needed by all, but a process of information selection is required. The function of an information system is simply to supply only that information needed by a user for him to fulfill his responsibilities successfully. The task of designing such an information system must be viewed as a sequence of activities that culminate in an implemented system. Experience has shown that this sequence can be broken into several definite steps: (1) system definition and requirement specification, (2) data collection, (3) system design, (4) system testing, (5) system implementation, and (6) evaluation.

1. It is impossible to develop an information system without defining and specifying the subsystems that are to be a part of the total system. System definitions and subsystem identifications are derived from organizational goals, the nature of tasks to be performed, and the nature of the relationships inherent in the organization. The definitional step is what makes an information system for a school different from an information system for a warehouse, a hospital, or a military installation. The system definitions form the building blocks that support the entire information system.

2. Data collection provides the what, who, when, and why of the information system. Data must be collected that indicate what users need what types of information at what time for what reasons. The data collection step is the one in which the system designer determines information needs and plans information flows.

3. The third step is the design process that makes the information system an operational system. Basic subsystems are identified, major inputs are specified, and general outputs are determined. This is the framework on which the information system operates. The design specifies the information to be prepared and processed manually or by machine, and the relationships between manual and machine operations. This is the step in which the "nitty-gritty" of each detail of the entire system is laid out.

4. Before plans for system installation are executed, it is wise to test system operations. This can be accomplished in a number of ways. Three such tests are: (1) parallel tests, using the new system without eliminating the system it replaces (the two systems for providing the same information are put into operation simultaneously on a small scale); (2) pilot tests, a small scale sample of the total system; and (3) simulation, using data typical of the data to be processed by the information system and manipulating these data exactly as if the system were in full operation. Testing rarely provides a flawless picture of the system after it has been installed. Rather, testing allows the designer to make alterations in procedures that would be problematic after system installation. This in itself is sufficient reason to develop and implement a sound testing program before the information system is installed.

5. Once the information system has been designed and tested, it is necessary to put the design into full operation. Since a system does not operate in a vacuum, it is necessary to consider personnel, hardware, facilities, and timing as crucial elements in this step. Personnel must be trained in the operations of the new system. Hardware must be installed and made functional. Facilities must be prepared and space provided. Finally a schedule for system implementation must be developed to provide a smooth transition to new system operations.

6. It has been suggested that a viable information system has three attributes:

(1) The system measures the impact of decisions, either before or after they are made; (2) the system measures the environment, because we can neither control or forecast the effect of changing the external circumstances; and (3) the system reacts in an appropriate time frame, to enable us to learn of the development of potential trouble areas in time to take appropriate action.[8]

To enable the information system to perform according to these three attributes, continuing evaluation of system operations is important. In reality, the information system is a tool that can be used to great advantage in the organization. The extent to which the tool fulfills this expectation is the proper focus of system evaluation.

Few school people have experience in designing information systems. Further, many have probably never considered information use as a conceptual basis for organizing a school. When designed and implemented according to the rationale of a school for tomorrow, this information system forms an organizing unity that provides directions for the delivery of educational services.

Designing the Information System

Defining the system and specifying the requirements is the first step in designing an information system. The proposed information system for a school for tomorrow is comprised of the following six subsystems: students, personnel, instructional technology, facilities, instructional components, and finances. Each of the subsystems represents a set of data or potential information, in other words a data bank. The data stored in these banks will be used in making decisions about instruction in a school for tomorrow. In relation to the earlier discussion of the school curriculum, students and personnel are actors; instructional technology and facilities are artifacts; instructional components are operations.[9]

In four of the six data banks, data will be stored about individual elements. In the student data bank, each student will be considered an element. Each person who might make a contribution to the instructional program in a school for tomorrow will be considered an element in the personnel data bank. The elements in the instructional technology data bank will be the individual pieces of instructional hardware including books, films, and so forth. The elements in the facilities data bank will be the instructional spaces and fixed equipment available to the school.

For each of the elements identified in these four data banks, three kinds of data will be stored. First, the attributes of each element will be listed. These attributes will consist of descriptions that identify each element and distinguish it from other elements in the data bank. In choosing the attributes care must be taken to ensure that the data meet the important information characteristics of value, validity, cost, and timeliness.

The second kind of data has to do with time or schedule. Since time will take on new meaning in a school for tomorrow, some elaboration is in order. In a traditional organization, school time is typically restricted to a five-to-seven-hour day (between 8:00 a.m. and 5:00 p.m.) in a five-day week as part of a nine- or ten-month term. In a school for tomorrow, such constraints must be lifted, because many of the potential opportunities for instruction will not be available within these time frames. As instruction is individualized, the scheduling problem will demand access to times other than those scheduled so "efficiently" in the traditional school. Thus time alternatives must be expanded greatly for students and for personnel working in a school.

The most valuable resource that exists in any school is student time. In a traditional school where a teacher works with a group of twenty-five to thirty students, the importance of student time is often overlooked, and teacher time is considered the major resource. This oversight is detrimental to decision making in traditional schools. The concept of "opportunity costs" is an important one. When a student is involved in a particular activity, he cannot be involved in another activity at the same time. One loses the opportunity to participate in one activity when he is engaged in another. Weighing the value of those two activities is essential. This concept becomes even more important and prominent as instruction is individualized.

In the traditional school, time is perceived to be best used by scheduling students into groups that meet during assigned blocks of time. In a school for tomorrow, however, the emphasis will be on scheduling resources according to schedule data on each of the elements in the student, personnel, instructional technology, and facilities data banks.

The third kind of data to be stored about each element in the data banks is that of "extra" costs. These data will be keyed into the finance data bank as well. Most of the available instructional resources will be on inventory in a school for tomorrow. In other words, some of the professional personnel will be under contract; there will be books in the "library"; there will be "classrooms" available. Some resources, particularly those in the community outside the school building, may have some extra cost associated with their use. Such cost data must be stored in the data bank. Because a school for tomorrow will have limited resources, costs of providing services must be considered in program planning. This point will be discussed further in the description of the finance data bank.

Subsystems

Student Subsystem. The student subsystem will be the heart of the information processing system of a school for tomorrow just as it is the heart of the information system in a traditional school. Most school systems have a rather well developed data bank centering on students; each student is an element in the data bank. Unfortunately these data are not easily accessible, and they do not have much impact on the instruction that takes place. Unless data can be organized in such a way that they will be used more effectively in a school for tomorrow, it will be difficult to go beyond our present achievements in individualizing instruction. There must be a greater capability to "mix" student data with other instructional resource data in making decisions.

The kind of attribute data stored in traditional systems will be stored and used in the information system of a school for tomorrow. Included among these data are the student's past record of academic work—test scores, indications of ability, aspirations, and learning difficulties—a record of "outside the school" variables that are important to the student's instruction, and biographical data about his parents and home community.

As indicated earlier, a most important aspect of the student data bank in a school for tomorrow is time. For each student, a complete record must be made of the activities in which he has engaged and those that are planned for him. When a student program is planned for the period ahead, this schedule of activities must be logged into the student data bank so that a record can be kept of what the student has done and is planning to do. Related to those data is a list of the objectives or targets that are set for each student. These targets or objectives, as well as the instructional treatment or curriculum prescribed, must be recorded. Data such as schedule of activities, objectives, and treatment record are a very important and obvious extension of the student data bank in the traditional school.

Personnel Subsystem. The second major subsystem of the information system will be personnel. Included as elements in the personnel subsystem will be a number of new and different kinds of human resources available to assist in the instructional process in a school for tomorrow. Traditional schools store data about personnel, particularly the professional personnel, but most of these data are not used in making decisions about instruction. In a school for tomorrow, a greater range of personnel will be dealing with the instruction of students. There will be instructors, diagnosticians, tutors, master teachers, curriculum specialists, personnel to seek out and catalog instructional resources, system analysts, administrators, aides, clerical personnel, paraprofessionals, and many others. A school for tomorrow will have a differentiated staffing pattern quite unlike that in traditional schools. Also stored in the information system will be data relating to "outside of school" human resources. These resources will include a wide range of community personnel who can make contributions to the education of students in the school.

For each of these personnel elements in the subsystem, the chief attribute data will consist of descriptions of the contributions each might make to the instructional program. In addition, a schedule for each will be maintained in the system. This schedule will be exceedingly important as resources are assigned to students. This complex scheduling problem calls for a very different information system from what now exists. These schedule data will also be stored for the "outside of school" personnel. Some of the personnel obviously will not be available to contribute at any hour of the day; data as to availability must be easily accessible to those planning instructional activities. Some evaluation of each person's contribution will also be stored in the information system. After having some experience with using these personnel resources (whether from within or outside the school), a record must be kept of the quality of their contributions.

Most of those working with students will be employed by the school. Quite often, however, there will be need to contract for outside services. The "extra" costs of such services must be known to the persons responsible for choosing from among curriculum treatment alternatives. A school for tomorrow will have financial constraints, hence the need for these kinds of data.

Instructional Technology Subsystem. The technology of instruction has developed rapidly over the last two decades. Major attempts have been made to establish data banks relating to this subsystem. Library and instructional materials center information systems are well developed. Included among the elements in the instructional technology subsystem will be the many mechanical, electrical, and optical devices used for instruction—photography, audio technology, language laboratories, radio music centers, talking typewriters, video transmitters, electronic data storage and processing machines—as well as programmed instruction, books, pictures, filmstrips, recordings, videotapes, slides, tape recorders, and films. Also to be included will be technology available in the community. This may be in the form of commercial television, movies, or library resources. Attribute data about these elements must be stored. One must know what a particular piece of technology is capable of doing, or what it contains. Another important bit of data will be the schedule for each particular element and a delineation of any special or "extra" costs associated with the elements.

Facilities Subsystem. The facilities for a school for tomorrow will not be restricted to a school building or school property, even though these facilities will continue to play a major role in instruction. Elements to be included in the facilities data bank might be a local fire station, a museum, an industrial laboratory, a warehouse, or a grocery store. For each such element in the system, the attributes must be identified and the schedule explicated. There may also be some "extra" costs associated with using some of the facilities, especially those in the community.

An important characteristic must be identified in designing the building that will house a school for tomorrow. Some progress has been made in the last decade to free building designs from the concepts that the school is organized around class groups of twenty-five to thirty students. The movement toward open classrooms and to large and small group instruction has led to the removal of some of the walls and barriers to instruction. In a school for tomorrow, much more emphasis will be placed on space for the individual. Each student in the school, as well as each person working in the school, must have an individual work space. This space may be in the form of a carrel or an office. It will be as important for a student in a school for tomorrow to have such an individual work space as it is for the teacher in the traditional school to have such a space. This student work space will be provided with some kind of remote terminal access to many elements identified in the instructional technology subsystem.

Instructional Component Subsystem. This subsystem of a school for tomorrow's information processing system typically does not exist in a traditional school. Stored in the instructional component subsystem will be the list of requirements that will be a part of every student's basic experiences. These might be in the form of experiences or objectives common to and required of all students. Obviously, these data must be available in planning a student's program.

In addition to the list of basic requirements, there will need to be a list of the objectives or desired results to be accomplished by students in a school for tomorrow. Associated with that list will be a set of treatments or instructional components available to students in the school. Objectives and treatments must be cross-indexed so that when someone gets ready to prescribe a treatment or set of experiences to meet a particular objective, he can go to the data bank and retrieve from it all alternative treatments that are recorded and available to meet this objective.

The major role of curriculum personnel in a school for tomorrow will be that of refining and updating this instructional component subsystem. The treatments will be keyed to different kinds of variables, such as reading level, maturity, sex, or some other human indicator, so that when a treatment is sought, the appropriate one for the particular student will be identified.

Some record must also be made in the curriculum data bank about the possible success of each particular treatment. For example, if two alternatives are provided to meet a particular objective—one involving a tutor and a particular bit of instructional technology, and the second involving a videotape—there should be some indication of the success of each alternative with different classes of students. Success can be measured in two different ways. One way is in terms of the probabilities that a person will master a particular objective in a certain period of time. In this case time is the variable and mastery is constant. Another way of viewing the success of the particular treatment is to indicate the percentage of mastery that can be accomplished in a given period of time. In this case, time is constant and the percentage of mastery is the variable.

Also to be included in this subsystem are the tests and evaluation instruments used to monitor progress toward the objectives. Parts of this data bank will be available to students so that they can monitor their own progress.[10]

This subsystem will be built on experiences as a school for tomorrow begins to operate. The objectives will be identified and recorded, and the treatments will be logged. Following up on an assessment of these experiences, the data can be expanded and modified.

Financial Subsystems. In the financial subsystem data will be stored in two categories, committed and discretionary funds. At the beginning of each fiscal year some long-term commitments will be made on the total resources available. There will be fixed charges, such as debt redemption, costs associated with building maintenance, and contracts written for personnel. These kinds of obligations or encumbrances will be identified among the committed resources. One will be able to modify these commitments, however, if conditions warrant such action. It might be possible, for example, to transfer resources from or to another school or to relieve personnel of assignments and hire new personnel as needs dictate.

The "extra" costs identified in the other subsystems relate to the discretionary fund category. The school administrator will have a fixed amount of discretionary funds for the year, and it will be essential to monitor the expenditure of those funds by using data stored in the finance subsystem. Each time an "extra" cost resource is used or encumbered, a charge will be made against the discretionary funds in the system. Information about these funds will be fed back regularly (at least once each week) to the persons charged with program planning and to the school administrator, so that they will know what resources are currently available to them.

An examination of the six subsystems and the data prescribed in each leads to the conclusion that while many of these data are stored in traditional school information systems, the data are exceedingly difficult to use in instructional decision making. The data are not integrated. The student data bank is one of the best developed in traditional schools, but it is practically impossible to put student data together with personnel data, or instructional technology data, or facilities data. Personnel data typically are stored in some central office filing system and are not available to those who make decisions about mixing students and "teachers." As indicated earlier, some instructional technology information systems are well established. Data about facilities in traditional schools are stored and updated, but the data are not used nearly as much as they will be in a school for tomorrow. A financial information system is maintained in all schools, but again the data are not readily available or used to any great extent by persons who plan individual instructional programs. The only real difference in a school for tomorrow's system is the addition of an instructional component, or curriculum, sub-system. Currently there are few records kept of curriculum treatments or their successes.

A new kind of personnel will be needed to design and maintain this system. Individuals will be included to seek out or search for instructional resources and opportunities available in the community. Information specialists will be needed to develop the software and refine the system. The school administrator's major role will be one of building and maintaining the information system. His major responsibility will be to establish mechanisms to coordinate information flow.

Many problems are involved in the complex process of integrating data in the proposed instructional system. While many of the data are currently stored in a multitude of places in traditional schools, there must be an automated, computerized system for handling the storage and retrieval problems in a school for tomorrow. The hardware is available; software becomes the major obstacle to system implementation.

Operational Model

Some attention has been drawn to information system design and data bank specification. A plan of operations must be considered to link the system to its users. Such a plan provides the rationale and the conceptual framework for operations. In a school for tomorrow with the information system design explicated earlier, there are probably a number of potentially viable operational models. One such model is shown below.

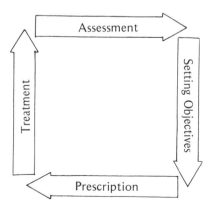

Instructional Decision-Making Model

In this model, four separate operational phases are suggested. Each phase occurs in sequence; the output of one phase provides input to the next. As an individual student progresses from phase to phase, the full resources of the information systems are tapped, and in turn additional data are generated for use in the data bank.

This model assures primary focus on the individual student. The student's first contact with the school consists of assessment and diagnosis. During the first phase, attention is given to discovering everything possible about the student and subsequently feeding these data into the student data bank. In the second phase, a skilled professional uses data derived from the previous phase, in addition to data from other available sources, to assist the student in setting specific performance objectives. These objectives then become the basis on which instructional prescription can be based. During the prescriptive phase, objectives are related to prescriptions of strategies to achieve the specified objectives. To accomplish this, the professional queries the data bank to determine if strategies exist for the stated objectives, whether facilities and personnel are available for implementing the strategies, what resources are necessary to use given strategies, and what "success" can be expected for each strategy under given sets of conditions. Once these data are made available, prescriptive judgments are made, and a scheduled course of action is developed with the student. These prescriptions and the conditions under which they are to be used are then fed back into the data bank to provide benchmarks against which future decisions can be made. In spite of the implied "perfection" of the system, judgments will often have to be made on the basis of inadequate and imprecise data just as in the case of traditional schools.

The fourth phase is that of instruction or treatment. During this phase, the prescriptions are followed and the schedule is implemented. Once treatment has been completed, the entire operation is set in motion again. Treatment provides input for a new assessment, for the setting of new or altered objectives, so that new or adjusted prescriptions can be made for additional treatment.

This brief description of the model and its operational characteristics is obviously incomplete. To provide a more comprehensive picture of a school for tomorrow, we shall present an illustration—a narrative of some of the events in the life of a student attending a school for tomorrow.

Phase One: Assessment

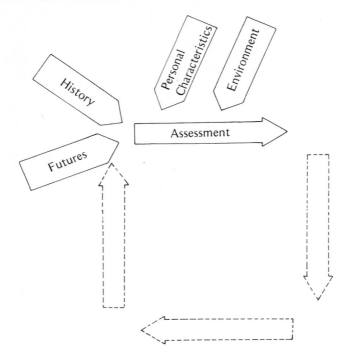

The first event in the life of the student, in this case a boy
named Adam, in a school for tomorrow is a conference with a professional skilled in collecting data. There are few limitations on the
amount of data to be collected during this conference. They include
personal attributes—such as personality characteristics, behavioral
mannerisms, abilities, interests, desires, previous successes and failures, physical features, and condition of health—and any other data
that help provide a complete picture of Adam as an individual.
Further, these data are obtained by discussion with Adam, by observation, by a broad-based battery of tests, by reference to existing
records, by conversations with others who know Adam, or by any
source of valid and reliable information.

Once these data have been collected, someone must build them
into the student data bank. These baseline data are related and compared to Adam's subsequent educational experiences. Without such

data, all hopes of making the timeworn educational cliche of "meeting individual needs" more than just a cliche are dashed.

The identity of specific units and types of data to be collected during the assessment phase will derive from several sources. First, Adam plays a major role in determining types of data to be included. Second, objectives of the school and the environment in which it is located will help in determining necessary data. Third, professional judgment and the wisdom of experience can assist. And fourth, the availability and reliability of collection devices must be considered. The intent during this phase is to learn as much about the individual as possible and to store that knowledge for future reference.

Phase Two: Objectives Setting

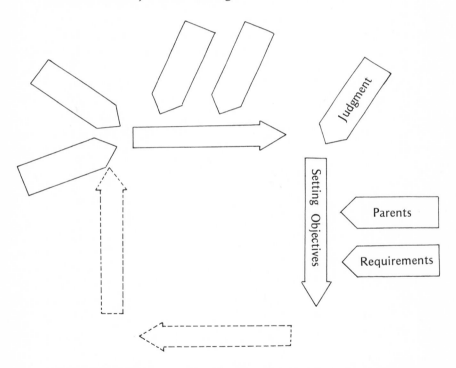

Data derived from the assessment phase form the primary data inputs to objectives setting. A professional staff member, who may or may not be the same person who met with Adam in the assessment phase, assumes primary responsibility for assisting him in developing a set of objectives that can be translated into prescribed treatments. This person performs a diagnostic function in developing Adam's school program.

The diagnostician retrieves all available information about Adam from the student data bank. He discusses possible objectives that Adam, his parents, and other professionals hold for his educational endeavors. The diagnostician also retrieves from the instructional components data bank the objectives established for all students of the school or for all students with similar characteristics. For instance, a general school objective might be that all ten-year-old students be able to make change on purchases of one dollar or less. If Adam is ten years old or older, and he cannot make change, then learning to do so would be an objective to be accomplished.

Setting objectives forms the very heart of the operations of a school for tomorrow. This is the phase in which problems are diagnosed, needs are identified, and educational ends are specified. This phase is essential to the assumption supporting a school for tomorrow.

Two objectives that might be identified are listed below. Assume that the identity of these objectives developed from analysis of all available data, from consideration of established objectives for students like Adam, and from consideration of Adam's own desires and wishes. The objectives are:

1. To gain a "knowledge of the reputation of a given author for presenting and interpreting facts on governmental problems."[11]
2. To gain a "recognition that there may be more than one acceptable point of view."[12]

These objectives are very general in nature and their attainment is difficult if not impossible to judge. It is therefore necessary to develop specifications that provide a basis for determining the degree to which each objective is or is not met.[13] After a list of objectives is developed, it is possible to prescribe a set of experiences designed to enable Adam to gain and demonstrate his knowledge of the reputation of a given author and provide proof that he recognizes the fact that more than one acceptable view does exist.

These objectives are then added to the student data bank. They form part of the growing set of data about Adam and his school experiences. They also add to a growing list of performance objectives being pursued in the school. This list in turn forms a bank of objectives that can be used for planning by other students, for providing data about the operations of this school, and for making an inventory of curricular offerings.

Phase Three: Prescription

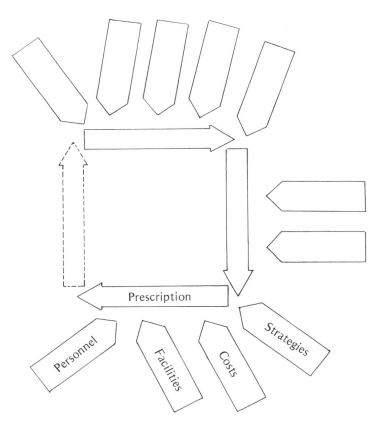

Prescription is the act of laying out a course of action to be followed by a student to meet the objectives developed earlier. This activity is essentially one of matching existing or newly developed strategies with objectives. This activity, like the objective-setting phase before, is performed by a diagnostician or by a professional whose specialty is devising instructional plans with the assistance of the student.

After surveying the list of objectives developed for Adam, the first task is to check the curriculum data bank to determine the prescriptions previously followed by students whose objectives were identical to those devised for Adam and students whose characteristics were similar. In addition, the data bank would reveal the degree to which the several prescriptions were successful in helping each student reach the objectives. These then become alternatives, based on experience with other students, that are available for use with Adam. From this list of alternatives, the diagnostician will be able to make a judgment about the appropriateness of each for Adam.

Each alternative or possible prescription selected can then be used to secure other types of related data. The data bank will include extra cost data for each prescription, facilities needed, special equipment required, professional personnel needed for implementing each prescription, and special conditions surrounding each alternative. What emerges from the data bank, then, is a list of alternatives that might be prescribed for each of Adam's objectives. This list will ultimately include all known information about each alternative including probabilities of success under given sets of conditions.

The diagnostician and Adam then examine the list to determine the most cost-beneficial prescription for each of the objectives. If, however, an alternative does not emerge from the curriculum data bank, it is the responsibility of the diagnostician to prescribe a course of action that he believes will assist Adam in meeting his objectives.

In reference to the two objectives listed above, two sample prescriptions secured from the data bank are shown for each objective. (It is assumed that the activities prescribed are within Adam's capacity to accomplish.)

Objective 1
  Prescription 1
    Check editorial page in *Daily News* to tally views of other writers about Mr. X.
    Subsequent inquiry indicates that: Six hours individual work required. No extra costs involved. School library files contain copies of *Daily News*. A paper and pencil test is available in file 1333 to test completeness of knowledge about Mr. X.
  Prescription 2
    Arrange field trip to discuss writing of Mr. X with Congressman Y.
    Subsequent inquiry indicates that: Two days travel required plus one-half day to meet at the Capitol. Extra costs estimated

at \$300 per student per trip. No special facilities required. A paper and pencil test is available in file 1333 to test completeness of knowledge about Mr. X. Has relationship to 422 other objectives, list available on request.

Objective 2

Prescription 1

Arrange debate between two students to consider the proposals of the Democrats and the Republicans for halting inflation.

Subsequent inquiry indicates that: Six hours individual study time required. One hour of debate time and one hour of discussion time also required. No extra costs involved. Library contains materials necessary to research the topic, list available on request. Room requirements depend on size of audience, list available on request. Postdebate interviews with debaters indicate growth of tolerance to other points of view. Has relationship to 83 other objectives, list available on request.

Prescription 2

Arrange field trip to discuss divergence of points of view in government with Congressman Y.

Subsequent inquiry indicates that: Two days travel required plus one-half day to meet at Capitol. Extra costs estimated at \$300 per student per trip. No special facilities required. Posttrip interviews with students indicate a moderate growth of tolerance to other points of view. Has relationship to 422 other objectives, list available on request.

From such a list, Adam and the diagnostician choose a set of alternatives that form the basis of a prescribed treatment. The alternatives are explained to Adam and plans for implementing the prescription drawn. In addition to the prescription, Adam and the diagnostician identify sources of help, develop a schedule, and determine the testing procedures to be followed.

As was the case in the previous two phases, the prescriptions are then added to the student data bank. During the subsequent assessment phases reference can be made to these prescriptions and to these objectives. In addition, these prescriptions add to a growing list of available alternatives that can be tapped in the future. The result is a historic file for use in assessing Adam's progress and a growing bank of empirically tested practice for use by other professionals and students.

One other type of input must be provided for the data bank at this point. The prescriptions developed for Adam require a specific set of resources for their implementation. Teachers, rooms, books, money, buses, or any number of resources may be required. Therefore, it is necessary to inform the personnel, instructional technology, facilities, and/or finance data banks that these resources are to be used at given times in order to keep an up-to-date tally of resources available for other students. As each diagnostician prescribes the use of resources for a student, the list of available resources for others is thereby altered. This "real-time" inventory of available resources is crucial.

Phase Four: Treatment

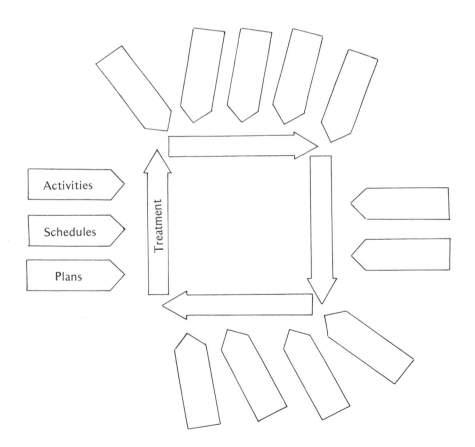

Treatment is the phase in which students follow prescribed educational strategies. Once a treatment has been prescribed, the student enters a time period in which the treatment is followed. Assignments are completed, "teaching" takes place, and prescribed plans are implemented, all according to a schedule produced in the prescription phase.

Supervision of students by adults will differ according to prescription. It is conceivable, for instance, that a given student would not be seen by a professional staff member throughout the period of treatment. Another student might be in contact with a staff member every hour of the day. Younger students would probably spend more time in direct contact with adults than would older students. In any case, the amount of contact is part of the prescription, not part of an assumption that all students need a specific number of "class contact hours."

An important aspect of the treatment phase is an early recycle option for the student. When prescriptions are developed, they contain, at best, only an estimate of the amount of time necessary to complete a given set of objectives. Since students differ and motivation is a sought after commodity, the possibility of a student's completing the prescribed activities earlier than scheduled must be considered. Students who complete one or more prescribed activities ahead of schedule must have the option of returning to the diagnostician for early assessment and recycling through the system.

Assuming that the first alternative was prescribed for Adam for each of the two objectives, it is quite possible that he can begin work on both immediately. He can collect the necessary data for the two projects and check with his instructor to arrange the details of the debate. While he is working on these two objectives, it may be advantageous for him not to come to the school building but to conduct his research in the library of a neighboring university (a resource that would be prescribed) or, perhaps, to work at home. Further, if his father is planning a business trip that would make it possible for him to visit the Capitol, the services of the diagnostician should be available to determine the feasibility of alternative two under each objective.

Thus, the treatment phase is the period when students follow prescribed courses of action, but in a manner that remains flexible, individual, and most contributory to attainment of objectives. This phase may be similar to or very different from the day-to-day operations of the typical school of today.

When all conditions prescribed have been met, or when a scheduled assessment period begins, whichever occurs first, the treatment phase is considered closed. It is closed for testing, analysis of treatment results, and evaluation during the next assessment phase. In reality, the treatment phase closes the loop in the information system, which brings the process back to assessment and subsequent recycling.

Group Relationships

As indicated in the introduction, it will be difficult, if not impossible, for a school for tomorrow to operate using the hierarchical authority model typical of many bureaucracies. By definition, the decision process in a school for tomorrow involves groups of people —students, professionals, paraprofessionals, support personnel, parents, and community resource persons. Each individual operating in this group setting is a key to the success of the school and therefore must be recognized for his own worth, not for the position he holds in the hierarchy. This is particularly important in correcting the traditional situation where students hold the lowest position in the hierarchy.

Blau and Scott cite three reasons why hierarchical differentiation curtails group processes: (1) status distinctions within groups reduce social interaction and social support; (2) status differences undermine the process of competition for respect, that is, in peer groups, the standing of any member is based on the respect of others; in groups with status distinction, members do not compete for respect of all others, because being respected by those of higher status is more significant than being respected by those of lower status; (3) status differences make it difficult to provide for error correcting in the social interaction, since group members will be careful in opposing the judgment of a person with superior power or prestige.[14] These factors, which have been confirmed by empirical study, lead to their conclusion that the more pronounced the hierarchical difference in a group, the less effectively it will perform.

A school for tomorrow cannot succeed unless individuals can work effectively in these group settings. Four basic conditions are vital to such teamwork:

1. The basic premise of a school for tomorrow, which calls for valuing individuals, must permeate the entire organization. Each of the persons working in and relating to the school must be considered with concern. While this may appear trite, its importance cannot be overemphasized. To expect a person—whether he be teacher, secretary, administrator, or parent—to provide this model of behavior, characterized by valuing individuals, in an atmosphere where individualistic behavior is not recognized or rewarded is an absurdity.

2. There must be group participation in decision making. The concept of group is important in a school built around individuals. There will be a need for a different kind of coordination and group involvement than is so often imposed in traditional schools. Many decisions affecting individuals must be made in the context of groups. Individual inputs must be weighed independently of the role of the participant. The control of decisions and/or the decision-making process cannot be in the hands of one person or a group of elites. All persons affected by decisions, including students, must have easy access to the information required in the decision situation.

3. Members of the group must share a problem-solving mind set. The concept of teacher as learner was advanced in an earlier portion of this book.[15] Individuals associated with a school for tomorrow cannot try to hide problems; rather they must try to solve those that come from any source. The identification of problems and the generation of alternative solutions are in the domain of anyone associated with a school for tomorrow.

4. Members of the group must accept the concept of professional autonomy and discretion. The range of professional expertise in a school for tomorrow will be broader than in a conventional school. If such a school is to succeed, professionals must be encouraged to make judgments and given the opportunity to try alternative strategies in an environment free of the traditional constraints of rules and regulations. While accountability and order are needed in any organization, the order (rules, regulations, etc.) must be derived by the individuals affected, not imposed from the top. For this to be accomplished, accountability must be at the school level. Individuals working in the school will be accountable to their clients—the students and parents—and to their colleagues, not to the central administration and board of education. The school as a whole

will be accountable to the board of education through the central office administration.

While no specific pattern for organizing can possibly be imposed on any school organization, the general pattern may well follow that described by Likert as the "participative group."[16] Likert suggests a group pattern of organization as opposed to a man-to-man pattern. The following diagram illustrates these two patterns.[17]

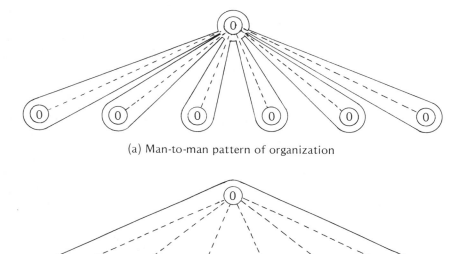

(a) Man-to-man pattern of organization

(b) Group pattern of organization
Man-to-man and group patterns of organization

The group pattern calls for a sharing of responsibility for decision making and of information. A school for tomorrow organized around the concept of information systems provides a natural environment for such organizational patterning. The man-to-man hierarchy is broken down in such an organization. The person represented by the circle at the top of the triangle is the linking pin to other persons outside the school but essential to the organization. Many different persons in the school may function as the linking pin. A teacher may provide the linkage to the school system's computer center; a student may provide the linkage to a certain community element.

Moeller and Mahan describe various examples of schools organized around such a pattern.[18] The faculty accept responsibility for the educational program, evaluate the program and develop new programs to achieve goals, monitor team progress, make decisions collaboratively, and ensure pupil-teacher partnership in learning. Students participate as full partners with parents and teachers in the development of school and individual objectives. Parents and community are linked to the faculty teams in goal setting as well as in operating the program.

Examples of Operations

Many functions performed in a school are not taken into consideration in the decision-making model proposed earlier in this chapter. These functions or activities are essential to the support of individual instructional decision making. Examples of such activities might be selecting staff; reporting to students, parents, and others; and acquiring resources. An attempt will be made to illustrate the differences between the operation of a traditional school and a school for tomorrow in two of these activities, selecting staff and reporting to parents.

Staff Selection

Selecting staff members is a crucial task in all schools. Large sums are spent in search of staff members who are perceived to hold promise of contributing to the goal attainment of the schools. Too often, however, the expenditure of funds and organizational energy are wasted because the selection process rests on a shaky rationale, a poor knowledge base, or, worse, no rationale or knowledge base of any kind.

Such a process is totally unacceptable in organizing a school for tomorrow. But, another alternative is available. That alternative is the generation of a selection procedure built around the information processing system. The contrast between such a procedure and procedures in use in many schools today is striking.

Staff Selection in a Traditional School. In the late winter or early spring, the principal of a typical school circulates a memo to all staff members inquiring whether they intend to return in the coming school year. In his files are evaluation reports about each teacher and the form on which he must list his recommendations for tenure, dismissal, or contract continuation. The principal has also accumulated a store of information about each teacher, derived from formal and informal observation, discussions, student behavior, parental comments, and secretarial complaints.

With these three sources of data, he sits down, sometimes with an assistant principal, a central office staff member, or even the teachers themselves, to formulate some sort of picture of staff needs for the ensuing year. What generally emerges is a list something like this: one third grade teacher, two fourth grade teachers, one art teacher, and so on.

His needs identified, he then notifies appropriate personnel in the central office, makes contacts with university and college placement offices, and initiates a whole series of informal contacts designed to elicit names of prospective teachers.

Soon thereafter credentials begin to arrive, each filled with glowing praise for the candidate and the wisdom of the school system that chooses to employ him. Somehow, these credentials are sorted, and two or three candidates for each position are invited to visit the school. The candidate's visits are marked by tours of the school building, interviews with central office staff members, and conversations with the principal and, in some schools, selection committees made up of other teachers. After all these data have been examined, someone or some group makes a decision about the identity of the new staff member. What results is a teacher whose responsibility it will be to "teach" students who are unknown except for their age, in a school with unknown colleagues, working for a principal who is a virtual stranger. (In some school systems the candidate may not have met a single teacher or even the principal.) What the school gets, on the other hand, is a self-styled "teacher," whose credentials indicate success in playing the education game to the extent of college graduation and who, by secondhand reports is a person of "sterling character" and a "good teacher."

The depressing fact about this process is that little attempt is made to get beyond the intuitive level for selecting staff members. No consideration is given to fitting teacher to prospective students. Little concern is shown for those few clues that research has given regarding teacher effectiveness. In a multibillion dollar industry, where the lives of millions of human beings are intimately involved and the future of a society is at stake, the process is still one of alchemy.

Staff Selection in a School for Tomorrow. The basis for selecting staff members in a school for tomorrow is found in answers to the following questions. What skills and knowledge and what personal attributes must professionals possess? What tasks need to be accomplished? What is the organizational setting in which these tasks must be accomplished? What are the characteristics of the specific number of individual children with whom the professional will interact? When decision makers can respond to these questions, the whole approach to selecting staff members is radically changed. In essence, the procedure for selecting staff members is one of finding a particular kind of professional who can perform specific kinds of activities located in a specific setting while working with a specific number of students.

As the staff selection team in a school for tomorrow approaches the task of selecting staff members, their behavior will be very different from that of such a team in a traditional school. First, they will probe the information system for data. They will probe the student data bank for information about the students with whom the new staff member will work. They will learn student strengths and weaknesses, student backgrounds, student likes and dislikes, and all the things that make for a comprehensive picture of that specific number of children. Second, they will base their projection of new staff members' competencies on analysis of the competencies and personality characteristics of the extant staff. They will base this judgment on data derived from continual evaluation of teacher and student performance.

They will identify ingredients of the setting that can assist in identifying new staff members. If the organizational setting requires a person to work very closely with a team, this forms a very vital piece· of information to be included when collecting data about a candidate. Similarly, if a staff member is expected to work independently, or with small groups of children, or with large groups of children, or with individual children, or under the direct supervision and control of another professional, these factors are also vital.

With the types of information listed above as examples, the team builds a composite picture of the desired staff member. They know the skills, attitudes, concerns, emotional state, and personality characteristics of the person for whom they are searching. Thus, the task is one of matching persons with a given set of attributes to positions in which these attributes are needed. The team attends to organizational health by attempting to determine probability of organizational "fit" before a staff member's employment. They are also attending to needs of individual students and providing a basis for psychic reward to the new staff member.

Reporting to Parents

Problems of educational accountability have received extensive national attention in the last decade. There are a number of impediments to accountability including philosophical and ideological impediments highlighted by the humanist-behaviorist conflict and by difficulties of quantifying educational goals and the primitive status of quality control devices.[19] There are political-legal impediments, including an uneasiness about the impact that accountability will have on local governance and control of public education. There are technological and economic impediments, including the need for a better definition of learning outcomes, the need for installing the technology to produce those outcomes, the need to measure the product, and the need to generate resources to install such systems. Reporting to parents, while only a small part of the accountability dimension, faces these impediments.

Reporting to Parents in a Traditional School. The problems associated with reporting in a school for tomorrow are much more complex than in a traditional school organized around group norms. Some school systems have made rapid progress toward providing group data to parents and to other publics.[20] While these reporting systems have been very useful in relating school building or district-wide data, this kind of reporting is inadequate in terms of providing accountability data to parents in a school for tomorrow.

In the traditional kinds of reporting, the emphasis is on groups, with data being provided in terms of some measure of central tendency and range or variability. The data are provided in group format and comparisons are generally made with other groups of students. Clearly, this practice is inconsistent with the emphasis on individual attainment. Group data that show growth or incremental gains come closer to the concept of individual attainment than do group achievement data.

This discussion will be limited to reporting to parents. Some progress has been made to change present reporting systems from simply providing comparative data about a student's achievement with respect to that of his peers. The most significant changes have taken place in the early primary grades where few comparisons are made with the group norms. As the students progress through the grades, however, and at a time when greater variability within levels should be expected and even encouraged, the tendency is to fall back on comparing a student's achievement to some norm group.

Reporting to Parents in a School for Tomorrow. Providing accountability data to parents in a school for tomorrow will depend in large part on regular and extended communication between parents and school personnel. The data that are stored about students, the educational opportunities available to them, the educational experiences they have had, and expected outcomes will have to be collated and shared with parents frequently. The frequency of such sharing will be the function of the age and decision capability of the students. In other words, the younger, less mature student will be more dependent on adults—his teachers and parents—for assistance in making decisions about the directions in which he will go and the kinds of emphases that will be placed on learning experiences. As a result of that dependence, there will be greater need for communication between the school personnel and parents. As the youngster matures and becomes more capable of making decisions himself, the communication will shift from emphasis on dealing with parents to emphasis on dealing with the student himself. In either case, there will be a need to spend much more time talking through these matters as opposed to merely providing written data about attainment or progress.

An example of such a reporting mechanism might be as follows. For a student who is in the five-to-seven-year-old range, it may be essential for parents to meet with some representative of the school professional team at least once each month. During those sessions, the school representative will be charged with providing an up-to-date accounting of the accomplishments during the preceding period and, with the assistance of the parent, projecting directions for the period to follow.

As the student progresses through the system, there will be a need to involve the student more actively in those sessions, so that student, school personnel, and parents share in this process. As students mature, there will be less and less need for parents to be involved in these kinds of sessions and more need that the student and the school personnel work closely on these matters. In all cases, the availability of data will be a key to the success of this endeavor. Without an improved information system, these sessions will be no more than present day parent-teacher conferences.

Notes

1. For an elaboration of the concept of differentiation, see Conrad Briner and Gerald Sroufe, "Organization for Education in 1985," in Walter Hack et al., *Educational Futurism 1985* (Berkeley, Calif.: McCutchan Publishing Corp., 1971), pp. 84-86.

2. A. D. Hall and R. E. Fagan, "Definition of System," *General Systems*, 1 (1956): 18-28.

3. Stephen J. Knezevich, ed., *Administrative Technology and the School Executive* (Washington, D.C.: American Association of School Administrators, 1969), p. 171.

4. Norbert Weiner, *Cybernetics* (New York: John Wiley & Sons, 1948), p. 187.

5. *Webster's New Practical Dictionary* (Springfield, Mass.: G. & C. Merriam Co., 1953), p. 332.

6. Adrian M. McDonough, *Information Economics and Management Systems* (New York: McGraw-Hill Book Co., 1963), p. 82.

7. R. L. Martino, *Information Management: The Dynamics of MIS* (Wayne, Pa.: MDI Publications, 1968), p. 54.

8. Ibid., p. 55.

9. See chap. 3.

10. Problems of confidentiality of information in a school for tomorrow will be more visible because of the ease of access to data. The same kinds of questions regarding who shall have access to what data are being raised in traditional schools.

11. Benjamin S. Bloom, ed., *Taxonomy of Educational Objectives, Handbook I: Cognitive Domain* (New York: David McKay Co., 1956), p. 67.

12. David R. Krathwohl, Benjamin S. Bloom, and Bertram B. Masia, *Taxonomy of Educational Objectives, Handbook II: Affective Domain* (New York: David McKay Co., 1964), p. 100.

13. Carefully constructed performance objectives are essential to the information system. A number of sources are available that can be of assistance in writing such objectives. One of these sources is: Robert Kibler, Larry Baker, and David Miles, *Behavioral Objectives and Instruction* (Boston: Allyn and Bacon, 1970).

14. Peter M. Blau and W. Richard Scott, *Formal Organizations: A Comparative Approach* (San Francisco: Chandler Publishing Co., 1962), pp. 122-23.

15. See chap. 4.

16. Rensis Likert, *New Patterns of Management* (New York: McGraw-Hill Book Co., 1961), pp. 223-33.

17. Ibid., p. 107.

18. Gerald Moeller and David Mahan, *The Faculty Team: School Organization for Results* (Chicago: Science Research Associates, 1971).

19. For an elaboration, see Stephen P. Hencley, "Impediments to Accountability," *The Administrator's Notebook* 20, no. 4 (December 1971).

20. An excellent example of such a product is entitled "The Columbus School Profile: A Report of the Columbus Public Schools to the Community." This annual publication provides data grouped by school building.

7

Professional Development and Self-Renewal

If the goal of rational autonomy is to be achieved, it seems likely that it will succeed in situations where teachers and support personnel have first achieved this goal for themselves. What conceptions of staff development will we need to help us become what we propose others become?

Charles Galloway
Edward Mulhern

No civilization other than ours has tried to educate all of its young, much less to do it thoroughly and well. Our problems today stem from two basic goals: to improve the quality of education and to make education possible for *all* members of society. Our nation's schools have been under bitter criticism and attack for their compulsory attendance laws and recently renewed efforts to educate all persons regardless of their ability. Nothing seems to be right.

Controversies have arisen from charges of racism in the schools, from uses of intelligence and achievement test data, from attempts of schoolmen to dictate norms and rules for student behavior, and from assertions of the advantages of the neighborhood school. Almost everything has come under attack: textbooks, teacher militancy, outmoded school buildings, learner apathy, reading programs, traditional programs, etc. Negativism and criticism have come from all directions, even from professional educators themselves. Few have been silent in their dissent.

In traditional classrooms, teachers remained aloof from students. Teachers presented information, gave directions, and doled out homework. Teacher activity centered around the territoriality of the desk, and student activity required book reading and pencil pushing. The distance, both physical and psychological, between teacher and student was immense. The student learned to do his assigned work without asking why, and he learned to see his teacher as something apart from doing and thinking. The environment was restrictive, impersonal, and distant. The student learned that his environment was not something to act on, but something to resist and reject.

Teaching is not simple; it is difficult and complex. Few people possess the talents, abilities, and dispositions to be called teachers. Even persons who are identified as teachers vary among themselves in their ability to teach. That is, they cannot teach all things and all students equally well. Some teach mathematics well but fail miserably in teaching history. We might be able to teach chess but not be as capable in teaching golf. Knowing the subject matter and possessing teaching skills facilitate success in teaching. Many professionals believe these are necessary conditions to teach at all. But learned experts and informed teachers can be quite impatient with beginning learners. An oft-repeated remark is, "He knows his subject matter, but he can't get it across to students." Information, knowledge, and skills are necessary for teaching, but having them does not guarantee results. Learners can still fail, even when they are under the tutelage of the most knowledgeable informed persons available.

In the past the teacher was seen as a fountain of knowledge and possessor of information. Whenever a student wanted to know something, he simply asked the teacher. The teacher was supposed to know, and he often did. This view of the teacher is no longer tenable. Increments of knowledge in every field have developed so quickly and fields of knowledge have changed so rapidly that no ordinary teacher can possess a full grasp of his subject matter. The most a teacher can expect of himself is a way of ordering and structuring his subject matter and inquiring into it. Today, the teacher is also a student of his field, differing from students only in experience.

It is well known that teachers who serve the young in our schools have varying degrees of educational experience. Their past experience represents the prime basis for believing they have something instructive to teach. Teachers soon learn that regardless of their degrees it is necessary for them to continue their professional development. A bachelor's degree is not enough, a master's degree is better but not sufficient, and a doctorate is laudatory but represents no guarantee of final preparation. In short, inservice education is necessary for all.

Inservice education has always been available to the aspiring and conscientious professional. It has also been made mandatory for those who chose to neglect its promise. Thus, inservice education has been self-selected and required for varying reasons. Inservice education has prevailed, and its purpose of promoting professional development has remained unquestioned.

The basic way of keeping records of professional development is to distinguish among college degrees, certification deficiencies, credits of inservice, and years of experience. These accounts are mechanical and routine measures for making head counts and categorizing teachers. Little is known about the differences that exist in the qualities and depths of experience. At the record-keeping level, they appear to be the same. So a teacher is requested to finish a degree, to meet a certification requirement, or to take an inservice course. It is assumed that the teacher will benefit, that teaching will improve, and that students will benefit. This is, of course, a spurious inference.

What happens? Teachers often go through the motions of improving their experience. They appear to benefit, but silently and stoically endure unneeded requisites. They learn to resent education. The major exception to this outcome occurs when a professor or trainer is extraordinarily gifted in surprising the teacher into realizing that something might be gained. On college campuses teachers continue to decry the irrelevancy of courses. Even courses and programs that originate from school settings suffer from teacher apathy and indifference. The message is the same: when inservice offerings are forced on teachers, they rebel. They resent the intrusion on their lives and on their current experience. They see little connection between what is promised and what is delivered. They have learned not to learn.

In this society most people acquire knowledge and learn skills because they want to gain a position in the occupational network. Indeed, most Americans recall their educational past as a necessary grind to achieve something else. Whether the desired ends were grades, units of credit, or matriculation, the net result was the same. Learning was something to be endured in order to obtain something else.

After graduation ceremonies, it seems easy to take this same attitude toward further education and preparation. Unfortunately, inservice education has been viewed as a necessary pill and as something to be either avoided or quickly taken. It is like bad-tasting medicine: it must be endured but can soon be forgotten.

Paradoxically, when you ask a teacher what is meant by the term, inservice education, he will reply, "To learn more, to become a better teacher, and to increase my own knowledge." While a teacher serves students in a school system, he inservices himself. If this statement seems nonsensical, it is not meant to be. Inservice education, staff development, and career opportunities are all names for the same thing: teachers have to continue to learn to teach. Inservice education is an unwritten contract that binds a professional to the further development of his educative powers.

Who Is Inservicing Whom and What Is Going On Out There?

Some time ago I had the occasion to visit a few school leaders from a medium-sized school system. Someone asked if any interesting, exciting things were happening in inservice. I responded by saying, "Oh, yes, a number of things."

Someone else said, "But is there anything new? You know what I mean. Is it just the same old stuff?" "Oh, no," I replied, "there are all sorts of training programs in value clarification, informal education, individually guided learning, behavioral management, etc., and teachers seem to be very excited about these new directions."

"Yeah," responded another school leader, "but will these things work? In the past, you know, we tried some of that new stuff, but it didn't turn out very well. You know what happened to nongraded schools and team teaching. We're not about to be guinea pigs anymore." I remarked, "You guys sound pretty skeptical to me. You must have been burned badly in the past."

"It isn't that, it's just that we get so tired of everybody believing we have to change. What's wrong with the way schools are? After all, we've done a pretty good job. I'm just sick to death of innovations. When in the hell are they going to stop?" "Listen, buddy," said another one of the group, "the school board is really on our backs. We're going to have to deliver. This accountability business isn't any kind of a joke. They want to know where every dollar goes, and what they are getting for it." "Besides," said another, "not only is money tight, but we don't have any funds for inservice. Teachers are just going to have to do a better job, or they're going to find themselves replaced. I don't mean to sound hardnosed, but I'll tell you, there are just too many teachers looking for jobs. We can pick and choose what we want."

During the course of the conversation I picked up some other notions and attitudes that were not too different. Although it seems overstated, these expressions were fairly representative:

What is the other guy doing?
What is going on that is new?
We are all very busy with what we do.
That theory stuff is irrelevant and impractical.
How can you know anything, nobody tells me nothing.
If it won't work, we won't try it.
Those consultants, who needs them, they think they're a bunch of
     hotshots.
Who needs an advisory committee, they're a waste of time, nothing
     gets done.
Who has money for inservice anyway?
If the college and universities would train them right, then . . . .
We would like to work with the university, but you know . . . .
Our problem is that teachers don't have the right attitude about
     inservice.

When the purposes and goals of inservice education are broached to professional educators, they often refer to the need for teachers to catch up. It seems that teachers are always behind. Whether the reference is to a recent innovation, such as open classrooms, or to an older notion, such as individualized instruction, the result is the same: teachers need remediation and training. The language of current emphases for inservice education sounds something like the statements below:

To keep pace with educational change
To expose most teachers to inservice
To use the latest teaching equipment and materials
To focus on the teacher as source of instructional improvement
To analyze teaching methods critically
To continue learning of teaching principles and practices
To learn diagnostic skills
To increase multimedia approach
To meet classroom teacher needs for instruction
To try innovations and experimentations

For too long, inservice education has enhanced its own future rather than teacher development. We have not sought a direction that focuses attention on the teacher as a person. We have not valued teacher development for its own sake. The following statements suggest a shift in direction for inservice.

To demonstrate that personal development is teacher development
To produce teachers who are change agents
To increase opportunities for emotional expression
To demonstrate that teacher growth is staff development
To increase teacher self-awareness and self-acceptance
To develop increased teacher sensitivity to students and self
To encourage teacher-initiated development activities
To create situations for identification and clarity of teacher values
To plan training sessions aimed toward total human development of
    teachers

Teachers are not unlike people in other vocations. They want and need free time, vacation days, and reasonable working hours. It is unfair to assume that teachers are unwilling to improve their skills and learn more about their teaching task. When teachers feel apathetic toward inservice, legitimate causes may be evident.

Inservice activities are usually held after school, on the weekend, or during a holiday—always on teacher time. Often teachers travel considerable distances to avail themselves of inservice programs. In fact, teachers go to great lengths to attend inservice sessions that are engaging and stimulating. When teachers exhibit an absence of motivation and when interest is low, the causes for such responses may be real rather than artificial. It certainly is unrealistic to expect teachers to persevere in the face of mediocrity. When negative feedback is offered, inservice trainers recoil in suspicion. The prevailing attitude is that teachers should be martyrs. Unfortunately, it is believed that teachers should be grateful and should unflinchingly endure the worst without complaint.

Most inservice days for teachers involve listening to lecturers, breaking up into groups for discussions, and regrouping for a question and answer session or panel discussion. As long as the subject of the day is given coverage, it matters little how it is accomplished. In fact, decisions regarding what teachers will do during inservice days are frequently made on the basis of convenience rather than on the basis of pedagogical soundness. For example, a teacher may hear umpteen lectures on the virtues and merits of the open classroom, yet fail to have the opportunity to see a teacher in an open classroom or to practice its possibilities. The difficulty for us is not that we need more and more ideas about the latest experimentations and innovations. Inservice education is not engaged in some kind of race to catch up and remediate every recent suggestion that can be conceived.

Advocates of inservice education dream the impossible dream. They fantasize that teachers will voluntarily enroll in college courses and that the latest innovations will finally bring the desired result: perfect teachers, flawless in their approach to teaching. Nothing could be further from reality. Teachers will continue to do the best they can, but they will never be able to satisfy everyone's criterion of perfection, much less their own. Inservice education is a way of becoming a better teacher, but no guaranteed perfections accompany its practice. Not only has it been impossible to specify when a person becomes a teacher (except legally), but also there is no precise time when a person becomes a complete teacher. That is, the process of becoming a better teacher never stops. All of us can be better, and it is true that each of us can temporarily suspend the process of being better by simply relying on the way we already teach. It is not that as teachers we should give up the tried and true practices of our past experience, it is just that we should not depend on them without question.

Each year teachers engage in inservice activities that have become as well recognized and as predictable as the holiday seasons of Thanksgiving and Christmas. There is the well-known orientation program, the election of college courses at nearby Cupcake University, and the perennial inservice options that count as more credit toward a higher level salary. Perhaps all of this really is not so terrible, but there is one consequence of these arrangements that truly undermines teaching improvement. Teachers are taken out of their natural settings where they should have opportunities to profit the most. That is, the presumption of too much inservice activity is that the teacher learns best away from his school. This is clearly an unwarranted assumption. Indeed, preservice education has long made the error of believing that an easy transfer exists between the training context and the teaching context. There are some connections to be sure, but far too many teachers need real help in their teaching contexts, in the laboratories of their practice.

What we can reasonably assume then is that most teachers have experienced varied efforts to improve their performance, with most attempts arranged outside of their natural learning environment. If teachers continue to make the charge that too much inservice education has proved to be impractical and unrealistic there must be something to the claim. Instead of building collegial relations with the teachers with whom he associates, a teacher too frequently finds himself separated from his teaching fellows. Not only is the teacher grouped with new acquaintances, but also he finds that the very information and attitudinal dispositions that are acquired in college courses and inservice classes (assuming that such positive claims can be made) become dysfunctional and suspect when he returns to his home base. Teachers have long claimed that they learn best when they are paired with their teaching peers.

Another inherent fact in the professional development of teachers is that they differ considerably. How to accommodate these differences has always been the most profound difficulty for inservice designers. Indeed we have ordinarily treated all teachers as one of a kind. But it is altogether too obvious that teachers vary markedly in their mastery of teaching skills, their intellectual understandings, and their personal humanity. We continue to need to differentiate growth opportunities for individual teachers, but recognizing the need does not solve the failures of the past. Therefore, any inservice model that intends to promote the continuing development of teachers must promote pluralistic and diverse modes of learning rather than lockstep programs for everyone. Such a direction would be marked by personalized choices rather than impersonal inservice assignments, and each teacher would begin at his own level of experience and progress at his own idiosyncratic pace. Any inservice model must represent the same philosophical spirit of teaching and learning that would be expected in the teacher's classroom. To grow and develop professionally teachers need to see the relationship between what is happening within themselves and what they are offering to youngsters. We can no longer expect the teacher to personalize and individualize his instruction for learners when the arrangements made for him violate his individual growth.

Teachers believe that administrators and developers of inservice programs are unresponsive to their real needs, that programs and courses are simply imposed. Officers of staff development decry apathetic and cynical attitudes they think teachers manifest toward inservice. But it is well known that effective programs are a result of teacher involvement in the planning and identification of problems. How often has the simple procedure outlined below been used by the advocates of inservice?

1. Circulate a communique of inservice options among faculty and administrators.

2. Ask teachers to select a few of the most appropriate.

3. Tabulate and resubmit the list to faculty.

4. Schedule a meeting for those who wish to make further suggestions.

5. Invite student groups and parents to offer suggestions.

6. Resubmit the list to faculty for their preference.

A Teacher's View of What Is Going On: Individualized Instruction

One of the more interesting notions promulgated and advocated by inservice educators for years has been individualized instruction and learning. While some success has been achieved in individualization, it must be admitted that the rhetoric has been better than the practice and that the controversy has been more interesting than the results. Many inservice educators would argue that it is irresponsible to criticize unless a better alternative can be offered. So it might be argued that inservice educators have done the best they can with individualized instruction and learning and that it would be unfair to criticize. Such a view is tantamount to expecting a football fan not to criticize the performance of a quarterback unless he is better at throwing passes.

More arguments and debates have centered on the question of individualization than on perhaps any other notion in education. Regardless of the positions taken, many expressed viewpoints seem pejorative. When an idea about individualization is offered, counterclaims and contrasting definitions abound. In the face of this controversy, little is achieved and understood by teachers. During inservice programs teachers hear one view, then another, and another, all of which are contradictory.

No idea in education has received more attention and invoked more controversy than individualization of learning. Its advocates have been exclaiming the virtues and values of variable learning rates for decades, and no idea has been more warmly received or more enthusiastically endorsed. Teachers visualize individualization as a one-to-one relationship. An individual conference or a tutoring session is believed to represent the essence of individualization. A recent emphasis on computer-assisted instruction, independent study, and programmed materials for students has steadily reshaped the vision of individualizing instruction, but the one-to-one view persists.

For teachers there has been the problem: How do you achieve one-to-one relationships in the midst of a class of thirty or more students? Teachers insist they need to forget individual students within the class in order to manage and teach the group. They believe that the classroom group as an entity must be the first priority. They realize that, in taking this view, different learning difficulties among students may be minimized and overlooked, but they believe the risk of ignoring individual students is necessary. They believe that in order to get anything done in school, the class or group must be preserved as the learning unit of instruction.

Teachers have replied consistently, "I cannot be everywhere at once. Too much noise and confusion results from trying to make varied and multiple contacts with students." A teacher recently said, "I lose control of the class. I know students are unique in their growth and development, but I cannot satisfactorily deal with the diversity and variability of thirty students. And I challenge anyone else to try." Teachers have remarked, "If I just had the time. There are simply too many students in my classes. It is impossible to get around to all the students during a day."

Maximum learning and achieving at one's potential are continually identified as the goals of individualization. This dictum is usually stated in terms of beginning the child where he is and permitting him to move as fast and as far as his ability will permit. This emphasis on developmental learning is ordinarily reserved for the learning of skills, which is assumed to be the most significant part of what schools teach. The skills required for reading, mathematics, language, and spelling are most often associated with individualized learning. Achieving at a maximal level, according to these enthusiasts, rests on two fundamental considerations: (1) learning occurs at different rates, and (2) learning occurs in incremental stages. Indeed, most proposals for individualized learning have been predicated on the differences of learning rate and on incremental stages from the simple to the complex.

Diagnosis and prescription have been in the forefront of suggestions that are usually included for individualization. With the use of various tests and observations, the teacher diagnoses what each child needs to learn. Making decisions in the best interests of students, the teacher prescribes and assigns appropriate learning tasks. These decisions are usually based on the need to pace and sequence learning activities at an individual rate of learning. Like a practicing physician, the teacher relies on measuring devices, consultations, and evaluations. Like the good doctor, the teacher writes just the right prescription and carries out the treatment. Borrowed from the concepts of preventive and corrective medicine, diagnoses and prescriptions are endowed with extraordinary educative powers. But this pedagogical stance goes beyond the medical analogy of diagnostician, for the teacher also plays pharmacist and nurse, filling the prescription as well as administering it. It is well known that patients are usually willing hosts to prescriptions for the cure of maladies. What is overlooked is that patients participate in the goal of getting well and cooperate with the physician. In schools, programs may be individually prescribed but fail to meet the test of learner participation in the goals and means of achievement. For instance, a student may be given the most appropriate prescription for his development yet fail to understand its purpose. Without shared participation in choosing a purpose, mutual consent may be missing and motivation absent.

The following polarities are not fully representative of the continuing debate that swirls around individualization, but they are indicative:

Learning occurs from within with reliance on individual powers and motivation/Learning is arranged from without and occurs through external stimulation.

Begin where the child is/Begin anywhere as long as you honor the child.

Individualization is skill training/It is general education.

Learners have their own style of learning/Certain techniques are appropriate to all learners.

A teacher can know the right time, speed, and tempo for learner/A teacher cannot know.

Time is the major variable (timing, speed-pacing, and sequence)/Time is irrelevant, not what you have learned or will learn, but what you are doing *now*.

Learning occurs in incremental stages from the simple to the complex/Learning occurs in leaps and bounds from intuitions, insights, and tacit dimensions.

Individualization is a one-to-one relationship between teacher and student/It is not.

Customized programs that are tailor-made for learners are best for them/Learners may reject programs that, in fact, may be completely appropriate for them.

Philosophy and theory are the key to individualization/The practices and techniques of individualizing are more important regardless of their theoretical base.

Individualizing is a method of instruction/Individualizing is a broad way of relating and working with learners.

Individualization is more humane and human/It is more manipulative and Machiavellian.

The more general kind of language regarding individualized learning suggests that programs must be designed and paced for each student according to his needs, that is, that curricula must be tailored and customized to fit. What is meant by these statements eludes most teachers. Such statements are lofty in purpose and fuzzy in their possibilities for implementation. Added to this is the view that it is the individual who matters and who needs to achieve at his highest potential. Teachers have a profound ideal but little direction. Few teachers know precisely what is meant by such statements, much less how to achieve it. The language of individualized learning has long suffered from such jargon. While no educator would want to relinquish his right to make high-sounding statements, there has been a tendency to state the cause of individualized learning in idealistic and romantic tones. Inservice efforts to exhort the teacher to individualize have been overdone. Individualization of instruction deserves attention, but past attempts to inservice teachers on this topic have suffered from vagueness and contradictory claims. Teachers deserve better.

A Model for Professional Development and Self-Renewal

Inservice workers are often tempted to use the latest terms and rhetoric that suggests something new and innovative. Recent references to performance criteria and competency-based instruction qualify for the latest in pedaguese. What goes on in inservice programs can often be hidden beneath the underbrush of semantic jargon. For inservice workers who wish to make a difference (and especially with teachers), a continuing check between rhetoric and reality must be made. The surveillance of what is real is always tough, but such a reality check is especially crucial for inservice education. For one thing, most projections and models of inservice activity are purer than their actual implementation. Plans and models usually stand unfettered by the impurities of human activity, but once you put the touch of human enterprise into action, the model gets shaky. This does not make it necessary to attack the model or lay the blame on people. The fault lies with neither. Conversely, the qualities of experience among teachers in an inservice activity may go beyond the elegance of a model. In a word, the process may be better. This is why it is so important to understand that the plans and projections of inservice activity are continually being reshaped in the light of experience.

Any inservice worker (whether teacher, administrator, or staff) must be prepared to apply his own individualized expertise and knowledge to inservice operations, but it is not just a singular and unilateral input. He teaches for change and is himself transformed by it; he guides other teachers, but is guided and directed by them; and he provides service to teachers but learns in the process as well. Although an inservice worker's specialized competency is needed and respected (whether outside consultant or formal leader), it is never inviolate within the arena of give and take with teachers. The inservice worker's role and function then is far more change oriented than his authority to impose.

In effect, inservice leadership and the professional development of teachers involves a transactional quality of teaching and learning. Inservice education is not something you do *to* teachers, it is something you do *with* teachers. And in the give and take of experience, both arranger and recipient are transformed by it. The heart of inservice operations is sharing and learning together through mutual exchange; the experience is that of the practitioner in the classroom laboratory, not the theorist in an ivory tower.

Within the operations of inservice activity, three phases of teaching need special attention, because the total teaching act is made up of three phases of experience: planning, instructing, and evaluating. In our model of inservice education we want to recognize these three phases of teacher activity as preactive, interactive, and postactive. Not only do teachers continually plan what they are going to do, do it, and evaluate its effectiveness, but also these are the very phases of teaching activity that need attention for inservice activity. It is well known that teachers have attitudinal sets, expectations, and goals that are planned or presumed before instruction (preactive); that they come into contact with students during instruction (interactive); and that they evaluate and weigh the value of instruction (postactive). A model of inservice education must accommodate these central phases that teachers deal with every day.

There are three other elements that provide the substance to teaching activity and behavior. These elements are the personal, task, and institutional aspects of educational contact. Whether we choose to discuss teacher behaviors, school life, or inservice education, it is apparent that the teacher is a person (personal) who performs skills (task) in the school (institutional). Each teacher must become aware of his personal abilities and shortcomings, improve his ability to perform instructional skills, and become more alert to the institutional pressures of school life. Teachers on the job are continually asking questions and dealing with problems that relate to the personal, task, and institutional aspects of teaching.

When we take the three phases of teaching (preactive, interactive, and postactive) and mingle them with the three aspects of teacher experience and influence (personal, task, institutional), we have our model. Indeed, the following model of nine blocks of teacher experience in schools constitutes a shorthand version of our rationale for inservice operations.

	Preactive	Interactive	Postactive
Personal			
Task			
Institutional			

Many examples of inservice activity from the nine foci of the model can be recognized. For instance, a teacher might engage in plans to personalize his instruction (preactive), involve himself in personal ways during classroom activity or workshop training (interactive), and discuss the results with a fellow teacher, confidante, or supervisor (postactive). An inservice activity related to this emphasis might involve sensitivity training, transactional analysis workshop, teacher effectiveness training, or classroom practice and trial. Indeed, inservice activity for the benefit of the teacher can take place in or out of the classroom context. Personal approaches to teaching and instructional change represent a large area of development for any teacher, and in the effort to become a better person, everything counts.

Within the task dimensions of teacher improvement, a similar sequence can be identified. Obvious examples are working on behavioral objectives, skills in question asking, and value clarification during instructional processes. Again, a teacher can take something as obvious as behavioral objectives and work through the planning stages, active phases, and evaluative aspects of writing and implementing these objectives.

The institutional pressures of school life are real and make considerable demands on teaching and instruction. While the debates and attacks on the realities of schooling continue to take place in a broader context of discussion outside the school, problems of institutional expectation and school life take place every day in the corridors and classrooms inside the school. Teachers need inservice activity, both in and out of the school, that provides opportunities for discussion, action, and reflection. In the past, teachers lacked a voice in deliberations on policies, rules, and regulations for the school, but this preactive influence on school life need not be omitted from teacher experience. Indeed, there are rich inservice activities to be had by attending and participating in school board meetings. More significantly, faculty meetings and formal discussions of school life for teacher and student have rarely been taken seriously. This is a grievous oversight, and the activity rightfully belongs within the sphere of inservice. Once again, it is obvious that prior decisions (preactive) make a difference in teacher behavior and attitude (interactive) that needs further reflection and assessment (postactive). Few programs need more current attention than the questions and issues that center on the nature of schooling and its influence on teaching and learning.

We have taken the three phases of teaching (personal, task, and institutional) and have shown their sequence and articulation (preactive, interactive, and postactive) through inservice operations. Nevertheless, within the possible activity of inservice experience, it might be desirable to focus solely on the preactive aspects of teaching and ignore the rest. The same can be said for interactive or postactive. The complexities of teacher improvement are too vast to deal with everything at once. Certain emphases may require attention now, but other foci may deserve temporary delay.

The improvement and advancement of teaching as a profession requires inservice activities that include emphasis on the nature of schooling; instructional tasks and skills; and personal values, behaviors, and attitudes. The distinction of the teacher as a person who shares himself has been ignored by inservice educators. The teacher can no longer be viewed as some impersonal entity who leaves his personhood at the door of the classroom. The teacher brings himself inside the classroom, and he needs to become more aware of what he is and how he can use himself more effectively. The myth of the teacher as nonperson has prevented self-fulfillment by the teacher. A further lack has been the neglect of teacher participation in the quality of school life and its institutional realities. We have sped past the day when the nature of schooling remains an unquestioned given for teachers. The quest for professional excellence includes the context of everyday practices as well as the arts and skills brought to it.

While the development of teaching skills has long been presumed to be a routine requirement for teachers, resources and leadership are often missing. Given favorable working conditions and change opportunities, teachers will improve their practice, but the rhetoric of inservice expectation can easily outdistance real improvement. The personal needs and professional interests of teachers must be considered if lasting change is to occur. We would place greater faith on teacher self-determination than on the single-minded agenda of administrators and staff developers.

Professional growth is a lifelong process, taking place cumulatively over time. Everything cannot be learned at once. No one teaching method or inservice approach can satisfy the development of all teachers. Multiple options for self-renewal must be available. What is essential for one teacher may represent an unnecessary and unwanted objective for another. Varied alternatives must be visible in order to overcome the tendency to impose a single inservice activity on all. Teachers do differ in experience and education.

An enormously promising source for inservice activity has been overlooked. The collegial relationships between and among teachers have been minimized and undersold as a means of growth. Given time and opportunity, teachers can not only learn from each other, but also serve as confidantes for feedback on teaching approaches and as respondents to teaching philosophy and style. Teachers do learn from each other, and every teacher needs a peer to listen to his latest speculation or plan. Fully functioning teachers need such confidantes. Without this opportunity, it is easy to retreat into a shell of secrecy and become defensive about teaching practice.

Inservice activity can profitably return to the natural habitat of the school and its classrooms rather than continue to overstress the advantages of unnatural settings. In the milieu of the teacher's classroom laboratory, much can be achieved. After all, it is teaching practice in its natural environment that needs attention. Whether by criticism or by the use of audio or videotape recordings, the teacher can profit by learning something of his own handiwork. It is here that the teacher learns the most, whether it be from students, colleagues, or outsiders. Collegial teams need to be organized to work together in mutually responsible activities.

As a final word, it must be recognized that our schools are not the same. Our teachers have not received similar training, and of course their levels of ability and skill development are marked by considerable variation. Teachers differ markedly. To be viable at all, inservice activity must accommodate itself to this difference. In a school for tomorrow there must be an open recognition of what is and what is not (an open accounting of strengths and weaknesses). To the mission of inservice education falls the lot of remediating the inadequacies that can be changed and accepting the realities that cannot be altered. Changing what can be altered and learning to live with current strengths and weaknesses without quarreling about the difference is the *sine qua non* of inservice education. It is this mood of acceptance of the way it is now and this article of faith in the willingness of teachers to change that characterizes a mature and just inservice operation. It is the difference that makes a difference.

Part 4
Reflections on the Problems of Change in Public Education

8

From Now to Tomorrow

What we have proposed is, in part, a hypothesis, but in a larger sense we have proposed a recommitment to a time-honored goal for education. But though we propose a recommitment, this in no sense denies us the responsibility to hold that both the means and ends we have explored must be viewed as tentative both now and in the years to come. What will a school of tomorrow demand of us?

Jack R. Frymier

Introduction

The concept of a school for tomorrow presumes a time line and changes over time. Previous chapters have described in detail some of the phenomena related to purposes and goals, curriculum, instruction, evaluation, and organizational and staff development. The general style has been advocative in a descriptive way. That is, we have attempted to adhere to one philosophical position, but we have also worked to describe in considerable detail the inherent realities of that particular value position.

Some will argue that is is both inappropriate and undesirable to attempt to describe what is being urged on others. We disagree. We realize that our descriptions are contaminated to a degree; that is the reality of human perception. What people believe in and feel strongly about is seen differently and described in different ways from what they reject or tend not to value or believe. We are not unmindful of that point. Our only defense is to acknowledge the fact and encourage the reader to test our descriptions against his personal experience and choose to use the ideas in ways that seem meaningful to him. This is what readers do anyway. Needless to say, the reader's values and his beliefs will also affect the interpretations he makes as he reads these pages. Our only request is that he strive to be as objective in his interpretations as we have attempted to be in our descriptions.

To this point in the book, our primary efforts have been theoretical rather than practical, abstract rather than concrete. In the following sections we have attempted to shift somewhat from a theoretical to a more practical point of view. Our concern is less with being "down to earth" than it is with being "helpful." In effect, we have tried to describe a plan of action that might be considered and adapted and modified by those who may be interested in trying to implement some of the theoretical propositions that have been set forth about a school for tomorrow. We feel very strongly that educational practice is always rooted in educational theory (whether the practitioner knows it or not), and the best test of theory is actually reflected in the extent to which it can be translated into practice.

The propositions for change described in this book are complex. Our proposal, in effect, is to change "the whole thing"—purposes, curriculum, instruction, evaluation, organization, staff development— the total complex of ideas and procedures which make a school a school. Changing the whole thing, of course, will be terribly difficult but unbelievably exciting. Changing even a minor aspect of the educational endeavor (the textbook for a course, grading practices, arrangements for grouping students for instructional purposes, preparing the agenda for faculty meetings, etc.) can cause real trauma and result in staff "choosing up sides," resisting the proposed change, or sabotaging the venture through inactivity or overt opposition. Just thinking about changing "the whole thing" will immobilize some persons, unless they can achieve genuine understanding and expect considerable help. No individual or faculty can accomplish all of the changes that have been set forth here working strictly on their own. They can, over a period of time, transform their present operation into a series of change efforts that will move them steadily and surely in the direction of a school for tomorrow. The films, film strips, cassette recordings, pamphlets, and simulation materials which are available[1] should prove useful, and over time a cadre of persons who have worked to bring a school for tomorrow into being in their schools today will also be available.

We think several factors will be in evidence among those faculty groups that are successful in weaving the ideas outlined in this book into the operation of their schools: they will employ an experimental attitude; they will capitalize on the surge of energy that always seems to accompany the "Hawthorne Effect"; and the full meaning of fostering intellectual and emotional growth in the direction of rational, autonomous human beings will be reflected in a variety of ways in what those educators actually do in their schools day after day.

The process of attempting to implement the ideas inherent in a school for tomorrow in a school today, for example, must be a process predicated on the experimental attitude of those who are involved. They must be willing to venture, to hypothesize, to try. They have to work at the business of generating alternatives, exploring assumptions, creating new materials, examining their own practices, beliefs, and teaching styles. There must be a continuous process of development and evaluation followed by feedback and further change. The staff in a school for tomorrow simply has to learn and grow professionally all the time.

If faculty can become excited about the ideas involved in a school for tomorrow, commit themselves to give the ideas a good try, and find a way to study their own efforts carefully and creatively, then the "Hawthorne Effect" will emerge. The power of the "Hawthorne Effect," of course, resides in the fact that when people who are a part of an experimental undertaking are studied as a part of the experimental effort, they work harder than they normally do. They know that they are important to the success of the experiment. They feel involved. Their commitments to the project take on new meaning; they expend more energy and are more creative and persistent than they would normally be. The challenge is to find a way to maintain a continuous sense of innovation and change along with enough stability to prevent chaos or a feeling of helplessness or dependency.

Finally, in the day-to-day endeavors of the staff in a school for tomorrow, a whole host of activities will reflect a rich understanding of what it means to foster intellectual and emotional growth in the direction of rational, autonomous human development. There will be a greater range of curriculum materials than in a conventional school. Further, there will be less compulsion on the part of the staff to insist that any or every student interact with and "learn" the subject matter that is imbedded in the curriculum materials that are there. Students will be learning to give direction to their own lives. They will help set their own goals. They will be encouraged to learn in ways that reflect their own personal and unique learning styles.[2]

Students will be creators, synthesizers, analyzers, consumers, users, and pattern builders of knowledge. They will become increasingly aware of the dimensions and structure of their own knowledge and will recognize the source of support for their beliefs and conclusions. They will be more open to experience, more accepting of themselves, more confident, and more accepting of others.

Teachers will be more patient; more skilled at listening and observing; and more flexible in their use of materials, teaching strategies, and assessment tools. They will spend less time restricting, controlling, and directing students and more time thinking, watching, pondering, conjecturing, and reflecting on what students do. The pace of teaching will be slower, even with more subject matter available and more complex "hardware" and "software" around. Paying attention to the individual learner, hearing him, and thinking about him and with him will be in evidence everywhere. Inducements, threats, reprimands, and rewards will not be apparent.

To think about working toward a school for tomorrow or plan for an educational change requires some understanding of "where we are now" and "where we ought to go." The *is* and the *ought to* problem confronts us head-on. Suppose we shift our focus at this point and try to get another perspective. At the outset we will review some of the previous efforts at educational change. After that we will describe in brief detail our own understanding of a "change model," which we think characterizes many current attempts to bring about educational change. Then we will set forth certain principles or concepts of change that we feel have merit and ought to be considered in any serious attempt at change. Included in this discussion will be a series of specific suggestions for persons who see themselves as agents or facilitators of change in an education context. Finally, a listing of some of the research that might be pursued, some of the problems that can be anticipated, and some of the resources that may be available will be outlined in a beginning way. Suppose we begin with the historical considerations.

A Brief Historical Perspective

Schools and schooling are not without direction in America today. Silberman was probably correct when he described the mindlessness of schools—the failure of educators to focus their attention upon the basic purposes of education—but that is not to say that schools and schooling lack direction.[3] They do not. The fact that educators have failed to be concerned about purposes and goals or have failed to examine them critically and subject them to logical and other kinds of scrutiny does not mean that schools and schooling have wandered willy-nilly from pillar to post and back again.

Even a cursory look at the history of American education makes clear the fact that the educational enterprise has proceeded determinedly if not thoughtfully along fairly narrow routes toward particular goals.

Historically there have been three basic sources from which the purposes of education have been drawn: the nature of knowledge, the nature of society, and the nature of the individual. Before the turn of the present century, only two of the sources were used to any appreciable degree. During the nineteenth century the common school assumed responsibility for helping the nation build its social allegiances and assimilate its groups, while the academies and high schools of that period were primarily concerned with the academic disciplines and the practical fields of knowledge directly related to preparation for the professions or other vocational pursuits. With the establishment of the Committee of Ten in 1892, and continuing through the time of the First World War, a concerted effort was made to shift the purposes of secondary schools from academic considerations to social concerns.[4] About the same time Montessori's work and what came to be called the "activity school" aspect of the progressive education movement were inclinations in the direction of individual considerations at the elementary school level. Beginning with the "curriculum reform" movement in the late 1950s, the focus in secondary schools shifted sharply from social considerations back to the academic disciplines again. By the late 1960s and early 1970s, though, concern for the individual as a basic source of purposes was emerging once again, this time at both the elementary and the secondary school levels.

Curriculum theorists during most of this time were continually writing about curriculum in terms of these three basic sources. Smith, Stanley, and Shores described "the subject curriculum," "the activity curriculum," and "the core curriculum."[5] Foshay dealt with the three areas in a slightly different way. Taba wrote in terms of preserving and transmitting the culture, transforming the culture, and individual development, but the concepts were the same.[6]

Tyler's description was similar, but he also implied that all three sources could be drawn on equally. For example, in the classic, *Syllabus,* Tyler argued:

> The point of view taken in the course is that no single source of information is adequate to provide a basis for wise and comprehensive decisions about the objectives of the school. Each of the sources has certain values to commend it. Each source should be given consideration in planning any comprehensive curriculum program.[7]

Herrick employed the same general frame of reference, but added the value component in curriculum when he suggested that certain sources inevitably came to be seen as more significant than others in the mind of the curriculum worker. This results in a "preoccupation" with some factors and a deemphasis on others. Herrick described the reality as follows:

> The preoccupation with subject fields leads directly to problems of generalizing, the cognitive processes, the logical structures of subject matter, transfer of training, mental disciplines, readiness, repetition, motivation, reinforcement, retention, the ability of the individual to learn. A preoccupation with a socially centered curriculum leads to an examination of the nature of persistent and recurring social and democratic processes, group dynamics, valuing and normative behavior, organismic and topological concepts of learning, and status- and role-determining processes. A preoccupation with the learner as the initial consideration in curriculum building leads to examination of the self-perceptive process, the mechanisms for the identification of persistent and recurring concerns of the individual, questions of creativity, phenomenological fields, biological growth processes, and what constitutes maturity and development in the human organism.[8]

The fundamental thesis in a school for tomorrow, of course, is predicated on what Herrick refers to as "a preoccupation with the learner as the initial consideration in curriculum building." And the term *preoccupation* describes the value position precisely. No either-or distinction is intended. What has been outlined in this book is a conceptualization of a school that presumes a preoccupation with the learner rather than with academic subject matter fields or social concerns.

The idea that the organizing center for education should be the individual rather than the disciplines or society is probably not widely shared. We realize most people feel that social considerations or academic considerations ought to be accorded positions of primary prominence rather than positions of lesser attention, but we would like to try to convince them otherwise.

Tradition and many of the "experts" are on their side, of course. In an analysis of the problems confronting educators today, Grayson insists that "Every analysis should begin by deciding what benefits should be gained, as determined by needs and values. *For the most part, the basic goals of education are rooted in the values of society.*" (Emphasis added.)[9] This does not mean Grayson feels that the individual is not important. He does. Even so, the following statement by Grayson must be interpreted in terms of the statement above.

At this time when there is growing demand for rendering education more personalized and more responsive to the needs of students, accurate determination of costs, benefits, and effectiveness are becoming of increasing importance to educational decision makers. The individualization of instruction, long a goal of American education, is one approach being investigated to meet that demand.[10]

What Grayson seems to be saying is that *society is demanding* that schools individualize and personalize their efforts to help young people develop and learn and grow. Williamson advances the same argument in a more forceful way.

Educational purpose must be based squarely upon a clear and insightful analysis of the needs of society. . . . As has been noted previously, many of the contemporary arguments of outrage criticize organizations and schools in particular for submerging basic humanitarian and democratic values to the needs of the organization. While many of these arguments are quite insightful and convincing, they provide little foundation upon which to take action, since they deal only with the needs of the individual. . . . Such arguments have little utility. As long as the dominant social and institutional needs are not consonant with individual growth, independence and creativity, these attributes will not be fostered, regardless of the idealistic pipe dreams of educators or social reformers. *However, the dominant social and institutional needs have developed to the point where these individual traits are critical to the viability of institutions and indeed to society.* (Emphasis added.)[11]

Williamson and Grayson both seem to be arguing that society now needs fully functioning individuals, and because of this social need, schools must provide experiences that will foster the development of individual potentialities.

Some might argue that this is what schools have always tried to do. Perhaps they have. Our general experience and the professional literature both suggest that the emphasis has never been operationalized quite that way. For example, a widely hailed experiment in general education at the college level over twenty years ago made the point for honoring the needs of society this way:

> Its function is to prepare young people . . . to deal not with the special problems parceled out in our society to the members of various occupations and professions—to the chemist and the carpenter, the architect and the accountant, the doctor, the merchant, and the housewife—but with the problems that confront all members of our society alike, such problems as our domestic and foreign policies, our political leadership, our individual relations with the physical universe, our personal philosophies. General education appears from this point of view to be the preparation of youth to deal with the personal and social problems with which all men in a democratic society are confronted.[12]

There is no doubt that this statement of educational purpose alludes to the *personal,* but the emphasis is unquestioningly on the *social* concern.

Curriculum development and educational practice, like other human activities, evolve in new and different directions over time. What seems to be emerging at the present time is a growing awareness of the necessity for institutions to focus on and further individual development, growth, and learning possibilities.

Consider one illustration. The concern for ecology, growing dramatically in recent years, can be examined in academic, social, or individual terms. All of these perspectives are important. Pollution kills individuals, however, not societies or academic disciplines. Individual people deteriorate or die from excess mercury in fish, strontium 90 in bone marrow, or contaminants in the air. Social institutions such as governments and industrial corporations must deal with the problems involved, but the problems are first and foremost very personal problems of particular men. The individuals who are affected need assistance and relief.

Our present social problems seem less pressing when compared to the ecological problems that mankind must resolve or die. One authoritative study concludes that mankind has only until about 2100 to come to terms with the forces and factors in nature, or catastrophe will ensue.[13] Furthermore, the steps necessary to prevent that catastrophe from occurring must be accomplished in the next twenty years or so, or man as a species may be doomed. The authors conclude their study:

> If there is cause for deep concern, there is also cause for hope. Deliberately limiting growth would be difficult, but not impossible. The way to proceed is clear, and the necessary steps, although they are new ones for human society, are

well within human capabilities. Man possesses, for a small moment in his history, the most powerful combination of knowledge, tools and resources the world has ever known. He has all that is physically necessary to create a totally new form of human society—one that would be built to last for generations. The two missing ingredients are a realistic, long-term goal that can guide mankind to the equilibrium society and the human will to achieve that goal. Without such a goal and a commitment to it, short-term concerns will generate the exponential growth that drives the world system toward the limits of the earth and ultimate collapse. With that goal and that commitment, mankind would be ready now to begin a controlled, orderly transition from growth to global equilibrium.[14]

In a report to the U.S. Commissioner of Education, Shane describes the results of his future research as follows:

A final crisis that most scientists interviewed in this USOE study felt to be a severe one was made up of three components: universal use of technology, rapid increases in world population, and consequential ecological problems. . . . It seems clear, in terms of the welfare of the planet, that we must recognize that there are limits to affluence, to technological exploitation and to population increase, and endeavor to move toward a policy that will reconcile people everywhere to the need to find satisfactions from sources other than acquiring material possessions. For the most part these . . . problems and the ineffably complex dilemmas they pose have not been thoroughly attacked or even widely discussed. Not unexpectedly under these circumstances virtually no serious thought has been given to what the problems or crises imply for curriculum change.[15]

This kind of thinking may account for society's insistence that schools focus on the fullest development of individuals. Helping children become sensitive, considerate, and humane may not be enough in the years ahead. Learning meaningless facts or unimportant social skills may in fact be woefully limiting in a world in which vast storehouses of information will go unused unless schools can help all people become inquiring, motivated, creative, intelligent learners who can discern the real from the superficial problems and use their energies and their abilities to tackle and solve the pressing, basic problems of human existence.

A school for tomorrow must include a commitment and a curriculum that reflects an awareness of and a consistency with these fundamental problems facing all mankind. The philosophical focus on the importance of *life* in a school for tomorrow and the goal of providing experiences and curriculum content designed to maintain and improve the quality of life for each individual is sharpened by our awareness of the possibilities for survival in an environment that is increasingly hostile to human life. A major thrust of curriculum content in a school for tomorrow must be related directly to the growing imbalance of the ecological complex. Other illustrations could be pointed out. The essence of our argument is that schools and schooling must define both the ends and the means for fostering the intellectual and emotional growth of all persons—young and old, rich and poor, black and brown and white, conservative, liberal, and in-between. The need is to facilitate educational growth for all people everywhere.

The point of this discussion is obvious: the purposes of education have changed in the past and they must change again in the future. Suppose now that we move to consider a model of "change" that has characterized our efforts in recent years.

The Logic of Many Change Efforts

In his study of educational change, Sarason concludes that many agents of change have employed self-defeating procedures.

The more I have read about and personally observed efforts to introduce change in the classroom the more clear several things have become. First, those who attempt to introduce a change rarely, if ever, begin the process by being clear as to where the teachers *are*, that is, how and why they think as they do. In short, they are guilty of the very criticism they make of teachers: *not being sensitive to what and how and why children think as they do.* As a result, teachers react in much the same way that many children do and that is with the feeling that they are both wrong and stupid. Second, those who attempt to introduce a change seem unaware that they are asking teachers to unlearn and learn. Third, if there is any one principle common to efforts at change, it is that one effects change by *telling* people what is the "right" way to act and think. *Here, too, those who want change do exactly that for which they criticize teachers.* [16]

We ought to be able to learn from Sarason's experience. At another point he states:

Good ideas and missionary zeal are sometimes enough to change the thinking and actions of individuals; they are rarely, if ever, effective in changing complicated organizations (like the school) with traditions, dynamics, and goals of their own. To change complicated settings requires, initially at least, a way of thinking not the same as the way we think about changing individuals. [17]

What are the techniques that have traditionally been employed by those working at educational change? There have been many, to be sure, but a major portion of the change efforts have reflected a similar sequence of activities when viewed in relation to time. In essence, anywhere from three to five stages or steps have generally been followed by those attempting to bring about change: awareness of the need for change; conceptualization of a change proposal; personal attempts to implement the change; institutionalizing the change; and finally, making the change a part of a new tradition. These five stages are simply points along a time line. Most efforts at educational change do not go through all of the various stages; some never get beyond the first or second stage, in fact. Each stage is described briefly in the following paragraphs.

Awareness of the Need for Change

The first phase of any change effort has typically begun with an awareness of the need for change. Some aspect of program or practice is obviously not achieving the purposes for which it was intended. Anomalies exist; discrepancies occur; sensitive people are dissatisfied and uncomfortable about the way things in the school seem to go. There may be empirical data or only vague feelings. The particulars may be small and apparently insignificant, or they may be traumatic and obvious for all to see.

For example, a careful study of achievement records of all children in a junior high school may indicate that the mean level of reading achievement is 2.9 years in grade level below national norms. Such data indicate something ought to be done.

Teachers in the teachers' lounge may discover the fact that several parents have reported separately to each of the teachers that they feel their children are developing negative feelings toward learning and school.

After four separate instances of arson and serious fire damage in a senior high school, the principal concludes that some students in the school feel extremely hostile toward school personnel and something needs to be changed.

The first step in the process of educational change begins with a sensitivity to the need for change. Something may be wrong. Dissatisfaction, anger, or frustration may have appeared. Expert assessment from the outside may have pointed out problems that those working regularly in the situation did not see. Every change effort begins with an awareness of the need for change.

Conceptualizing a Proposal for Change

Once it has become apparent that things are not quite right and they need to be changed, somebody has to conceptualize a proposal for change. Many times school people are aware of the need for change, but no one sits down to develop or reaches out to select a new and different way of doing things. If they do, the proposal may come forth in either simple or grandiose terms; it may be the product of a single individual or a large working team; it may be easy to implement or very difficult to achieve; take more money or less; require special equipment or training or both, or it may require neither. The conceptualization for change may be elaborately developed in written form, or an idea carried around in the innovator's head. But there must be an idea. There must be some conception of what could be done. In effect, there has to be a kind of hypothesis about how education could be better if it were changed.

One Person Spearheads the Change

In almost every change venture in education, one person leads the way. Such people have sometimes been referred to as "curriculum heroes." They carry the burden of responsibility for change on their backs day after day.

This one person is generally pulling, pushing, leading, coordinating, encouraging, prodding, and pressing the proposal for change. One person leads the way, showing, telling, listening, suggesting, answering, helping in any one of a hundred ways. Changes do not come about unless one person works at the business of change regularly. In effect, this typically means that that one person assumes primary responsibility and expresses basic concern about the proposal for change. It may be a committee, but more frequently it is a charismatic leader who strives in innumerable ways to help people give the proposal for change a good try.

Institutionalizing the Change

Eventually the proposal for change may be formally adopted, policies revised, and procedures formalized. Because schools are formal institutions, if change attempts transcend the personality of the one person who has carried the proposition into the school, they must be institutionalized. To say it another way, the decisions about the change go beyond the immediate interests of particular people if they survive. Too many proposals for change evaporate or die if the person who spearheaded the change moves on to another position. Insuring that the change will survive requires that it be institutionalized.

Traditionalizing the Change

Sometimes proposals for changes are adopted and institutionalized to a degree that they become a new tradition and are projected into the future because "that's the way we do things here." Most proposals for change, of course, never reach this stage, and one might argue that change ought never to become stabilized and traditionalized, but sometimes it is. The adoption of the change proposal language, a view of the change as "part of the regular scene," a fading of change from "figure" into "ground" with a preservation of its essential features: all of these instances are illustrative of proposals for change becoming more or less permanent parts of the educational endeavor. "Grade level," "electives," "report cards," "recitation," "workbooks," "audiovisual aids," and other examples are traditionalized changes that persist today. "Team teaching," "mini courses," "nongradedness," "modern mathematics," and "modular scheduling" are well on their way to becoming traditionalized, too.

This description of stages is arbitrary, of course, but those who have worked closely with change efforts in education will have little difficulty in recognizing these stages as a kind of logic in many proposals that have been attempted in educational change. Unfortunately, many efforts at change have failed. Following a time line has been an inadequate tool in bringing about significant change. Sarason's conclusion that "the more things change the more they remain the same" suggests that change efforts that employ the logic described are apt to fail. We need another conception or model for educational change. We need to plan carefully and creatively if we hope that a school for tomorrow might come to be.

A Strategy for Change

Perhaps we might begin again with Sarason's conceptualizations. His insights have been particularly helpful as we have thought about the problems and possibilities of educational change. Much in the following discussion draws from and builds on his notions about change, as we understand those concepts, if only because his experience regarding change efforts generally "squares" with ours. For example, from our reading of Sarason we infer the following about educational change attempts:

1. Ideas are important.
2. Schools are terribly complex.
3. The building principal is the key person in educational change.
4. The culture of the school is both more influential and less understood than is generally acknowledged.
5. Schoolmen tend to equate "what is" with "what ought to be."

Those *descriptive* ideas about educational change are followed by these kinds of *prescriptive* notions:

1. The place to initiate change is at the building level.
2. Change strategies must vary from building to building.
3. Change efforts must deal with the complexities of schools and schooling.
4. Change efforts must discourage the development of dependent relationships.

Gross' description of difficulties in implementing an innovation in one elementary school suggests the same kinds of considerations.[18] Piecemeal change efforts that do not have the vigorous and thoughtful leadership of the building principal, are not precisely tailored to the unique complex of factors within the building, and do not honor the concerns and expectations of the teachers involved will probably not change anything.

We would like to propose a six-phase change process that we feel is worthy of consideration by persons interested in implementing the ideas inherent in a school for tomorrow. Again, the phases represent a time line. However, the sequence of events described below also reflects attention on the motivations of people who participate in change efforts and tries to deal with those motivational problems directly and realistically. We acknowledge the fact that there is no one sequence of events that is "just right" for every situation. Situations differ, and change strategies must differ, too.

But change efforts do take place as specific events that occur in a particular sequence over a period of time. By drawing attention to the notions of sequence and time line, and by emphasizing the complexities that exist within every individual school, we hope to get those who want to work at the business of educational change to organize their efforts, their ideas, and their resources in ways that will insure that the problems inherent in change are both rationally and creatively engaged. The sequence outlined below, therefore, must be viewed as illustrative rather than definitive; suggestive rather than final; a hypothesis rather than a blueprint for change.

Briefly, the six phases are as follows: awareness of the need for change; conceptualizing a range of alternatives; exploration and consideration of the alternatives; commitment and institutionalization of the proposal for change; preparation of staff; implementation, evaluation, and modification of the change. Each of these six phases is discussed in more detail below.

Awareness of the Need for Change

Ascertaining inconsistencies or inadequacies in the educational effort suggests the need for change. Awareness of the need for change may emerge slowly in the minds of concerned persons, or it may be thrust on them forcefully, but dissatisfaction with existing programs or a sense of irrelevance of effort would probably be involved. This aspect of change has been discussed before and will not be described at length again.

Conceptualizing a Range of Alternatives

Once the need for change has become apparent, those who would like to modify existing practice must generate a range of alternative possibilities. A school for tomorrow is one such alternative. Others must be articulated, too. Sarason suggests that educators study the programmatic and behavioral "regularities" in their school, and from a consideration of these regularities—events and processes that repeatedly recur and are typically assumed to be "a natural part of things"—set forth a series of alternative ways of doing things.[19]

Since most of the existing regularities in school have been part of the fabric of schooling for many years (students raise their hands before they speak, teachers talk and students listen, everybody studies mathematics, students are assigned to instructional groups according to age, etc.), it is terribly difficult for most persons to question their existence, let alone their purpose. Even so, a thoughtful examination of existing assumptions and regularities is absolutely essential if change is to take place. And from this examination, a series of alternative ways of doing things must be created.

Because most schoolmen unconsciously equate "what is" with "what ought to be," this process of generating alternatives is usually terribly difficult. One purpose of this book has been to expedite that activity for the reader by spelling out some alternative ways of thinking about educational purposes, curriculum, organization, and the like. But a range of alternatives is imperative if meaningful change is to be brought about in schools.

Exploration and Consideration of Alternatives

Once several ways of doing things have been described, it then becomes the responsibility of those interested in change to "think through" the possibilities carefully and completely. Those who are responsible for implementing any change in educational program must have a thorough understanding of that program in relation to available alternative programs if the change is to be successful. They must have an opportunity to explore in detail the basic assumptions, the theoretical dimensions, the practical problems and possibilities, and the unknowns that are involved. They have to argue about these things, turn them over in their minds, meet with expert consultants on a "face-to-face" basis over extended periods of time, and "mull over" and "muddle through" the variations and ramifications.

The leader's role during this period is crucial. He must listen to their questions and hear their concerns, expedite the flow of communication, share his understandings and frustrations, make new information available and meaningful, press basic assumptions out into the open, and help all persons articulate their understandings of "how things are" and "how they ought to be."

Adopting an educational change because it was "mandated by those above" or "because everybody else is doing it" makes no sense at all. The people who will have responsibility for implementing any program must have an extended opportunity to explore and consider a range of alternative ways of doing things, including the way things are done right now.

Commitment and Institutionalization

Following an extended period of time in which a range of alternatives are considered and explored, some kind of commitment will have to be made by those who are going to be involved. Unanimity is not required, but unless three-fourths or so of the people who will be directly affected are in agreement with the proposal for change, it probably will not be possible to give the innovation a good try. Certainly any proposal that is as complex and far reaching as the proposal for a school for tomorrow will have to have the allegiance and commitment of many people just to get the ideas off the ground.

In addition to the teachers and administrators in the particular building involved, members of the central administration and board of education must be apprised of and committed to the venture if it is to have a chance to succeed. In all probability this should probably require formal board action and allocation of special funds. We feel that school boards ought to allocate additional funds out of the regular operating budget rather than simply approve proposals that outside agencies are willing to fund. School boards that authorize projects funded by other agencies are actually saying, in effect, "We do not really believe in change. We will let you try out those new-fangled ideas if somebody else will pay the bill, but we are not going to use any of our regular money for change. We have confidence only in the programs and policies we already have." Needless to say, such comments are seldom actually stated aloud, but the thought processes involved follow along those lines. By laying their policies and regular operating budget "on the line" and formally commiting themselves to the venture, school boards can assure the teachers and building principal that they have confidence in their proposal. Further, they are also communicating to the parents and the rest of the school community their intention to support well-thought-out proposals for change. Board members and central office administrators must understand the proposal and the alternatives fully if their commitments are to be more than a formality, and their commitments must be much more than that if the change is to succeed. It goes without saying, of course, that seeking and using resources in addition to those included within the regular operating budget is important on occasion, too. No school board members worth their salt can ever hope to achieve all of their hopes and dreams for the students and staff in the schools they serve without deliberately soliciting financial and other kinds of help. But they dare not allow themselves to slip into the role of approving only those changes that other agencies are willing to help educators finance. School boards have a responsibility to support worthy proposals for change at the policy level, the financial level, and the psychological level.

Preparing the Staff

While the proposal for change is being considered and explored, staff members will be learning about the proposal and developing new insights and attitudes. Once a commitment has been made to "go," however, more extensive preparation of the staff must be undertaken. Summer workshops, regular inservice meetings, college courses, and individualized and personalized training sessions must get underway. In all likelihood specific answers to specific questions will not always be known. Those who have responsibility for implementing the proposed change must work regularly and seriously at the business of acquiring new skills, understandings, materials, and ways of doing things if the venture is to be effective.

This means, of course, that extra money, time, materials, and help will be essential, particularly in the initial days of the effort at change. Even if everybody involved understands the proposal for change and is committed to it, it still will not "go" unless they get highly specialized assistance and materials when problems arise, as, inevitably, they will. Therefore, staff development must be seen as an integral part of the change venture: regular, available, and relevant.

It might be helpful to think about preparing staff in relation to four fairly discrete blocks of time: summer, autumn, winter, and spring.

During the summer months before a building faculty attempts to implement the ideas involved in a school for tomorrow, a workshop of two to six weeks' duration probably ought to be held. Such a workshop would follow several months of deliberate consideration of the concept and an expression of commitment, but it would precede attempts to put the ideas into practice within a particular school. At least five kinds of activities should be included in the workshop: exploring the theoretical propositions, collecting materials, simulated teaching and practical experience, deciding on organizational arrangements, and keeping a daily log. Let us begin with the last item first.

Teachers and administrators who are going to attempt to implement the ideas about a school for tomorrow in their school will have questions. They will have concerns. There will be particular ideas, materials, assessment devices, skills, or understandings that they need. We feel that it would be terribly important for every professional person involved in the effort to maintain a daily log. If the principal would simply purchase one hard-cover, blank-page ledger for each staff member, the practical problems of where to keep a record would be solved. Further, if every teacher's log is comparable in size, carefully bound, and durable, they can be carried home, handled, and used in many ways without being destroyed. Looseleaf notebooks are inappropriate. If every staff member is encouraged to write just one page each day, then books can be collected periodically, analyzed, and used as a basis for improvement and change.

In our judgment, teachers ought to record the kinds of problems and accomplishments they encounter. What would they like to have available that was not in the school? What materials or equipment or assessing devices did they want that they could not find? What successes took place? What seemed to work? Where did the significant events occur?

A daily log of problems, accomplishments, questions, insights, frustrations, and the like can be very helpful for the individual professional who records his concerns and for leadership personnel who want to be of assistance to all involved. Obviously such a device might be perceived as "prying" or as a tool for evaluating teacher's performance. Such thoughts must be dispelled in every way known. The difficulties inherent in making a school for tomorrow operational are so many and so complex, getting bogged down with false staff reports simply cannot be allowed to occur. Those who are working at implementation need good information and accurate data, not the "cover-up" comments or incomplete reports that are likely to be submitted if people feel that their own problems in working on a school for tomorrow may be interpreted as ineffectiveness on their part at the least or as cause for dismissal at worst. A school for tomorrow can succeed only if there is genuine commitment to give the proposal a good try, free and open access to all information, and full and frank sharing of both successes and failures. Keeping a daily log can be one way to record a history, one procedure for generating experiential data, one technique for sharing insights and questions.

Beginning to keep a daily log ought to start during the summer workshop. The log should be maintained daily throughout the school year, but it ought to be initiated when those who have already committed themselves to the change begin to work seriously at learning how to bring about the change.

Another thing that probably ought to occur during the summer workshop is further discussion and exploration of the theoretical aspects of a school for tomorrow. Listening to experts lecture (in person or on tape), holding discussions, reading, and watching films are all useful. An in-depth approach is important. Reviewing the ideas encountered when the consideration phase was taking place is appropriate, but some time should be devoted to learning in a cognitive way about what a school for tomorrow could be.

A third thing that teachers probably ought to have a chance to do is collect curriculum materials. According to the concepts set forth in this book, an elaborate curriculum system would characterize a school for tomorrow. That is certainly true. But it is also true that such a system does not exist today. Persons interested in moving that way, in working toward a curriculum system such as has been described here, can take both a short-term and a long-term view.

From a short-term point of view, teachers can begin to build collections of curriculum materials, assessment instruments, and the like. If these are so collected that they are theoretically consistent with the general ideas described, they can become a part of the larger system when that becomes available. In the meantime, they can draw from their own experience and acquaintance with materials; search out new sources; contact publishers, supply houses, and the like; and begin to build what used to be called a "resource unit" for themselves. Eventually all of these materials could be put into a larger, more elaborate system, but in the meantime the collection process can go forward.

It may be that employing some type of conceptual rationale would help. For example, a conceptual scheme for collecting materials in the general area of ecology is described in figure 8-1. In this diagram we have listed down the left-hand side five topical areas, which Meadows sets forth as the crucial variables that must be considered in coming to grips with the complex ecological problems in the world today.[20] Meadows' work is based on Forrester's analysis, but the point is that one can start with an acknowledged expert's conceptual framework and use it as a basis for collecting curriculum materials for use in school.[21] The framework needs to be reasonably accurate and relatively complete, but it need not be perfect. If there are serious conceptual voids, difficulties will eventually arise, but by employing several scholars' conceptions teachers can avoid most of the problems.

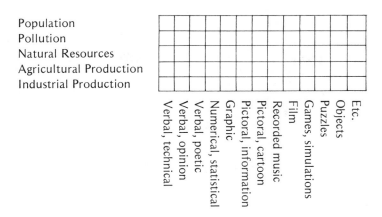

Population
Pollution
Natural Resources
Agricultural Production
Industrial Production

Verbal, technical
Verbal, opinion
Verbal, poetic
Numerical, statistical
Graphic
Pictoral, information
Pictoral, cartoon
Recorded music
Film
Games, simulations
Puzzles
Objects
Etc.

Figure 8-1. Conceptual Scheme for Collecting Curriculum Materials
in the Area of Ecology

The horizontal axis of the matrix has been laid out to suggest varied types of materials. Working directly from the premise that children are different, it is very important that the materials generated are varied in both substance and form. A comprehensive approach can be accomplished by selecting some artifacts that are printed, verbal materials of a technical nature (e.g., scientific reports), others that are verbal opinion (e.g., newspaper editorials or "letters to the editor"), and others that contain poetry, music, statistical graphs, problematic situations, puzzles, games, recorded music, films, and the like. Further, if several "items" could be identified for each cell in the matrix (e.g., some items might reflect a liberal point of view, some a conservative position, and others be "middle of the road"), a deliberate approach to generating artifacts can be employed by several teachers to collect literally hundreds or even thousands of artifacts in a fairly short period of time. Ultimately, a considering, sifting, "editing" process must occur, and items that are felt to be inappropriate can be eliminated or placed in another file.

If teachers prefer not to use this kind of conceptual scheme, they can invent their own. The point is, if curriculum artifacts are to be small, discrete, varied in content and form, and valid and are to meet the other criteria set forth in chapter 3, teachers must begin somewhere. *Creating* curriculum materials through writing textbooks is one way to develop curriculum. Another approach is to *select* materials that have been created by others but can be used by teachers in one or more ways. In a summer workshop, at least, the *selection process* is both practical and possible. Something can get done. Other arguments also suggest that the selection approach has merit (e.g., materials can be diversified, highly valid, and original rather than "watered down"), but those will not be argued here. What is being suggested is a simple but powerful conceptual scheme to guide teachers in their efforts to select curriculum materials from any sources they can find.

A fourth activity during the summer months ought to focus on organizational arrangements that may be possible in the school. Various approaches to the organizational aspects of a school for tomorrow might be considered, depending on the kind of organizational concepts employed in the school in the past, the size of the school, the degree of satisfaction and comfort that people have felt with previous organizational arrangements, the age and characteristics of students, and the amount and type of expert assistance and technical help available. Our suggestions center on the idea of ascertaining what the existing "regularities" in the school have been, and generating a range of alternative ways. Asking consultants to set forth possibilities would be one approach, and brainstorming among the staff would be another. We feel that it is important to come up with and consider a variety of ways of organizing the time-space-staff-resources complex of the school to meet individual student's learning needs.

For example, if the school involved happens to be a K-6 elementary school now organized around the concept of self-contained classrooms, we might consider various patterns of staff-teaming that cut across grade level or subject matter lines or both: K-6; K-3; 4-6; language arts/social studies; science/mathematics/industrial arts; etc. If the school has immediate access to a computer, then "loading" the data bank with various kinds of pertinent information would be one place to begin. In every arrangement the various assignments and functions for individual staff members could be identified and even simulated or role-played. That is, teams could meet and work together for several hours at a time, then be reformed according to another scheme and simulate the work activities again. The mere process of organizing and reorganizing into different kinds of working groups for practice purposes may "open up" people's minds about the possibilities available. And if there could be the "real" problems to deal with in these various groupings of staff, practice in an interactional setting could be especially helpful.[22] There is no one way of organizing a school for tomorrow apart from a consideration of the factors inherent in the particular school to be involved. To incorporate data into an information system requires careful specification, collection of information, and trial and modification *before* school opens in the fall.

A final thing that might take place during a summer workshop would be direct experience with students or simulated interactions by means of portable video recorders or simulation materials of various kinds. This experience might also include watching physicians diagnose a patient through a one-way mirror, studying video recordings of split image pictures of himself with an individual student (i.e., half the screen showing the teacher's face and behaviors, the other half showing the individual student's face and behaviors), or practicing item analysis with the intention of ascertaining strengths and weaknesses of particular students by studying their specific responses to particular items contained on a given achievement test form.

The point is, teachers and administrators who are moving toward a school for tomorrow need to work together for a reasonably extended period of time to hear more about the ideas and discuss them in detail; to collect materials; to practice some actual teaching behaviors in fairly "safe" surroundings; to explore various organizational possibilities; and to begin to record their questions, problems, expectations, and concerns. They would also need to set forth in fairly precise ways their own goals and objectives in relation to time. How much can we accomplish by Christmas? How far can we move toward that point by April 1? Will it be possible to "phase" our efforts so we attempt some things early, make more changes about January, say, and then try for a further shift in philosophy and means about the end of March or early April?

Retraining an entire staff, reorienting one's whole philosophy, and changing the operation of an entire school is extremely difficult to do in a short time. Some persons argue that it cannot be done. We do not agree. The task is terribly difficult, we know, but we are absolutely certain that it can be achieved. Some kind of intensive workshop experience in the summer when the children are gone is a good time to begin.

Implementation, Evaluation, and Modification

Certain basic decisions about organization, staff assignment, curriculum materials, and planning procedures must be arrived at before school begins. In our judgment, the decisions made at that time must be seen as tentative. However, in order to get things started and try out the new ways of working, it would probably make sense to begin school with the understanding that the new arrangements and the new procedures will be maintained within reasonable limits at least until January 1. That is, if staff members can feel assured that any major changes agreed on in the summer will be held fairly constant for three or four months, a stability should be possible that the threat of continuous change would not allow. In a theoretical sense, continuous adaptation and modification are desirable; in practical terms that is simply more than most hardworking professionals can cope with until they have had considerable experience and at least some success with efforts at change.

Specific activities for the entire school year will not be suggested here. Daily planning sessions for members of teaching teams, regular inservice opportunities for all persons, visits to other schools, attendance at conferences, and an ongoing reading and study program are absolutely essential. The precise nature of these events must be shaped by the experience and needs of the particular professionals who are working to bring a school for tomorrow into being in their school today.

It would undoubtedly be helpful for the professionals involved to have one or more process evaluators working with them every day collecting data, making video recordings of assessment efforts, analyzing curriculum materials use, and synthesizing expressions of concern and requests for assistance of various kinds. If such a process evaluator could have direct access to a university nearby, he might also serve as a liaison between theoreticians and practitioners who are mutually interested in evolving new and better ways of doing things in schools.

Implementing the ideas of a school for tomorrow requires careful thought and meticulous planning, but it also requires flexibility and willingness to change. The basis for change, of course, must include a thoughtful examination of pertinent facts assembled in terms of the plans that were made, but it must also include a consideration of the accomplishments and processes that occurred in relation to the plans.

Stufflebeam's proposals for using evaluative data as a basis for decision making in education seem particularly sound to us, but we are aware that other conceptualizations would probably work equally well.[23] Sarason's notions have been described at length already, but Goodlad's propositions for working cooperatively with other schools in a rigorous developmental effort are equally exciting.[24] In other words, there are many roads to change, but almost every road that leads to successful innovation in schools will include data collection, analysis, and use as a basis for meaningful change. Implementation, evaluation, and modification of a school for tomorrow demand the energies of many persons over an extended period of time. And though we have not spelled out the kinds of detail we know would have to be employed, we have tried to set forth some of the factors that we think ought to be considered.

One final note before we proceed. Implicit in everything that has been written in this book is the concept of a school for tomorrow as a *hypothesis* for change. What we have tried to argue for is an experimental posture, a willingness to try, an open-minded approach to the problems and possibilities inherent in this proposal for educational change. We should also state at this point that we firmly believe that those professional educators who decide to move toward a school for tomorrow in their school today ought to predicate that decision on a reasonably long-term commitment to change. To say it another way, because a school for tomorrow involves complex and far-reaching changes, it will not be possible to give the ideas a good try unless there is an initial commitment to work at the business of fostering change over an extended period of time.

We are not arguing for many months of effort with strict adherence to a particular concept of plan. Quite the opposite. We are suggesting that because a school for tomorrow presumes dramatic transformations of attitudes, assumptions, policies, procedures, and materials, it will be possible to work at the business of such a change only by taking "a long view." What happens in the short run may or may not work out. We realize that the difficulties and lack of know-how will be immense. Our proposal, therefore, presumes that intelligent, dedicated professionals ought to work at changing their schools steadily, deliberately, and thoughtfully. As they go about clarifying for themselves the criteria they intend to employ and choosing the courses of action that seem most likely to help them move toward the ends they seek, they will, in effect, be functioning as rational, autonomous, professional persons in search of building a school and a program designed to help children become rational, autonomous persons, too.

But it will take a long time. There are no quick and easy answers to an endeavor as complex as education, despite what others have sometimes said. We must be learners. We must try, observe, modify, and try again. Our style must be inquiring and our position one of perpetual growth.

Research and Problems

If a group of concerned professionals explored the kinds of ideas that have been outlined in this book and decided to work toward translating those ideas into educational practice, what kinds of problems would they encounter? What kinds of research would help them answer the questions that will emerge?

We do not know for certain what might be involved, but several things will probably impinge on their efforts. In the next sections we have attempted to sketch in at least some of the research possibilities and some of the problem areas that we feel may be important. No in-depth discussion of these topics seems appropriate here. We will learn more as we go along and work with educators to implement a school for tomorrow in their schools today. As of now, the following seem likely handles with which to begin to grasp the realities that are involved.

Research Possibilities

Research in any area always begins with a gnawing question or worrisome concern. Listed below are some of the research possibilities in question form. The listing, of course, is little more than a beginning. More questions will arise as schoolmen probe the depths of the propositions in this book and work in schools to see whether the ideas can be made operational.

1. What do individual learners need to know?
2. How can we distinguish human "needs" from "wants"?
3. How can teachers ascertain students' needs?
4. Are there sequences of experience or stimuli that will facilitate the development of rational, autonomous persons?

5. What qualities of personality or behavior among professionals are most likely to facilitate the development of rational, autonomous persons?

6. What is the function of group activities in developing rational, autonomous persons?

7. What kinds of change strategies will be most effective in helping a faculty move toward a school for tomorrow?

8. Which curriculum materials will be most useful in helping children develop into rational, autonomous persons?

9. How do pathological factors affect growth when certain curriculum materials or organizational arrangements or methodological procedures are employed?

These kinds of questions, of course, are pregnant with further possibilities for research. For example, question four can lead to many other kinds of researchable questions, such as, Is there a relationship between Piaget's concepts of intellectual development and Kohlberg's concepts of moral development? If so, should teachers arrange subject matter in particular sequences designed to foster such developmental stages? To what extent will children differ in terms of such developmental stages? How can such differences be ascertained? What subject matter, what relationships, what experiences are most likely to facilitate such developmental growth? Are such developmental stages consistent with helping children become rational, autonomous persons?

Take another illustration, question three: "How can teachers ascertain students' needs?" A whole host of questions spin off, such as, Can we develop instruments and procedures for identifying particular human needs? Will these instruments or procedures be sufficiently reliable and valid to use in school? If we find that there are no specific human needs that relate to particular subject matter fields, can we identify a variety of experiences or stimuli that will satisfy a given student's particular need? Is there a hierarchy of human needs that can be accurately and reliably observed in a school setting? In what ways do professional persons' experiences or qualities distort their perception of students' needs? For example, do insecure, inadequate teachers tend to see a student's request for information as movement toward a dependent relationship on the student's part?

These questions are illustrative, of course. They simply suggest something about the range of questions that might be explored by thoughtful researchers interested in pressing ideas related to a school for tomorrow in empirical ways.

Needless to say, untold numbers of new observational devices and assessment procedures (i.e., "tests") must be developed and validated for use in a school for tomorrow, too. Since most of the existing devices and techniques for assessing people are appropriate either for groups of persons or for qualities related only indirectly to rational, autonomous behavior, they are, by definition, not relevant in a school for tomorrow. Adaptations of existing instruments or procedures could undoubtedly be made, but most of the so-called standardized tests now available would have limited applicability in a school for tomorrow or in research related to a school for tomorrow.

Let us shift our discussion at this point from research possibilities to a consideration of some of the problems school people would undoubtedly face in their efforts to bring a school for tomorrow into being in their school today.

Problems That Might Be Anticipated

The problems and difficulties inherent in a school for tomorrow are many. Some persons would probably estimate that such problems would overwhelm a building principal and his staff. We do not think so. We know that the problems a professional group will face will be both severe and real, but we also feel that school people who face those problems head-on and deal with them professionally and on the basis of sound reasoning and valid data will have a sporting chance to resolve them satisfactorily. Further, they will grow to be more rational, autonomous persons themselves in the process and serve the youth in their school more effectively and humanely.

Briefly stated, we guess that problems may arise in relation to any or all of the following institutions or groups: state departments of education and regional accreditation agencies, groups concerned about educational costs, colleges and universities, community groups, members of the teaching staff within the school involved, teacher organizations, and textbook and curriculum producers. There will also be the usual expressions of concern: "Are children going to learn to read?" "Will they know their multiplication tables?" There are no simple solutions to problems such as these. Each must be dealt with before it arises, if possible, but always in a manner that will enable those involved to keep their eyes on the purposes and goals of a school for tomorrow rather than unrelated peripheral concerns.

For instance, accreditation by state departments of education and regional accrediting agencies are typically related to input rather than process or output factors. As a result, such things as teacher-pupil ratio, number of books in the library, number of degrees held by teachers, adequacy of support personnel, and recreational or cafeteria facilities available are given primary attention. These are appropriate areas of attention, of course, but if adhered to slavishly they force school people to allocate resources, space and energy in equitable rather than educational terms. They are formulated in relation to both subject matter areas and the group rather than the individual. That is understandable, of course, considering the fact that such standards were devised by conventional educators and meant for conventional schools. Fortunately, most accrediting agencies permit—in fact, encourage—experimentation, so if the staff of a school interested in moving toward a school for tomorrow will agree to adopt an experimental frame of reference, collect data, and report back to the accrediting agency, the deviation from the established set of rules will almost always be allowed.

The cost of a school for tomorrow will be somewhat higher than the cost for a typical school of today, and for that reason extra funds will need to be made available for materials, staff training, travel, research personnel, and consultant help. We dealt with this problem earlier in this chapter, so it will not be discussed here again at length. Extra funds will be important. Somehow, such funds must be made available to a principal and his staff.

Parental expectations and concerns are a very crucial consideration. School people must work to help parents and others understand the basic concepts of a school for tomorrow: devotion to the individual child, increased amounts of subject matter available, dedication to rationality and autonomy, variability in procedures available, emphasis on growth rather than control, and so forth. Parents and members of a local school community have been asked repeatedly to let school people innovate, to go along with change. Understandably, their suspicions have been aroused when so many of the change efforts have not made the difference in children's learning or satisfaction that was hoped for and sometimes promised.

But parents are still terribly concerned about their children and the schools. They desperately want education and schooling to be improved; they hope and pay for what they think will be better learning situations for their children; and they want a part in determining where the schools are going and how they will get there: that much is certain. If school people and school boards will share their plans, their expectations, their dreams, and if they will encourage parents and other community members to do likewise, serious problems can always be overcome. Communicating with out-of-school community persons always increases the time required for change and the number of criticisms that will appear, but it is worthwhile. Community members have important information they can add to the effort at change. Honesty in great quantities, full and complete sharing of expectations and plans, and genuine involvement and participation at a variety of levels will generally insure both better understanding and a broader base of community support than would otherwise occur.

Teacher organizations may object to some aspects of a school for tomorrow, because it would require role differentiation and variation in such factors as class size, time for planning, and the like. Negotiated agreements might include attention to such things, but in all probability dedicated professionals who are working to improve the quality of education for young people will be able to devise their own solutions to such problems.

Colleges and universities will not immediately be geared to provide teacher education programs for persons interested in teaching in a school for tomorrow, and some may actually oppose such changes. Even within college and university programs for preparing teachers, the primary interests are for subject matter or group concerns. However, collaborative relationships between public schools and teacher education institutions can always lead to reciprocal developments.

In general terms, college and university programs *follow* changes that occur in public schools rather than precede them. Many college professors like to think that they are in the vanguard, leading the way for educational change, but the reality of the situations in public schools is such a pervasive force, it actually functions the other way around.

There will be a growing body of expertise available. Many schools have already begun to adopt and adapt the concepts of a school for tomorrow into their schools today. The Association for

Supervision and Curriculum Development will facilitate the development and dissemination of a variety of training materials that professional educators might use. This book, of course, is one such piece of material. Films, film strips, pamphlets, cassette recordings, simulation materials, and other things will be available, too. The authors of this book have also pledged themselves to assist in whatever ways they can to help school people think through the concepts, realities, research, problems, possibilities, materials, and hardware that would be associated with these propositions in their local situations.

We fully expect—in fact, we hope—that the ideas described in this book will evolve and change with time. It is in the nature of intellectual things to grow. One of the members of our writing team has said, "It takes time to grow an idea. Ideas never emerge full-blown. Like cattle or corn or men, it takes a while for an idea to grow. And it takes support, too." We accept that point, and acknowledge the fact that this book is a seed. We hope the seed will fall on fertile ground; we hope that it will flourish and grow. We hope, too, that responsible educators will nurture the notions and provide the encouragement to help the ideas expand and multiply.

Criticism can be especially helpful, and our sincere hope is that those who find these ideas provocative and useful will press their examination and prod their colleagues to do so, too. We realize that searching examinations will force us all to modify our conceptualizations and alter our assumptions, but that is the stuff of intellectual and professional growth. And a school for tomorrow is concerned with growth: student growth, professional growth, theoretical growth, and growth in competence and skill. If men can learn to become more rational, autonomous human beings because of the ideas outlined here, our goal will have been achieved.

The function of a school for tomorrow, as we see it, is to create a relationship of ends and means that will further the development and growth of every human being who comes into contact with the school—male or female, young or old, black or white, rich or poor, bright or dull, professional or nonprofessional. However, the leadership to accomplish that function must come from the professional group. This book has set forth a series of propositions about schooling and the future. It is not a model to be imposed, but a set of ideas to be tried. The schools of tomorrow can be better schools, if we start working toward that objective today.

Notes

1. For additional information about where to purchase these materials, write to: Executive Secretary, Association for Supervision and Curriculum Development, 1201 Sixteenth Street, N.W., Washington, D.C. 20036.

2. Adapted from J. R. Suchman, "Some Criteria for Assessing Qualitative Improvements of Learning Environments," mimeographed (Berkeley, Calif.: HumRRO Briefs, n. d.).

3. Charles Silberman, *Crisis in the Classroom: The Remaking of American Education* (New York: Random House, 1970), pp. 10-11, 182.

4. Gerald Gutek, *An Historical Introduction to American Education* (New York: Thomas Y. Crowell, Co., 1970); Edward A. Krug, *The Shaping of the American High School* (New York: Harper & Row, 1964).

5. B. O. Smith, William Stanley, and Harlan Shores, *Fundamentals of Curriculum Development* (Yonkers-on-Hudson, N.Y.: World Book Co., 1950), chaps. 10, 12, 14.

6. Arthur W. Foshay, "A Modest Proposal for the Improvement of Education," in *What Are the Sources of the Curriculum* (Washington, D.C.: Association for Supervision and Curriculum Development, 1962), pp. 1-3; Hilda Taba, *Curriculum Development: Theory and Practice.* (New York: Harcourt, Brace & World, 1962), chap. 2.

7. Ralph Tyler, *Basic Principles of Curriculum and Instruction: Syllabus for Education 360* (Chicago: University of Chicago Press, 1950), p. 4.

8. Virgil Herrick, *Curriculum Development Strategies* (Columbus: Charles E. Merrill Publishing Co., 1965), p. 6.

9. Lawrence P. Grayson, "Costs, Benefits, Effectiveness: Challenge to Educational Technology," *Science* 175 (1972): 1217.

10. Ibid., p. 1216.

11. John N. Williamson, "The Inquiring School: A Study of Educational Self-Renewal" (Doctoral diss., Harvard University, 1971), pp. 30-31.

12. Clarence H. Faust, "The Problem of General Education," in *The Idea and Practice of General Education* (Chicago: University of Chicago Press, 1950), chap. 1.

13. Donella H. Meadows et al., *The Limits to Growth* (New York: Universe Books, 1972), chap. 5.

14. Ibid., pp. 183-84.

15. Harold G. Shane, "The Educational Significance of the Future," mimeographed (Bloomington: Indiana University, 1972), pp. 8-9.

16. Seymour B. Sarason, *The Culture of the School and the Problem of Change* (Boston: Allyn & Bacon, 1971), p. 193.

17. Ibid., p. 213.

18. Neal Gross et al., *An Attempt to Implement a Major Educational Innovation: A Sociological Inquiry Report Number 5* (Cambridge: Harvard University, 1968), chaps 6-7.

19. Sarason, *op. cit.*, chap. 6.

20. Meadows, *loc. cit.*

21. Jay W. Forrester, *World Dynamics* (Cambridge: Wright-Allen Press, 1971).

22. For example, see Donald R. Cruickshank, Frank W. Broadbent, and Roy Bubb, *Teaching Problems Laboratory* (Chicago: Science Research Associates, 1967).

23. Daniel L. Stufflebeam, "Evaluation as Enlightenment for Decision Making," in *Improving Educational Assessment and an Inventory of Measures of Affective Behavior,* ed. Walcott H. Beatty (Washington, D.C.: Association for Supervision and Curriculum Development, 1969), pp. 41-73.

24. John I. Goodlad, "Staff Development: The League Model," *Theory Into Practice* 11 (October 1972): 207-14.